If a Tree Falls

❖

Rediscovering the Great American Chestnut

Douglas J. Buege

ISBN:	Hardcover	978-1-4363-1609-5
	Softcover	978-1-4363-1608-8

This book was printed in the United States of America.

To order additional copies of this book, contact:
Xlibris Corporation
1-888-795-4274
www.Xlibris.com
Orders@Xlibris.com

42826

Introduction

"I think I'm so educated and I'm so civilized
'cos I'm a strict vegetarian.
But with the over-population and inflation and starvation
And the crazy politicians
I don't feel safe in this world no more
I don't want to die in a nuclear war
I want to sail away to a distant shore and make like an ape man."

—Raymond Douglas Davies, "Apeman," on The Kinks' *Lola versus Powerman and the Moneygoround*, 1970

"For in the end, we will conserve only what we love. We will love only what we understand. We will understand only what we are taught."

—Baba Dioum

I stole into the grove with a handful of misconceptions and a truckload of expectations, foolishly stopping to photograph the first sapling I saw. The tulip-like flower emanating from a ring of five-inch leaflets must be the mysterious chestnut I'd come to see. Later, as clearer thoughts prevailed, I admitted my zeal coerced me into quivering in the presence of the common hickory, a tree never decimated by epidemic blight, a tree I'd known since youth.

Winding my way through the newly-leafed growth, I avoided the researchers expecting me, hoping to crystallize first impressions without taint of their knowledge. The mighty American chestnut, *Castanea dentata*, had all but disappeared from Earth nearly two decades before my conception. Though I accepted as fact that one out of four trees in a tract from Maine to Georgia had once been an American chestnut, I still had difficulty believing that the largest remaining stand of this fabled species, which some immodestly called "the Redwood of the East," could hide in the rolling topography of southwest Wisconsin. This "driftless" region, where the southern-most lobe of the last glacier, the Wisconsonian ice sheet, left a corner of state untouched, held many botanical wonders, relicts of plant populations found well outside of Wisconsin, to the west and south. Noted plant ecologist John Curtis, in his epic study of the Badger State's vegetation, held that the Driftless Area served as reservoir for almost all of Wisconsin's species that repopulated regions north and east at the end of the last Ice Age. An eastern species like chestnut, though, proved an unlikely resident. The nearest native chestnuts would have once been found in contiguous populations in southeastern Indiana or possibly in isolated pockets of Illinois hundreds of miles away. Trees would take hundreds of years to migrate that far, and they'd leave a number of their species along the way.

If not for the whim of one Martin Hicks, a settler from New York State, these chestnuts might have never found their way west. Sometime around 1890, he planted ten or so chestnuts in a row behind his new home, undoubtedly hoping to benefit from the wood and nuts that served as staples of life out east. In his youth, like many boys of his day, Hicks probably earned a decent autumnal income from the nuts he gathered near his home. Or else he just liked the taste of the chestnut's fruit. His passion for the tree drove him to transport seed or, less likely, saplings to his new home not far from the mighty waters of the Mississippi. That original stock multiplied over the years, becoming roughly 2,500 trees covering 60 acres of land owned by three separate owners.

I felt as if I were entering one of those legendary displays of Ripley that dared me to believe it or not.

A staunch lover of the botanical world since childhood, I'd been pulled to these trees by a series of coincidences. In a chance hallway encounter, a fellow educator and orchardist mentioned a curious chestnut grower he thought I'd find of interest. When I visited that grower, he mentioned the West Salem trees and gave me some seeds to play with. References to chestnut blight popped up in my readings. On a visit to the University of Wisconsin's herbarium, I found a sample of American chestnut from this stand of trees. The drive to learn more led me to contact researchers who invited me to the grove on this Sunday morning.

I should mention that I'm not a devout tree person. In a college forestry course, the rote memorization of the various trees on our campus held little importance to me. Instead, I'd always taken intrigue in the oddities of the plant world—the carnivorous, the oddly-flowered, the stinky, the poisonous and the edible, and the rare. The first plant I remember growing, a begonia—purchased from a rural greenhouse when I was maybe eight, caught my attention for the chocolate "X" inscribed in each hairy leaf. Entering college, I admitted to myself that cycads excited me; hostas did not. Certain trees like live oak inspired while red oak bored me. I learned to identify bladderworts while I let someone else spend their time keying out rushes. A fussy botanist, I held a fascination for the survivors who'd evolved desperate means to counter the ravages of animals, particularly humans.

American chestnut caught my attention for several reasons. First, the whole sad story of its decline appealed to my concern for the underdogs of the world. The fact that chestnut had not given up the fight for survival suggested that the species had some hidden strengths, lending mystery to the story. And the shape of the tree's leaves triggered my aesthetic sense; the sweeping curves rounding in wave-like teeth offered a visual harmony to which I succumbed. My interest only grew as I immersed myself in this species' odd tale.

Though I highly doubt humans will leave more than a dismal collection of weed species in their tragic wake—roaches, rats, crabgrass, poison ivy, in my epic fantasies, Kingdom Plantae in all its diverse glory eventually wins its showdown with *Homo sapiens*. I smile when I see that Far Side with a ring of bugs dancing on a leaf while mushroom clouds in the distance signal the destruction of civilization. You could definitely call me a species, if not kingdom, traitor. I show little interest in my affiliation with the race of humans or mammals or even vertebrates. It's the realm of the green for which I root. My highly fictional scenario where plants, and possibly insects, prevail receives occasional boosts from real world events, these strange Eastern survivors being a case in point.

While working toward my doctorate in philosophy, I honed my anti-anthropocentrism on various authors positing animal rights, respect for ecosystems, rights for trees, and a variety of other views many humans dismiss as silly or unrealistic. Pulled to environmental ethics like a gnat to a fly trap, I tended to think that none of these theorists went far enough. In my estimation, humankind proved the worst plague that Earth had ever seen, fitting Alex Lifeson's telling lyrics describing "New World Man": "He's old enough to know what's right, But young enough not to choose it. He's noble enough to win the world, But weak enough to lose it." Humans had the ability for complex thought necessary to act responsibly in the world but retained the reptilian brain so adept at acting sub-rationally, so keen to grab the quick gain without batting a neuron toward contemplation of the future. I found difficulty in building much optimism for us, concerned so much with winning the human race and ignoring the costs of our ravages. The rest of the biotic world needed champions; humans would survive without my support.

The way I measure human society, I see quite a few people blasting forward with little regard for the consequences of their actions. Making a buck, or a million, or a billion, heralds victory in the American mindset. Some of us, though, stand as speed bumps to this so-called progress, reminding humanity of the sacred aspects of the world—the hidden bogs, the endangered species, the natural systems bringing us the air, water, and food we need. Likely to suffer penury for our ideals, we battle against the torrent of greed because losing our natural world would prove a fate worse than death. The long, slow decline of planet Earth weighs heavily upon us, though we refuse to relinquish the future of humanity or the natural world. For me, a defense of this non-human bounty proves a moral imperative, not a way of advancing personal benefit. I'm defending my home against the true ecoterrorists—those who would take dollars to sacrifice environmental health in my backyard.

Many a dogmatist would cast aspersions upon my favoring non-humans, noting a litany of reasons why Kingdom Plantae remains undeserving of the respect we heap upon species occupying hard-earned positions among Animalia, particularly those in Class Mammalia, and a handful of genera including *Homo*. I respond by noting that some of these creatures, particularly humans, have clawed their way up the metaphorical tree of life, and from high perches, quietly or vociferously argue their special status, barely aware that their esteemed position relies heavily upon the plants and those single-celled organisms from which we devolved.

A quick perusal of the workaday world reveals the minor place we reserve for our photosynthetic cousins, the plants. Excluding the Toronto Maple Leafs, no major league sports team adopts herbaceous or woody mascots. College athletes mass under the aegis of humorous tokens such as the billikens or banana slugs but I'm unaware of any daring to call themselves the Vindictive Pteridophytes despite the innate aggression packed into the name. Yes, Ohio State has its Buckeyes, but one must search the lower echelons of college sports to find other photosynthetic mascots. Most people remain unaware that Chaminade University of Honolulu's nickname, the Silverswords, refers to a plant indigenous to one of Maui's dormant volcanoes, rather than a weapon. And I cannot accept the Delta State Fighting Okra as a true mascot as the school administration officially recognizes their teams as the Statesmen and the seemingly contradictory Lady Statesmen. If I had a college soccer team, I'd name them the Hemlocks, just to terrorize opponents, particularly Greeks and Socratics, with the deadly appellation.

Lion tamers and their ilk merit special attention in our annals of the brave; those who train hedges garner little but yawns.

Just recently, as automakers burn through their finite list of aggrandizing titles for the noxious vehicles we operate, have the names of plants become candidates for those obnoxious chromium advertisements gracing our trunks. The Toyota Sequoia, accepted undoubtedly because "King Kong" and "Godzilla" were protected by copyright, proves an insult to the majestic tree. Yes, the vehicle is massive in relation to its four-wheeled brethren, like its namesake. The SUV, though, irresponsibly consumes petroleum at fantastic rates. That fossil fuel comes from the demise of the sequoia's leafy ancestors. To me, the name proves offensive in the same way a vehicle powered by Native American remains called the Apache would.

I could rattle on like this for pages. Despite our obvious dependence on the herbs, shrubs and trees, we denigrate them at nearly every opportunity. Consider, though, a few of the ways plants surpass us.

Longevity has never been a human strong suit. The recurring news story that the oldest living human died at 113 seems laughable when we consider the 5,000 years of change one bristlecone pine has witnessed. While humans continue their on-going aim of shortening the lives of other humans, as well as ancient trees the world over, we should examine the stolid pacifism of our woody elders. Remember, someone aged the bristlecone by counting its rings after mistakenly cutting it down.

Humans have been known to approach heights of eight feet, possibly exceeding that measure in cases we label as medically dangerous gigantism. Excessive height is linked with reduced longevity.

We reserve the term 'sapling' to refer to eight foot tall trees. Non-woody plants, including grasses, commonly exceed the extreme of human growth. Perhaps this explains the perverse enjoyment plastered on the lawn mower's face. Plants also dwarf humans when comparing girth, even in the carbohydrate-rich Midwest of the United States.

Plants enlisted solar energy thousands of millennia before Jimmy Carter drew up tax incentives to promote the non-fossil fuel dependent form of power. Indeed their knack for using light to synthesize complex sugars from ambient gas and liquid molecules made possible the life forms we term 'higher.' Though we depict plants at the bottom of food chains, such intellectual short-cuts reveal more of our anthropocentric culture than they do of the plants' essences. A more telling analogy would be of plants as lifeboat and all animals as reliant passengers, not really a foreign concept in Western tradition given that even Noah's ark was allegedly crafted from wood.

Without doubt, though, Kingdom Plantae's greatest accomplishment is manipulating the various members of Kingdom Animalia.

For the most part stationary, the clever green race needed a way to accomplish their numerous errands without lifting a root. And they didn't cheat by developing brains. Instead, they lured messengers, delivery experts and technicians in a strategy to shame the postal service.

Assistance with intercourse became an early priority for evolving flora. Wind, an excellent medium for pollen transfer in species dominant in size, number, and pollen production, would never allow for the teeming diversity that has flourished since the Triassic Era when cycads and ferns ruled. Low density rarities like orchids would never have evolved their intriguing shapes if wind proved adequate for their pollination. Many conifers and grasses, still satisfied to broadcast their sperm on a stiff breeze, deserve credit for their independent nature, refusing to entrust mere animals with their genetic legacy.

As any Sunday afternoon jaunt to the conservatory shows, animals will rally from miles around to glimpse a few oddly-colored petals arranged temptingly, particularly if they smell good. Insect pollinators, one of the few animalian groups to rival flora, evolved alongside the angiosperms, performing an inter-kingdom ballet from which both pollinators and pollinated benefit. Botanists prior to 1900 proffered "phanerogamous"—an odd term derived from Greek and translating loosely to "visible marriage"—to refer to true flowering plants. Ancient Greeks had considered the act of pollination a form of marriage between insect and plant, a cross-kingdom arrangement probably deemed too risqué for modern defenders of the sanctity of marriage.

Once pollination's goal is met, our foliar friends had to devise means of dispersing their seed. Of course, quite a few turned to air currents to carry specially evolved packages. For dandelions, this strategy proved ingenious; cousin coconut, though, contrary to the claims of Monty Python, could rely on neither swallows nor tropical breezes, and, thus, turned to gravity, ocean waves and currents, and a tough fibrous hull for expanding its range.

Burrs, spines, and illustrious hook-like hairs fooled unsuspecting fur bearers into transporting seed so endowed far from the parent plant. Delectable berries prompted consumption from herb—and omnivores, with quiet dung dispersal post-digestion. In such a way, many a wingless seed took flight to distant lands and islands in an avian gut. Nut trees enlisted frugal rodentia to gather and plant their progeny, playing the odds that a few of the beasts would forget their cache or die before exploiting the protein source. Thus, the non-witty plants tricked the mobile forces of nature into delivering their priceless packages.

Plants excel at numerous other tasks. While humans struggle to keep their plumbing fit to deliver essential water, roots draw moisture and minerals from the soil itself. Conifers and select deciduous species have learned to survive harsh climates of excessive cold. Cacti and their comrades evolved spiny defenses, while poisonous plants developed the ability to synthesize toxins to detract consumers.

A group of the green ones have even turned carnivore, drawing scarce nitrogen from bug carcasses.

Thus, I walked under the trees an ally, hoping to find a way to ply my skills to help these few remaining American chestnuts. Climbing a hill, I searched for chestnut. The largest specimens I quickly identified as oak. The trees, apparently tertiary growth or worse, composed a woods like most others I'd seen near La Crosse. They'd been clearcut multiple times since settlement as each wave of pioneers sought lumber for their houses and outbuildings.

The woods' first difference proved the spiky husks dotting my path. Chocolate brown with three spined lips pulling back, these pods sheltered the chestnut's famous nuts, esteemed for their roastability over open fire. The closest connection I could make was to Ohio's favored buckeye, another imposing seed case rarely found in Wisconsin. Husks littered the trail, long devoid of their precious cargo.

I also noted codes spray painted upon the trunks of several leafless trees. Some plants appeared ready to burst forth in green; others looked deader than George Armstrong Custer. Others sported healthy trunks boasting decrepit, skeletal branches stretching skyward.

In 1987, this isolated stand came down with the blight that had wiped out the eastern trees prior to 1950. The tagged trees, numbered for identification, flashing multiple colors of paint for the multiple groups studying them, came in clumps. None seemed surpassingly large and I lacked the knowledge to recognize chestnut saplings.

Imagine a bomb exploding in a pipe leaving the metal around the blast thrust outward with cracks appearing in the once-solid tube. Several of the trees sported similar damage, cracked bark extruded as if some great pressure had build up in the heartwood and finally escaped. These lesions, visibly the worst signs of the blight, can appear anywhere above ground on the chestnut, almost certainly evidence of a dying tree. The woods, littered with dead and decaying subjects, triggered in me a sense of despair. Having little more than an academic understanding of the eastern chestnuts' demise, I had already dared to consider the Wisconsin grove a last hope.

Even in their diminished state, these ragtag soldiers, engaged in ongoing battle against a smaller, faster devious enemy, held a heroic air I respected.

I wasn't alone. Faint voices drifted in from the west. I forged my way to meet up with Jane Cummings Carlson of Wisconsin's Department of Natural Resources, my contact for this excursion. She and three others, students from nearby UW-La Crosse, meticulously examined marked trees, comparing current signs of disease with recorded data.

Originally, Cummings Carlson hoped to treat afflicted trees in the few days she had in the grove but government snafus held up the necessary permit to use the treatment agent. This visit was simply an inventory.

Fifty yards away, UW-La Crosse mycologist Tom Volk also examined trees with a pair of his devoted students. Volk, bearing a glacial flat-top—three inches of snow white hair punctuated with a shock of electric blue—knows the world of fungi better than anyone else I've met. Endowed with earrings and a swarm of tattoos on both arms, fungal hyphae on report, the professor might be termed the "punk plant pathologist," but as one graduate student informed me, no one would say this to his face. His voluminous knowledge garnered their respect.

Volk's expertise with plant diseases brought him on this visit, just one of many. He knows more about the fungal cause of the blight, *Cryphonectria parasitica*, than he does of chestnuts. In general, the realm of the fungi is one of the least understood kingdoms in the traditional division of living organisms. In a sense, Volk is akin to Lewis and Clarke, penetrating new ground in an underappreciated branch of biology. Volk's intimacy with the fungi sometimes goes to extremes as in his bout with a dreadful flesh-eating fungus that ate at his foot.

The group convened and decided to complete two more areas before breaking for lunch. I wandered with Cummings Carlson's contingent, trying to remain out of the way while they tallied cankers. Glancing carefully at the bark of diseased trees, I noted the tiny red points like dense freckles dotting the bark. Being spring, the blight was less active than it would be in the heat of summer. I envisioned fungal mycelia penetrating the outer bark and flourishing in the soft inner bark or cambium where the tree's major physiological processes, water and sugar transport, occur. Like a kid left free in a candy store, the blight goes crazy in the cambium, rapidly growing and producing the next generation's spores which spread throughout the forest.

Over lunch, I exchanged words with the researchers, gaining insights into their attitudes toward the trees. Cold scientism hid a deeper fear that this stand faced doom. Despite nearly twenty years of treatments, experiments conducted in this living laboratory, the trees succumb to the blight. Government agencies slow the flow of funding and equipment needed to address perpetual fungal attacks, leaving the researchers to ruminate on the decline of once healthy chestnuts. Your average Washington factotum, seeking to rise in the ranks by saving the government money, has little clue to the importance of the work performed in the West Salem stand. I sensed that the crew went through the motions, straining to ignore the ultimate fate of their stand.

Before returning to their cataloging, Bernadette O'Reilly, one of Volk's undergraduate students who shares his passion for mycology, offered to show me the original line of trees, or at least what remains of them. We strolled down another trail running alongside a farmer's field and climbed a gentle slope. A few larger chestnuts marked the site of Hicks' onetime backyard. A procession of stumps, some nearly eight feet across, denotes the original trees, veritable giants for the land surrounding us. A possible original survivor stands tall, though the blight has denuded much of its greenery.

I looked around, realizing that I was really not there. Instead, I stood in the Brooklyn Botanical Garden one-hundred years ago, wondering why, why must these beautiful nut trees die so quickly. I faced a sea of questions concerning the terminal diagnosis of a species more distinctly American than the baseball or apple pie remembered as rural legend. The carelessness and greed of humans appalls me as I understand the depth of the ecological catastrophe to follow the introduction of a supposedly harmless fungus.

Tasting the loss of this remarkable species, I realized that I'd been initiated into the cult of the American chestnut.

Chapter 1

"What has really happened, so far, is that [the American chestnut] has been reduced from the status of a most useful forest citizen to the Kindergarten grade of a forest shrub."

—Arthur Graves, 1937

85 million years ago, the eventual evolution of humankind would haunt the nightmares of only the most imaginative and prescient of the sentient creatures. The late Cretaceous period of the Mesozoic Era would have had everyone talking, had there been anyone to talk. The written word would wait another 84.994 million years to appear in ancient Sumer. Proponents of Biblical stories claiming the Earth as only 4000 years old would appear even later, wielding their odd Eurocentric arguments that tend to paint those brilliant Sumerians and their precursors out of historical existence. Evolution proved an open door through which most species would pass and eventually disappear long before the members of the genus *Homo* would intrude upon the Darwinian process like a tribe of stegosauruses in a glass factory.

On a time scale vexing such ephemeral creatures as humans, Earth's visage has expressed dynamic changes. 85 million years ago, the moon would set on much steeper Appalachians while the juvenile Rockies still formed. Pangaea had begun to dissolve into continents 200 million years ago, the tectonic plates moving in their varied directions. Over the millennia, varied land bridges came and went as continents drifted into and away from one another like extremely slow-motion bumper cars.

By 85 million years ago, when chestnut-like plants first appear in the fossil record, kangaroos had already hopped around Earth for nearly 50 million years. Modern sharks patrolled the oceans. Mammals had existed in some form for 110 million years, though critters recognizable as squirrels and mice had yet to show up, according to available records. In another 37 million years, monkeys would appear, followed by those beloved pigeons 30 million years later. In 20 million years, a large chunk of space rock would put a dent in the planet where the Yucatan peninsula now sits, sending the Cretaceous out with a bang and bringing in the Paleocene Epoch.

Katherine Willis, who heads Oxford University's Long-term Ecology Laboratory, and paleobotanist Jennifer McElwain, of the Field Museum in Chicago, cite the earliest evidence of chestnut in their *The Evolution of Plants.* This original appearance 85 million years ago—only a cameo, followed by a greater abundance starting roughly 55 million years ago, shows that today's chestnuts have an incredible evolutionary history that dwarfs recently contrived species such as *Homo sapiens.* Chestnuts survived the cataclysm that destroyed the bulk of dinosaur-like organisms populating both land and sea, drawing the curtains on the Cenozoic. Like other nut trees, chestnut would evolve over millions and millions of years, differentiating into varied species and capturing an encyclopedic range of information within developing genomes. When one considers the number of errands one can complete in the odd day off, the potential for genus *Castanea*'s accomplishments starts to come into focus. But, of course, human beings fail to fathom the depth of these numbers, particularly those who grow restive waiting for their microwave popcorn. We have little comprehension of the adaptive strategies coded in *Castanea*'s seemingly repetitive strings of nucleic acids—adenosine, thymine, cytosine, and guanine arranged to code for key proteins that would help individuals survive the odd calamities that might strike, from insect incursions to ice ages.

Of course, much of this evolutionary development remains highly speculative. From our perspective, we've just walked in on the last second of a movie's credits and we want to reconstruct the film's entire story line. The problem lies not in Darwinian theory which proves incredibly useful; problems arise because plants and small creatures like rodents tend to decay, leaving few fossil records. Squirrel bones, being rather small, tend to be overlooked while mastodon remains more likely trip up the itinerant paleontologist. Smaller creatures play greater roles in chestnut's evolutionary history than the behemoths populating the halls of natural history museums. Like these small mammals, plant parts—leaves, wood, and bark—decompose fairly readily. Ever wonder why museums have more arrowheads than wooden spoons? Only in rare circumstances do plants leave tell-tale fossils of their ways of life. We need to draw large conclusions from scant evidence.

Also, human beings tend to be rather hasty, consuming the bulk of the world's coal beds before those ancient plant remains can be examined for microfossils that might help us sketch in some details of life's progression. Our pusillanimous devotion to fossil fuels refuses us the luxury of slow, methodical research.

Ironically, some of the most telling evidence concerning the evolutionary history of plants comes from some of the smallest fossils available. Most pollen grains, the tiny packages of male gametes sent forth in on-going attempts by organisms to multiply, have tough outer walls that withstand acidic, low-oxygen environments well. Coal beds and peat bogs offer exceptional opportunities to delve into the distant past, to explore the historic ecology of plant types. Thanks to pollen and spores, we can trace the history of plant-like organisms back an astonishing 3.8 billion years! The science of fossil pollen, paleopalynology, developed in the Twentieth Century, in league with paleobotany, the study of megafossils—leaf imprints, fruit castings, and fossilized wood, allows us to draw some interesting conclusions, particularly for larger specimens like chestnut.

The woody titans in class Fagaceae—the home to oaks, beeches, chinquapins, and chestnuts—leave many samples throughout the fossil record, perhaps only surpassed by birches and walnuts in their bulk sum. But the fine details of flower architecture, leaf structure, and other anatomical features, particularly those related to softer tissues, remain shrouded in theoretical fog, with few widely-held agreements among paleobotanists and palynologists. Often called 'holes' in the historical record but really more areas of minimal visibility, these unknown areas create an evolutionary story for chestnut that's at best fragmentary. Future findings may change this state of affairs.

We have learned more about the big picture, the large-scale phenomena offering the conditions for plant evolution from which we draw generalizations about genera and species. At the end of the Cretaceous period, the angiosperms—true flowering plants—began to diversify as they increased in numbers. Willis and McElwain explain that a warm temperate zone, stretching from 45 degrees to 65 degrees latitude—a strip including northern North America, southern Greenland, northern China, Russia and parts of western Europe in the north, and Australia and coastal Antarctica in the south—served as home for early chestnuts, as well as elms, birches, and walnuts, which competed with the more primitive ferns for ecological dominance.

The angiosperms gained momentum in conquering North America as climatic changes heralded a new age of seasonality. Instead of fairly consistent greenhouse conditions that had predominated the Cretaceous, cyclical temperature variations came to dominate, giving the continent something approximating the seasons we know today, though temperatures ran much warmer due to high atmospheric carbon dioxide levels creating a greenhouse climate. Such conditions pushed plant adaptation toward deciduousness; plants that strategically lost their leaves during drier and cooler annual periods would have greater chances of surviving compared to their ever-green fellows, especially in regions experiencing more severe seasonal changes. (Today's evergreens which hold on to their needles experience altered metabolic rates, an evolved advantage allowing them to survive seasonal changes.)

Though deciduous trees expanded in kind and number, one must remember that they survived without many of the luxuries their ancestors exploit today. Relationships with Kingdom Animalia were essentially competitive. The bizarre assortment of herbivores, rather than gratefully acknowledging their photosynthetic kindred's brave settlement of terrestrial environments that paved the way for land animals, simply consumed as much of the greenery as they could reach. Plants could retain their evolutionary foothold by producing defenses—toxins, thorns, and tough coverings for their tender parts over millions of years.

Another survival strategy involved rapid growth. Quick vertical assent, where tasty vegetation soared above the height chewing mouths could graze, high atop inedible stalks or trunks, benefited many green species. Others employed rapid vegetative expansion using techniques exploited by horticulturalists today. Chestnut developed ways to exploit all these options.

The rise in vegetative real estate provided incentive for ground fauna to learn to climb, both to reach sky-born meals and to escape carnivores down below. Squirrels and nut trees underwent a long process of co-evolution, both pushing one another toward their modern ecologies. Once canopy-dwelling herbivores ascended, trees could benefit by finding ways to employ these new pests. Nuts satiated the beasts, preventing them from eating the individual's needed flesh, while opening new doors for perpetuating the species. The bark dwellers became diligent dispersal teams for the seed. Statistically speaking, though the trees sacrificed some of their biological energy in feeding the proto-squirrels, they benefited because a share of nut seed would survive to grow into new trees, particularly given the rodents' propensity for caching seeds underground and then succumbing to predators' jaws.

Over the course of time, genera and species within the Fagaceae, like modern fashions, appeared and disappeared with little fanfare. The oldest American record of chestnut-like species, in the long-extinct genus *Tricolporopollenites*, dates to 83 million years ago. A swamp inhabitant long gone from Earth, *Cupuliferoipollenites pusillus*, lived in California 70 million years ago. A leaf fossil from roughly 35 million years ago, found in the Oligocene Florissant Formation of present-day central Colorado, has been identified as *Castanea dolichophylla*, a species long since extinct. The leaves, long and slender, in some ways willowlike but more tapered, feature less evident teeth on the leaf's edge than today's American chestnut. (Willis, p. 209) More than 30 million years ago, during the Eocene Epoch, *Castanea ungeri* grew on North America's west coast—land currently in California. The species also pops up in Greenland's fossil record. The John Day Basin in eastern Oregon revealed that 26 million years ago chestnut species composed 5 to 10 percent of the forest, along with other species now restricted to the southeast—sweet gum and beech. Idaho housed *Castanea spokanensis* some 7 million years ago. Another chestnut-like genus, *Castanoxylon*, disappeared in the upper Pliocene—approximately 3 million years ago.

For most of these long-gone species and genera, pollen samples only illustrate existence in the fossil record. We have no way to recreate a tree from its pollen. I find it amazing enough that scanning electron microscopes allow us to examine pollen grains in such detail that we can reconstruct tiny parts of the evolutionary record. It remains highly unlikely that we will ever have a detailed picture of Earth's distant biological past.

While fossil pollen has limited use in recreating chestnut's history, today's species may harbor secrets hidden deep in their genomes. Nucleic acid sequences, properly studied, can yield information of ancient conditions if scientists choose to explore them.

One fact made clear by our comparatively extensive knowledge of climate change throughout Earth's last few billion years is that tree species required mobility. With temperature variations, natural cataclysms—particularly volcanic, encroaching and retreating glacial ice, continents creeping about on tectonic plates, and changing ocean currents, any species without the ability to migrate to less harsh conditions likely went extinct. A stop motion film of Earth's vegetation in which each second represented a million years would feature rapid, abrupt maneuvering of forests, prairies, deserts, and oceans, with land bridges appearing intermittently as species ushered across.

Researchers at the National Climatic Data Center, in Asheville, North Carolina, devised a web-based viewer to watch the rises and falls of notable North American plant species since 21,000 years ago—an extremely brief time in chestnut's history but, given our increasing myopia as we look back in time, a time for which our data proves fairly accurate. Using pollen records from cores drawn from well-preserved sites such as bogs, their software translates lots of tedious raw data into a visual re-enactment of plant migrations.

Looking at the 21 millennium progression of chestnut, I see that chestnut once claimed a foothold on huge non-glaciated parts of North America, from present-day Alaska to a wider Floridian peninsula. Depicting conditions only 13,000 years ago, the program details a small patch of green, an area of chestnut, somewhere near the modern Virginia—North Carolina border. No chestnuts had appeared there a millennium earlier. By 12,000 years ago, this range expanded northeast and southwest. By 4000 BC, the species reached the Atlantic and had grown in range and density, a black cloud of established groves with a green lining showing a rapidly increasing population. 2000 years later, the tree's heart range sent a pseudopod into New England where the species grabbed hold to increase its numbers up until blight struck. Chestnut almost reached the Gulf of Mexico but retracted by 1000 AD. 500 years ago, the species' range shrank once again.

Fred Paillet, a chestnut researcher who has paid close attention to history, notes that somewhere in the last 8000 years, chestnut took off in New England. He offers conjecture that cooler and wetter conditions prompted chestnut's descent from mountainous refuges to colonize the broader plains of the region.

Evolution produced an American chestnut quite different from its varied kin on other continents. Chinese and Japanese species, far shorter than the American, have endured a longer period with humans who have cultivated the trees to meet their requirements. Southern Asia features cold-intolerant species. Europe's chestnuts have the closest ties to American chestnut, likely making European expansion in North America a bit more comfortable for chestnut aficionados.

Once humans reached North America, the American chestnut's story began a new chapter. Native Americans certainly found the chestnut a tremendous source of protein, the perfect companion food for carbohydrate-rich corn. The mix of corn and chestnut would provide full dietary amino acids. The Cherokee, for example, used American chestnut for food, medicine, and dye.

Europeans also accepted chestnut's largesse. As the newcomers cut the woods for shelter, heat, and agricultural space, the chestnut employed its remarkable ability to repopulate the forests with suckers. Many trees simply die when cut. Others, though, send up new stock from the root that grows more quickly than species growing by seed. Like the fabled hydra, cutting a chestnut prompts the tree to put up several new shoots that, given open air with plenty of sunlight, race for the sky. And chestnut grows faster than oak. A sixty-year-old chestnut would often be the same size as an oak twice its age.

Clearing fields for homesteads and agriculture certainly would favor a fast-growing sprouter like the chestnut. A year after cutting a stand of trees, chestnut's sprouts would take off unless the roots had been killed or removed. Thus, human settlement created prime conditions for American chestnut to out-compete other tree species. Folks would welcome the adventitious trees for their multiple uses, allowing chestnut populations to take off.

As technological knowledge advanced, chestnut's uses multiplied. Well into the 20th Century, chestnut, a fairly rot resistant wood, provided telephone poles and railroad ties, helping Americans build a growing technocracy. The wood found use as interior trim, in crafting furniture, and in constructing long-lasting outbuildings. The tanning industry relied upon chestnut as its main source of tannin for curing heavier leathers. And, of course, the nut itself entered into folklore, a fixture of the winter holidays. Chestnut's utility made it the most valuable tree throughout Appalachia and New England.

David Hume argued that aesthetic taste proved one of the key areas in which humans would never find consensus. The American chestnut, though, failed to agree with this philosophic truism. Americans loved the flavor of their very own chestnut. With a thinner shell than other nuts, the chestnut, upon roasting to free aromatic oils, would be extricated from its paper shell with a slight incision and some prodding with thumbs. A slight buttery taste combined with hints of newly-shelled peas and a subtle sweetness all its own made the nut an addictive indulgence.

Hume never considered evolution's role in influencing the flavors of natural foods, an unsurprising fact as his work pre-dates Darwin's by nearly a century. By the time humans arrived on the scene, fruits and nuts had endured a lengthy selection process, points out Tim Flannery in *The Eternal Frontier: An Ecological History of North America and its Peoples.* (p. 239) Squirrels and other nut eaters preferred the tastier nuts, giving those species reproductive advantages. Successful species would also tend to have greater nutritional value and easily accessed fruits. Flannery concludes that nut trees, upon human contact, were "an already domesticated crop, but it was squirrels rather than humans that had done the selecting."

Throughout Appalachia, kids would gather the nuts, earning up to $10 per bushel. Autumn became a time of relative wealth for the laborious many willing to scoop up the fruit. Given the tree's penchant for dropping all its nuts simultaneously, fiscally sharp youth would sneak out windows at night to check their trees. Once ready, the nuts fell like rain, a sound some elderly citizens recall wistfully. Pounding on and shaking trunks helped loose stubborn nuts clinging to their burs. What the kids missed fattened domestic and wild hogs, turkeys, and other woodland creatures consumed, contributing to their bulk in time for the cold winter.

Train cars filled with the nuts wended their way to New York City and other dens of urbanity where curbside venders wielded portable roasters, hawking the delicacy to passers-by. Given the October and November ripening, chestnuts appeared just in time for the Christmas holiday, earning their fame in the popular "Chestnuts Roasting on an Open Fire." Today, children sing that carol without ever knowing a chestnut or, perhaps, an open cooking flame.

Of course, little if any of this vast history came to poor Herman Merkel's mind as he perused the New York Zoological Park's stand of American chestnuts in the summer of 1904. Scattered yellow and ochre tracks dotting the bark of chestnuts caught his attention; these colorful blotches had not been observed before. By 1905, what was evidently an epidemic had spread to an estimated 98% of the chestnuts with the tell-tale markings evident below girdled trunks and branches. Merkel, the park's head forester, suspected a fungus of some sort which "attacks the live and apparently sound bark of twigs, branches, and limbs. The age and thickness of the bark present no obstacle, nor does the fungus seem to have any preference for susceptible points, such as crotches and eyes." He reported these findings in the pages of the New York Zoological Society's annual report and spread the word to colleagues.

Merkel's description of the disease, possibly the first written account—at least in English, offers a graphic depiction of afflicted trees:

> "To the casual observer the first visible sign that the disease has fastened itself upon the tree is the wilting of a portion of foliage for no apparent reason . . . . Upon closer inspection there will be found a ring of dry bark completely encircling the base of the wilted member, and in a short time the spore bearers of the fungus will be scattered thickly over the entire surface of the dry bark. These spore bearers are about the size of a pinhead, and at first are of the color of raw sienna, turning a dark umber with age."

A careful observer, Merkel watched one infection take only 21 days to girdle and kill its host tree.

Little did Merkel know that his observations would still be read a century later. His writings heralded what is arguably the greatest ecological and one of the worst economic catastrophes of the 20th Century, focusing its blow upon the environmentally resourceful citizens of Appalachia.

Flora Patterson, the US Bureau of Plant Industry's mycologist, examined samples of the fungus which she placed in the genus *Cytospora*, the first of a litany of genera claimed by the tricky ascospore fungus. She recommended that all infected branches and limbs be cut and burned and all trees be sprayed with a common panacea for plant diseases of the day, Bordeaux Mixture, a solution of lime and copper sulfate.

Merkel followed her advice, requesting $2000 to begin chopping and spraying. Pruners attacked 438 trees with alacrity, leaving many standing as bare trunks. The

Niagara Gas Spraying Company provided a sprayer complete with a 150-gallon tank and an 8-foot tall, platform-mounted tower for $175. With carbonic acid gas supplying 1,200 pounds of pressure per square inch, the device launched a mist of "potato strength" copper sulphate solution—4 pounds of copper sulphate to 10 gallons of water—to the injured trees. A crew of three, two sprayers and a driver, could treat an average of four trees per day—not exactly a rate speedy enough to save the East's great forests, let alone the thousands of chestnuts in New York proper. A photo from Merkel's original publication shows the horse-drawn contraption, some sixteen-foot ladders and one pruner 20 feet up the tree hosing down the specimen.

Merkel remained skeptical of the costly and time-consuming treatments: "Just how far we have checked the progress of the disease is a matter of conjecture until the growing season reveals the facts." As countless farmers, landowners, and chestnut lovers would learn soon enough, the treatment had little or no effect on the deadly fungus.

William Murrill, mycologist with the New York Botanical Gardens, began early work to identify the fungus responsible for the new disease and describe its mode of killing trees. By testing pure cultures of chestnut, Murrill concluded that the fungus could only attack trees through abrasions of the bark or through lenticels, pores in the bark that allow gases to pass to the cambium. The fungus was baptized *Diaporthe parasitica* by the mycologist, in conflict with Patterson's identification.

Murrill's description of the disease's epidemiology reads like the script for a horror film:

> The fungus works beneath the cortex in the layers of inner bark and cambium. Its presence is first indicated by the death of the cortex and the change of its color to a pale brown, resembling that of a dead leaf. Later the fruiting pustules push up through the lenticels and give the bark a rough, warty appearance; and from these numerous yellowish-brown pustules millions of minute summer spores emerge from day to day in elongated reddish-brown masses, to be disseminated by the wind and other agencies, such as insects, birds, squirrels, etc.

Despite all this information, Murrill had few ideas on how to conquer the fungal invasion.

By the time Murrill's writings hit the press, the blight had been reported in Connecticut, Massachusetts, New Jersey, Maryland, the District of Columbia and Virginia. Further south in Georgia and Alabama, several chestnuts succumbed to unidentified maladies, though Murrill's research of die-offs at the Biltmore Mansion in North Carolina found no sign of the fungus, leading him to believe that death was caused by "poor soil, forest fires, the chestnut beetle, and the disturbance of natural forest conditions in various ways." The American chestnut did not stand alone in its susceptibility. Closely related chinquapins (*Castanea pumila*), a smaller shrublike native, and Japanese chestnut (*Castanea crenata*) showed signs of the disease.

Murrill offered rather pessimistic advice for owners of chestnut: "Owners of standing chestnut timber within the affected area are advised to cut and use all trees, both old and young, that stand within half a mile of diseased trees." His goal, to retard the progress of the disease, while honorable, had little effect on the rapid spread of blight, in part because so few took his advice. He also advised Europeans not to import any stock from the States to preserve their chestnuts.

For denizens of the cities, the American chestnut provided both aesthetically pleasing greenery and cooling shade. Roads lined with the trees served as vehicular cathedrals as the similarly doomed Dutch elm did in my youth; driving down the emerald tunnel of arching branches offered a transcendent security, a womblike feeling of oneness. The trunks and foliage helped disguise urban existence, supplying a park-like atmosphere not easily replicated by smaller trees.

American chestnuts also boosted property values and helped maintain class distinctions in the money-centric world view developing in these former colonies. A grove of giant chestnuts announced status the way a classic Steinway or bottles of Moët & Chandon would, though the trees stood out better from a distance. Needless to say, wealthy chestnut owners would never let their treasured trees disappear without a fight.

Murrill and Merkel's concerns about the disease were not shared by all. In 1908, New York State Botanist Charles Peck waxed optimistically:

> Wherever I have been this summer the chestnuts are free from the disease. I do not think the chestnut is doomed. There are antidotes in nature to the excessive increase and ravages of such destructive agents, and, so far as I know, no such agent has ever been able utterly to annihilate any other member of creation. (Country Life in America, 1908)

The agreeable professor obviously lacked the knowledge of extinction one would assume of a person in his position. Likely, he held a rather Biblical theory of species as natural kinds, permanent and necessary cogs in the workings of Nature. Nonetheless, the historical record notes a multitude of extinctions, many in Kingdom Plantae. His placid demeanor would be readily denounced by anyone familiar with severe epidemics. His blind optimism serves as example of how an educated man can be willfully ignorant.

Not all approached blight from a biological perspective. The early Twentieth Century had its share of citizens ready to blame the chestnut death on the general moral depravity of the United States. The New York Times reported that a few wrote to the Botanical Gardens to argue the blight was "a scourge for sinfulness and extravagant living"; they maintained that personal prayer or religious revival might stop the disease in its tracks. Other less-than-scientific minds suggested filling holes in chestnut bark with sulfur or rusty nails, as if any nostrum dreamed up might alleviate the trees' condition. Perhaps every age has its opportunists ready to claim AIDS as

God's wrath on homosexuals or plant diseases as that same divine power's revenge against blaspheming dilettantes.

The laity also offered up a grand array of explanations for the death of chestnuts. As forestry historian George Hepting noted in the Journal of Forest History, "The blight was said to be due to burning the woods or not burning the woods; to too little or too much lime; to bugs, the weather, the moon, and various other strange agencies." Like any unexplained phenomena, absurd explanations abounded. Philosopher David Hume's conception of causality remained, for many, a foreign notion, and Occam's razor proved equally useless when fantastic conjecture provided more popular foolishness. Why favor reason when so many apocalyptic theories hold such great intrigue?

General paranoia over chestnut started a particularly frightening rumor of human deaths in Connecticut. Newspapers and the rumor mill circulated stories of several confirmable deaths bearing a slight correlation with consumed blighted chestnuts. When asked about the alleged deaths, J. Franklin Collins told those assembled at the 1913 Northern Nut Growers Association annual meeting, "There have been, so far as I know, about 15 cases of supposed chestnut poisoning in the vicinity of Hartford with five deaths . . . . [All] that I can say is that there is no doubt about the cases of illness and it is impossible to dissociate the eating of chestnuts from the possibilities." (NNGA 4 (1913), p. 29.) No connection between blight and deaths ever surfaced; these deaths were isolated incidents.

Numerous less than honest souls sought profit from chestnut's imminent demise. Self-proclaimed "tree surgeons" scoured towns for easy marks, warning the poorly informed that their chestnuts would certainly die without treatment. While the claim proves patently true, it rhetorically hid the sad fact that the treatments offered no benefits. Indeed, many actions would actually hasten the trees' demise. Any dramatic healing—a mysterious powder sprayed over the ground surrounding the tree, dyes injected into the wood, sprays applied to branches and foliage—would impress the owners who'd pay an inflated sum to save their beloved shade producers. Placebos, though, have minimal effect on organisms lacking the cognitive ability to be deceived. The huckster trotted off to the next willing fool, nimbly stuffing the newly-gained folding money into deep pockets.

By 1911, the blight had spread to at least ten states. At first, focus had been on saving individual ornamental trees at great cost. Skeletons of dead chestnuts proved an aesthetic blight on the homesteads of Long Island, where large trees had provided shade and beauty. Teddy Roosevelt's Sagamore Estate, appearing as some ghostly woody graveyard, had more than 1,000 afflicted chestnuts waiting to be destroyed. Proving a democratic disease, the blight even ripped through the wealthy estates of John D. Rockefeller and Helen Gould. Able to throw lots of money at the problem, these millionaires hired foresters and laborers to carefully examine and treat their trees, all to little effect.

Eventually, strategy switched from saving individual ornamental trees to determining a means of rescuing the vast forests of chestnut across the eastern seaboard.

Haven Metcalf, a forest pathologist with the US Department of Agriculture, weighed in heavily with a plan to save the forests. He noted that while the blight moved slowly in a line over the landscape, like a forest fire, oftentimes the fungus would jump several miles, just as the fire would send forth embers on the wind, to establish a locus of infection ahead of the line.

Metcalf proposed establishing a network of "scouts" who would patrol the woods for isolated infections by the fungus. Because spotting the fungus proved tricky, the scouts would need advanced training; Metcalf wanted trained plant pathologists and botanists to lead this mission. College students could also be enlisted "for the summer vacation at least" though their training would need to be extensive as any failures to spot isolated infections could destroy the whole project. In addition, the scouts would take samples to be analyzed in laboratories set up for just such purposes.

Foresters would need to remove all signs of fungus: "The marked trees should be cut down . . . . The bark and brush should be piled over stumps and, as soon as practicable, burned." By having foresters enact one task and botanists another, Metcalf hoped to create "rivalry" between the groups to promote efficacy. Each group would compete with the other to prove their effectiveness. These workers performing their work on a large enough scale, Metcalf believed, would "result in the control of the bark disease."

Impractical as it may seem, this plan—requiring an army of plant experts and labor tramping through the woods in an on-going quest to eliminate every chance occurrence of chestnut blight—became the foundation for the most significant effort to fight chestnut blight. The Commonwealth of Pennsylvania enacted legislation establishing "The Commission for the Investigation and Control of the Chestnut-Tree Blight Disease in Pennsylvania" with hopes of arresting the blight. Their naiveté concerning forest pathology becomes evident when we recognize that no one condemned this plan for introducing herds of wood-bound specialists likely transporting blight spores on their own boots and clothing.

Metcalf admitted structural problems with his plan. Most importantly, he recognized that the federal government lacked the legal power to address chestnut blight at a national level. Instead, states held the power to tackle the problem. Naturally, some states would be more or less inclined to address the blight than their neighbors, decreasing the chances of stopping the blight's spread. Likewise, individual landowners might not cooperate with state officials. "A single indifferent or obstinate person can nullify the efforts of an entire community," notes Metcalf, of the limits of communal action. Awareness of these issues would later prompt the US Congress to enact legislation to more effectively deal with epidemics; chestnut, though, would never benefit from such laws.

Metcalf had one ace up his sleeve. A preliminary test of his methods performed in the region within 35 miles of Washington, D.C. had apparently eliminated the chestnut blight. The test, initiated in 1908, removed all infected stock and, as of 1911, disease had not resurfaced. The pathologist noted that the extreme measures would only work if carried out on a large enough scale. Like surgeons removing all traces of a cancer, workers would need to eradicate all chestnut blight in the United States. If not, spot infections could expand to re-infect blight-free zones.

Like other plant pathologists, Metcalf advised owners of chestnut woodlots within infected areas to "convert their trees into lumber as quickly as possible." Owners listened and, subsequently, earned short-term profits. The real downside of this advice, though, may lie in the destruction of any resistant trees in the region. When an epidemic strikes, be it plant blight or human influenza, biological differences may offer protection to a fraction of the population. We will likely never know if a few of those millions of trees held the genetic key to surviving the fungal plague.

When the blight struck Philadelphia in 1911, Pennsylvanians began to organize their opposition. Before then, the Federal government had kicked in a few hundred dollars a year to fight the blight, not enough to be a pittance. Americans garnered a meager $5000 from Congress in 1911, followed by appropriations of $80,000 for each of the two following years. Employing the Federal Reserve Bank of Minneapolis' Consumer Price Index calculator, $5000 in 1911 would translate to roughly $100,000 in 2005. $80,000 then translates to $1.5 million in 2005.

The government funded too little too late. R. Kent Beattie, who had served under Metcalf and led federal initiatives to stop the blight, noted that in the decade from 1913 to 1923, the blight spread over Virginia, moving 24 miles a year. Metcalf's attempts to stop spot infections had little or no impact on the line of plague marching slowly yet steadily across the landscape. Metcalf's crews may have won some battles but they had no strategy for winning the war. The blight simply overwhelmed them.

In 1911, plant diseases and insect pests of foreign origin finally pushed the US Congress to pass a law, the so-called Simmons Bill named after the Niagara Falls Representative who introduced it, limiting importation of foreign plant stock. Chestnut blight was only one of many plagues attacking US crops and forests. White pine blister rust, gypsy moths, the San Jose scale, the Mediterranean fly (now called the "Med-fly," a serious threat to Californian citrus crops), and potato wart were a few of the big name problems already established or threatening to cross US borders. Overall, insect damage alone caused an estimated loss of $1 billion annually in 1911 (roughly $20 billion in 2005 dollars). Plant diseases, including chestnut blight, probably accounted for another $1 billion in losses.

Charles Marlatt, of the USDA's Bureau of Entomology, described the various threats to US agriculture in an article, "Pests and Parasites: Why we need a National law to prevent the importation of insect-infested and diseased plants" that appeared in the April 1911 *National Geographic.* He credits a small number of nurserymen prioritizing the "freedom of their operations" over national welfare for preventing Congress from establishing quarantine laws. The United States, Marlatt argued, became a dumping ground for other nations' waste and diseased plant stock; almost all other countries had laws to forbid or restrict importation of plants.

Finally, in 1912, 14 years of work led the US Congress to pass the Plant Quarantine Act. While chestnut blight had been one of the reasons for the law, the American chestnut earned no benefits from the legal action which came too late.

The 1914 and 1915 Congressional appropriations to fight the disease declined significantly, as vigilant fighters abandoned the battle. Writers often cite 1915 as the year that Americans conceded their war against chestnut blight, though individual landowners continued to wage personal campaigns.

From 1915 on, hope for saving the chestnut waned, with brief interludes of excitement over some miracle cure that quickly failed. Over 300 articles made the reference bibliography for chestnut from 1900 to 1920. The following two decades had barely fifty articles, several which dealt solely with utilizing dead trees.

The price of chestnut timber remained strong throughout the blight years as supplies steadily dwindled. The Forest Service identifies a peak of 663.9 million board feet cut in 1909. Twenty years later, 269.9 million board feet were produced, dropping to 84.7 million in 1943, and 4.4 million in 1960. Railroad ties dropped off more drastically, from 8 million sold in 1908 to 115,000 in 1931.

Wall Street's crash of 1929 coincides with a brief moment of hope for chestnut. At a Mont Alto, Pennsylvania forester's conference, research forester John Aughanbaugh enumerated several reasons for thinking the tree was bound for a comeback. He cited healthy shoots, some even providing nuts, a key sign of chestnut's recovery. The blight seemed to attack second and third generation growth with less vigor as several more cankers were needed to kill these emerging shoots. And some cankers appeared to heal partially. Professor J. F. Collins speculated that the surviving chestnuts might have higher degrees of resistance than their dead predecessors. Nonetheless, Aughanbaugh tempered his excitement, noting, "The disease is still too heavily entrenched in the forests of Pennsylvania to hope for a speedy recovery of the chestnut."

THE PENNSYLVANIA CHESTNUT TREE BLIGHT COMMISSION

Pennsylvania Governor John K. Tener, in the absence of federal leadership, pushed to organize a coalition of states to eliminate chestnut blight. On April 10, 1911, he sent a letter to the Commonwealth's Senate and House of Representatives. Since the blight had not established itself west of the Susquehanna River and north of the Blue Mountains, Tener hoped, "by prompt action on the part of the State, to prevent further damage." He continued:

> "If this disease can be held within the southeastern portion of the State, it will mean the saving of the wild chestnut trees in the other parts of the Commonwealth, the value of which extends into the millions of dollars.
>
> "I therefore recommend that the Legislature give immediate attention to this important subject and that a Commission be created with sufficient power and appropriation of moneys to determine upon and employ efficient and practical means for the prevention, control, and eradication of this disease." (Final report of Commission, p. 22.)

The legislature introduced legislation creating the Commission the very next day, giving the body $275,000 and "almost plenary power" to meet the Governor's mandate. Tener signed the bill on June 14, 1911, and on August 23rd, the Commission began its work.

The legislature granted the Commission "power to use all practical means to destroy the chestnut tree blight." These means included the ability to examine trees on any private property for the blight. Property owners needed to follow the Commission's suggested remediation, with the right to appeal any findings within ten days. If commissioners or their employees established a quarantine zone or destroyed any trees, owners would be reimbursed at the prevailing stumpage rate. Anyone failing to meet the Commission's requirements could face misdemeanor charges, punishable with a $100 fine or a month in jail.

Written accounts note that private landowners worked diligently to meet the Commission's requests. People held a united front in the quest to defeat the fungal invader, even when asked to sacrifice their prized trees.

The Commission hired 30 field operatives to cover the entire commonwealth which, having driven across Pennsylvania a few times, strikes me as a rather small number. Given that about one-third of the state had already fallen to blight, inspectors looking for new loci of infection would only need to cover two-thirds of the state, approximately 30,000 miles square. In other words, each inspector faced the daunting task of examining 1000 square miles, an area equivalent to a square measuring roughly 31 miles on a side.

The commissioners and their crew labored to educate the public of the blight's presence. Museum exhibitions, talks to civic groups, work with children's organizations all helped spread the word. Oftentimes, agents would correct poor practices, such as tree surgeons who climbed tall chestnuts with spikes, stabbing many new holes that would promote infestation. They also listened to the many folks offering nostrums to counteract the blight, never finding a truly effective means from the concerned citizens and hucksters offering these alleged cures.

Immediately, Pennsylvanians enlisted a hybrid of Metcalf's and Murrill's early plans to fight the blight—removing all chestnut within established disease zones, most of southeastern Pennsylvania, while removing any infected trees outside those areas. Word spread to private landowners who, in most cases, followed suit.

Individual trees, mostly the larger specimens surrounding homes, received the utmost care. Owners were advised to employ gouges to remove any blighted bark, keeping the implements "scrupulously" sharp at all times. Then, by applying tar or paint to cover exposed cuts, workers could protect the tree from insects and blight. Like grafting, this procedure required careful concentration and a practiced hand to remove the fungal infection without damaging the tree. Only those wealthy enough to field a crew of trained workers to monitor and treat their prized chestnuts would be able to employ this treatment that, ultimately, saved the treated trees for a year or two before blight finally prevailed.

Governor Tener knew that Pennsylvanian's labors would prove futile unless other states also fought the spread of the fungus. He sent invitations to representatives of all chestnut-bearing states, the Canadians, and several government agencies for a conference in Harrisburg in February of 1912. In his opening remarks, Tener stated his goal directly: "Unless this disease be stopped by concerted action among the States, it is certain that within a few years very few living wild chestnut trees will be found in America." The conference drew the attention of President Taft who sent a letter of support, along with suggested readings.

Dr. Raymond A. Pearson, unanimously selected as Chairman of this Pennsylvania Chestnut Blight Conference, led the delegation with a rousing speech, quickly attacking some pathologists who urged waiting until researchers developed an effective plan. Characterizing such positions as "un-American," he drew audience applause with his observations:

> "It has been suggested that we should wait patiently until the scientists have succeeded in working out these questions in all their minutiae; that thus we may be able to accomplish our results more quickly. But that is not the way that great questions are solved. If we had waited until the application of steam should be thoroughly understood, we would be still waiting for our great trains and steamboats, which are the marvel of the age."

Thus did Pearson establish a false dichotomy of chestnut blight's opponents, those wanting more knowledge before acting, and those acting despite insufficient knowledge. He and many audience members trusted that a solution would present itself as half-cocked hatchets, axes, and saws echoed through the besieged woodlots of the country. Their faith that technological progress would offer up a miraculous solution bears resemblance to people today assured that declines in oil production will magically be augmented by new oil-replacing technologies. Collected evidence supports neither view.

Choosing a plan of action proved no small task. Plant pathologists, foresters and other experts all had their opinions, many of which contradicted one another's' views. Murrill's early views and those of Metcalf later both had significant impact upon the Commission's members.

Murrill, though, had changed his tune. Instead of promoting careful trimming of young trees to remove signs of blight, the mycologist believed, according to the New York Times ("States Are to Act on Chestnut Blight, Feb 18, 1912), that "large sums of money appropriated to check [the disease] at the present time will be practically thrown away." No means of countering the disease had surfaced to date, Murrill argued, so any Herculean efforts would be wasted.

The Washington success story touted by Metcalf drew Murrill's criticism as well:

> "The publication of the extermination of the chestnut canker in the vicinity of Washington, D.C., upon which experiment the requests for appropriations elsewhere are said to be founded, cannot be relied upon. Within less than a month after Bulletin 467 appeared the disease was located at several points near Washington, some of the trees affected being of large size and apparently having suffered for several years from the attacks of the fungus." (NYT, Feb 18, 1912)

Instead, Murrill repeatedly argued that not a single grove or tree had been saved by Metcalf's or anybody else's methods. Throwing money at chestnut rescue was akin to "a doctor called to a bad case [writing] a prescription knowing at the time that it would be absolutely useless." Unless a proven practice with a good chance of achieving positive results was developed, Murrill would oppose funding further chestnut rescue operations.

Murrill became a target for advocates of action; his knowledge of the chestnut blight had little value as a jingoistic "let's get the blight" fervor developed. Professor J. Franklin Collins of USDA closed his slide presentation with an interesting analogy with fire fighting in the congested downtown of New York City. Given the city's increasing density, fire brigades of the day met greater challenges in arresting blazes. Despite a commission called to devise more effective ways to fight fires, the New York Fire Department continued to respond to fires. Likewise, Americans, he maintained, should act upon the chestnut blight disease: "The fire is burning too fast for us to wait for the reports of experiments which will take from two to ten years time to carry out."

Then Professor Fred Stewart from the New York Agricultural Experiment Station entered the fray with a well-reasoned paper addressing the developing dichotomy of immediate action versus research. Establishing the problems with Metcalf's claims of eradicating blight around the District of Columbia, Stewart went on to show the scientific problems with Metcalf's approach. First and foremost, Metcalf failed to establish a control population to determine if his method worked. "Weather conditions may have been unfavorable for the spread of the disease," argued Stewart, citing the fact that fungal diseases often have periods of inactivity. Metcalf's findings meant little in scientific terms; his work should be seen as anecdotal at best. Then Stewart raised the *coup de grace* to his argument—soon after Metcalf released his paper, Stewart discovered blight at several sights in the alleged blight-free zone.

Without responding to Stewart's careful arguments, J. W. Harshberger repeated the general call to action fueling the conference. Ignoring scientific knowledge, Harshberger appealed to his listeners' patriotism and beliefs in conservation:

> "Pennsylvania is the Keystone State. She is so situated with regard to the other states of the Atlantic Seaboard that she occupies a central position, halfway between the North and the South. It would be the lasting shame of

> Pennsylvania if she would let the opportunity pass of taking some means of attempting to check the disease . . . In the future, when we look back on the history of the conservation movement in the United States, this movement in Pennsylvania will be held up as an example of a patriotic movement of the entire people in an attempt to prevent the destruction of our native forests, which are going all too fast."

He couldn't help himself from concluding with a profoundly racist comment to play to the audience. Explaining how a botanist friend had noticed a correlation between tree deaths and Italian immigrant settlements, Harshberger implied that perhaps the Italians held responsibility for tree maladies and even offered a newly coined term for this condition, "Dagoeatis." "So perhaps," he concluded, "the trees which were killed on Long Island suffered from a form of 'Dagoeatis." Harshberger's comments, while racist and falsely placing blame, captured the sentiment of many participants in the conference.

Another recurring theme in the conference centered on extremes of weather and their impact upon chestnut. Some presenters blamed the entire blight epidemic on an on-going severe drought that eroded the constitutions of American chestnuts enough to allow the common fungus to kill them. George Clinton, of Connecticut's Agricultural Experiment Station, alongside denials that the fungus could have come from Japan, cited the severe winter of 1903-04 in conjunction with five years of drought as reasons for chestnut's susceptibility. Noting that fungal diseases usually prove more potent in wet conditions, he worried that his predictions might prove wrong: "What a deluge of trouble we may expect with the return of a few moist years!"

Concomitant with these climatic claims were beliefs that better weather conditions would end the pandemic. Optimists clung to such news as it offered a shred of hope needed to prevail against the overwhelming bad news concerning the blight. What better way to solve the problem than to think that blight will simply run its course? Professor George Barrus, from New York's Conservation Commission, expressed such a view: "I think that if favorable weather conditions are going to help to bring the chestnut back to increased vitality, so that it may be able to resist this disease, I think it should encourage us to eliminate as much of the infectious material as we can . . . ."

Professor Charles McCue countered these drought claims; his observations across wetter and drier stands in Delaware led him to conclude that all trees suffered equally in that state.

Discussions also turned toward other plant diseases and infestations. Massachusetts' claimed success at countering the destruction of gypsy moths which were denuding pine forests became a rallying cry to increasing appropriations for chestnut blight; only through liberal spending had Massachusetts earned its success. Peach-yellows, another fungal disease, had been defeated; some speakers claimed that chestnut blight could be dealt with the same way. Dr. J. Russell Smith, an expert on tree crops still spoken of highly by fruit and nut tree growers, used peach-yellows as well as San Jose scale and foot and mouth disease in cattle as examples of epidemics successfully challenged in order to inspire the audience to seek such a victory against chestnut blight.

As the conference wound down on February 22nd, the rhetoric heated up. William Murrill found himself under attack by several speakers, not the least being I.C. Williams, Deputy Commissioner of Pennsylvania's Chestnut Blight Commission. Murrill made a point-by-point rebuttal to criticisms aimed his way. His key point, that advanced infections would always escape the eyes of inspectors and that the disease could not be stopped by visual inspection, irked many a fellow attendee. But finding all signs of fungal blight would be equivalent to finding an indeterminate number of needles in thousands of haystacks, many which stood more than fifty feet tall. Ultimately, Murrill's view proved accurate once the blight wiped out the largest stands of chestnut in the country.

Harshberger offered a novel suggestion at the end of the conference, suggesting that some body establish a grove of pure American chestnuts, perhaps in Germany, to ensure a supply of nuts in the future. He argued that if the chestnut was doomed, then the parasitic fungi's days were numbered as well. Once the fungus was extirpated, the seed bank could provide new stock. This insightful idea received no recorded response at the conference.

In the end, the two-day conference passed a list of resolutions to direct the future of the States' dealings with the chestnut blight. The resolutions advised that each state, the Federal Government, and the Dominion of Canada all procure funds to wage economic war on the chestnut blight. They recommended that the US Congress appropriate $80,000 for that battle. Other resolutions covered: limits on the transport of diseased chestnut, plans to have "the Interstate Commerce Commission permit railroads and other transportation companies to name low freight rates so that chestnut products not liable to spread the disease may be properly distributed," and recommendations to have governments distribute information to landowners and the general population to educate people of the chestnut crisis. The most controversial recommendation, after appropriations, directed each state to establish boundaries "beyond which limits an earnest endeavor should be made to stamp out the disease."

After passing these resolutions, discussion continued with Murrill fielding many questions. One interesting person, amateur forester E.A. Weimer, offered his personal observations of chestnut blight, drawing laughs from some of the professionals in the audience. His novel way of locating blight in the canopy, though, made evident his skills at observation:

> "I want to tell you how you can see the blight even ninety feet in the air on what we call top-infected trees. You place your back directly towards the sun, half close your eyes and then look up along the top part of the tree, and if there is any blight in the cracks of the bark in a direct line with the rays of the sun, you will find the yellow spores highly illuminated. Under any other condition you would not see those spores, as they would be hidden by the shadows cast by the bark."

Weimer's knowledge supported Murrill's claim that careful inspection would still miss many infections, particularly those high up in trees.

Murrill left the conference despondent. The New York Times reported on February 22nd: "Dr. Murrill was the only delegate who voted against the adoption of the resolutions, which were drafted by representatives from fifteen States and the Dominion of Canada." The following day the newspaper quoted more details of Murrill's disappointment:

> "I was sorry to note that the delegation from New York gave so little heed to the excellent address of Prof. F.C. Stewart of Geneva on the subject. This is a technical question, and the State deserves and should have the guidance of the best authority in settling it. The opinion of one man competent to judge of such matters may easily outweigh the resolutions of hundreds of men who feel urged 'to do something' at once without properly considering either the methods or the consequences.
>
> "Many foresters present at the convention believe that the principles of conservation could be invoked in this case, and that if the chestnut tree were kept in a healthy condition it would resist the canker, but this is by no means the case. All native chestnut trees are attacked and killed regardless of this condition. The only kind of conservation that can be practiced is the gradual replacement of the chestnut by other trees not subject to this or similar disease."

Most conference attendees, though, derided Murrill's apparent surrender to the blight. They came for action and they left renewed to fight the disease—no matter how deficient their strategies proved. A victory would establish their reputations as astute citizens while eventual loss would prove their mettle as fighters and patriots. Such heroic aspirations meant little to the secretive fungus which quietly continued doing what it did best, girdling and killing American chestnuts.

In August of 1912, the US House of Representatives approved an appropriation of $80,000 requested by Representative J. Hampton Moore on behalf of the Pennsylvania Commission.

In the wake of the conference, the Commission continued its research and attempts at eradicating the blight. But, on July 17, 1913, Governor Tener dealt the death blow to Pennsylvania's chestnuts by vetoing a bill appropriating $100,000 to continue the Commission's work. The Commissioners told Tener that this sum would be inadequate to fight the blight effectively. Their original request for $275,000 had been reduced by the Legislature. Tener reasoned that insufficient funds would simply be wasted.

The Commission's Final Report, released in December of 1913, opened with Chairman Winthrop Sargent's reflections. He recognized the importance of Murrill's early warning: "In 1908, Murrill advocated cutting out all chestnut trees within half a mile of diseased trees, but this plan was never put into practice in New York." Then Sargent made the following accusation:

> " . . . the greatest conservatism has prevailed regarding the seriousness of the disease. The view that the fungus was native to America, and its great virulence due to winter injury and other temporary climatic effects upon the trees, has been strenuously advocated."

The Commission considered the fungus a "dangerous invader" and designed their plan of attack accordingly. But, alas, their efforts proved ineffective since the blight had already achieved too great a foothold on American shores.

Of the Commission's ultimate success, General Manager Mark Carleton commented, "it is a great satisfaction to be able to report constant progress to date, and the attainment of good, practical results." No novice to plant work, Carleton had successfully obtained a hardy variety of wheat from Russia earlier in his career, helping farmers respond to the stem wheat rust ravaging America's breadbasket. Was he simply trying to put a positive spin on the Commission's and his accomplishments to secure his position? One must wonder given the dissolution of the Commission after only two years. With hindsight, we can affirm that many of Carleton's claims in that report proved utterly false or short-sighted.

Carleton claimed that the blight had been "checked" in the west half of Pennsylvania which helped stop the disease from establishing itself in Ohio and parts of New York and West Virginia. Following Murrill's recommendations of 1908, before the mycologist became a doomsayer, allowed the Commission to delay the progress of the blight by five years in the western half of Pennsylvania, by Chairman Sargent's estimates. While a sizable pause in the fungus's march, that time did not allow for the determination of a cure. Sargent knew the blight would take those trees soon enough. He noted, "The Commission closes its work with regret, knowing well that the blight will now spread over the State without hindrance."

From this tragic loss that weighed so heavily upon the people of Pennsylvania, Sargent hoped that one lesson would be learned, "the necessity of more scientific research upon problems of this character; to be undertaken early enough to be of some value in comprehending, if not controlling, the situation." If only the chestnut blight had been stopped at customs or wiped out early in its North American career, the species might have remained vital throughout its range. "But instead [the blight] was permitted to enter, and to spread for many years without scientific notice, and for several more years without any organized attempt to control it, or even to study it seriously," bemoans Sargent, who asked the penetrating question still of import today: "Are we doing any better now with reference to the future?"

The Commission enumerated a list of unfinished tasks upon its cessation. Besides continuing research on various pests of chestnut and determining how removed wood should be utilized, the most significant project involved breeding experiments. By 1913, the chestnut blight had been found in China on trees determined to be resistant to the fungus. Chinese and Japanese chestnuts were imported to begin cross-breeding with remaining American stock. This early work would literally sow the seeds for contemporary missions to save our native species.

In 1920, Pennsylvanian E.A. Ziegler who had attended the Chestnut Blight Conference offered some perspective on popular views. He noted that chestnut blight had disappeared from the public's collective awareness. The situation had become hopeless: "There is absolutely no information to rest a shadow of a hope on, of [the blight] dying out from any cause except the exhaustion of food supply—the blotting out of all native chestnut." While prices remained good for the wood, he recommended selling all harvestable chestnut timber as quickly as possible.

THE BIRTH OF THE BREEDING PROGRAMS

Many researchers realized that the American chestnut's days were numbered early. Plans to help chestnut endure in North America fell into two categories; those that sought to find new chestnut stock from Europe and Asia to replace our native trees and those that hoped to save our tree in some form by breeding.

Chestnut propagation in North America predates the United States. In 1773, Thomas Jefferson, at home in Monticello, grafted a French Marron cultivar onto some American Sweet chestnuts. (The term 'Sweet' affixed to chestnut was often used to differentiate the American chestnut from the similarly-named, though quite different, horse chestnut—*Aesculus hippocastanium.*) Twenty-six years later, Eleuthere Irénéé du Pont de Nemours, settling in New Jersey from France, began collecting American chestnut stock which he forwarded to his friend, Madame Bonaparte, who eventually became Empress Josephine. Du Pont, who established his namesake Powder Mills, wrote to a French neighbor at Bergen Point, New Jersey, Mr. Prudhomme: "I greatly regret that all the chestnuts which were sent from France were spoiled, but I hope that we will be luckier next season, and I have taken steps to procure not only French chestnuts, but young trees as well, from different sources." The entrepreneur, upon relocating to Delaware in 1802, became a reliable source for European chestnut stock, providing saplings to affluent friends throughout Wilmington and Philadelphia.

The late 1800s found a resurgence in foreign chestnuts' popularity. The Japanese species, *Castanea crenata,* was first imported, according to chestnut historian Sandra Anagnostakis' careful records, by one S.B. Parsons in 1876. Known as the 'Parsons Japan' cultivar, these trees sold well and can be found throughout New England. New Jerseyite William Parry also imported 1000 grafted trees from Japan in 1882. Noted breeding wizard Luther Burbank brought in loads of Japanese chestnut stock he planted on his California farm. He's rumored to have grown ten thousand trees, selling various seedlings through the mail.

The natural next step, crossing the various species of chestnut to create hybrids, began in the 1890s, according to existent records. Anagnostakis identifies an amateur breeder in Illinois, George W. Endicott, who began introducing American chestnut pollen to Japanese stock. The 'Daniel Boone' tree resulted, a rarity given its ability to self pollinate. Dr. Walter van Fleet, a trained botanist, also started making crosses between chestnut varieties in 1894, starting with the cultivar 'Paragon', itself a potential hybrid of European and American species, pollinated with American pollen. Van Fleet would make hundreds more crosses, experimenting freely with chestnut and chinquapin species up until 1921. Some of these crosses may have contributed to later breeding projects in Connecticut and at Beltsville, Maryland.

When the blight struck, some of the hybrids from these early crosses showed resistance to the blight. Colonel Coleman K. Sober had 400 acres of 'Paragon' chestnuts at Paxinos, Pennsylvania. At the Chestnut Blight Conference, a representative for the micromanaging Sober showed a series of glass slides of Sober's operation. The good Colonel ran a meticulously clean orchard and boasted of eliminating some of the more pernicious pests from his chestnuts. He believed that his superior trees had resistance to the blight due to their heritage; he hypothesized they'd survive the scourge impinging upon his property.

Sober, sure of his success, continued to make his trees and nuts available throughout the country. At the 1916 meeting of the Northern Nut Growers Association, Haven Metcalf read a rather disturbing letter from Michigan Agricultural College botany professor Ernest Bessey:

> "Last December, the forestry department of the college ordered of Glen. Bros., Glenwood Nurseries, Rochester, New York, five 6-foot trees of the Sober Paragon chestnut . . . . I examined the trees in company with Mr. J.H. Muncie, one of our assistants, and found all the external appearances of Chestnut Blight with, however, only a very few imperfectly developed pycnidia.
>
> "I am calling this to your attention as the trees were doubtless infected when shipped. I feel that you ought to know that his firm is sending out diseased trees."

This case suggested that the blight's spread was accelerated by infected nursery stock moving within the United States. Plant quarantine laws would have little effect on such inter- and intrastate traffic in plants.

Another botanist in Albuquerque, a Dr. W.H. Long, inquired of Glen Bros. Nursery whether or not their chestnut had blight resistance. John Mayo responded for the company with some rather confusing rhetoric:

> "In regard to the blight . . . [I] would say that this tree is practically immune from [*sic*] this disease, and you would stand no more chance of having your chestnut trees infected with the blight should you plant them, than you would if you planted apple trees, of having them infected with the San Jose scale or peach trees, of the Peach Blight.

> "There are over half a million trees at the famous Sober orchard in Paxinos, Pa., none of which have the blight, and yet the blight rages all around them in the American Sweet Chestnut groves that are all through the mountain. Further evidence of its immunity from this disease we cannot guarantee. We think this speaks for itself."

Far from a proof of blight resistance, Mayo's words allow us to see how one individual might disregard public policies out of ignorance or hubris, perhaps fueled by greedy interests. Sober and others thought they knew better than the experts, erring on the side of danger (and, not coincidentally, profits) rather than caution.

Colonel Sober passed away in 1921, preceded by those half-million trees whose resistance he'd so proudly defended. No one really knows how effectively his assumed resistant trees accelerated the blight's march across Pennsylvania and into isolated groves far away in Michigan, Virginia, and southwards. The Michigan Agricultural College at East Lansing was spared due to observant botanists inspecting their stock. Certainly not all who purchased those Sober Paragons shared such powers of observation, unnecessarily putting their own plantings at risk.

THE AGE OF EXPLORATION

In the early years of blight, experts speculated on the original source of the chestnut blight. Given the blight fungus' similarity to known native species and the fact that mycologists had yet to establish a reliable taxonomy based on genetics, several specialists suspected that one of Appalachia's common fungi had mutated to become lethal. Others sought a foreign source for the deadly agent with eyes focused on "the Orient," most particularly China and eastern Asia.

Cornelius L. Shear and Haven Metcalf at USDA enlisted a young man, Frank N. Meyer, to scour the provinces of China for sign of the fungus. Meyer, while not a trained plant pathologist or mycologist, had a lifelong love of plants he had nursed under the tutelage of botanical great Hugo de Vries in his birthtown, Amsterdam. Coming to the States in 1901, the 25-year-old Dutchman traveled widely collecting plant samples and laboring in public gardens. A wanderer with keen powers of observation, Meyer caught the attention of David Fairchild who had founded USDA's Foreign Seed and Plant Introduction Section. Fairchild hired Meyer to explore the relative wilds of Asia for novel plant varieties, a job Meyer performed admirably until 1918 when, due to influenza, he fell from the rail of the Yangtze riverboat carrying him to Shanghai and drowned. Among the novel plants he sent back from Asia were soybeans and *Ginkgo biloba*.

Shear and Metcalf provided information of the chestnut blight fungus, along with a sample, to Meyer with hopes that he just might find sign of the fungus. Meyer had already completed several tours of duty collecting specimens throughout Asia, suggesting his usefulness in finding a source of the blight. Traveling the mountainous region north of Peking—an area where for most residents he would be the first

American met—Meyer found what he believed was the blight fungus on June 4, 1913. A small square bark sample two inches on a side, along with photographs of the fungus, sent to Shear and Haven confirmed Meyer's identification. Three months later, experiments showed that cultures of Meyer's sample killed American chestnut trees. Voila! Asia became the assumed home of the chestnut blight. Metcalf wrote Meyer, commending him for "the most important work done in plant pathology in the past ten years."

Meyer's essential work had hardly begun. In 1914, he sent scion wood (for grafting) from chestnut trees he thought showed resistance to the blight. A year later, he found the blight fungus in Japan. Upon arriving in Seattle on ship, as immigration officers and the press flocked toward him, Meyer yelled from the ship's ramp to Fairchild that Japan must be the source of the American blight. News of this discovery would put to rest much of the debate over the blight's origins. More importantly, though, information concerning the relative resistance of Japanese and Chinese chestnuts to the blight would pave the way for future breeding programs; perhaps that resistance could be bred into our American tree, rescuing the species from certain extinction.

Others also searched for favorable chestnuts throughout Asia. An interpreter and licensed guide who showed visitors the sights of Beijing in the 1920s, Peter Liu met R. Kent Beattie, the American researcher, on a tour he was leading. Beattie found in Liu an intelligent multilingual agent to expand the search for chestnut varieties. In one letter to Beattie dated November 4, 1929, Liu described some challenges he faced:

> "I beg to inform you that I went of Fa Hua Ssu on the October 12th, and get back to Peking on the 15th in case to catch the 'Malolo.' I got all the three different kinds of chestnuts you required. Altogether I bought 30 catties [one cattie equals approximately one pound] of 'Tiger Paw,' 30 catties of 'Pailu,' and 120 catties of 'Hanlu.'"

Liu employed his skill with languages to deal with fastidious customs agents, eventually delivering the sought-after nuts. The interpreter also provided long, detailed letters, giving a fortune in information about chestnuts and other cultivars of interest to Beattie and others.

BREEDING PROGRAMS

Walter van Fleet, who had been breeding chestnuts since the 1890s, worked for USDA's Division of Forest Pathology. In 1909, he undertook a project to produce blight-resistant chestnuts. Two years later, the work moved to an experiment station near Glenn Dale, Maryland. This program, the first official attempt at breeding new chestnuts, ran for 50 years, establishing a body of knowledge to direct later work.

In 1925, Russell Clapper began crossing American and Asian stock, working to develop blight-resistant stock. The goal of the program is best told in Clapper's words: "The objective during the first several years was to develop blight-resistant chestnut trees, and to accept whatever favorable characteristics, such as productivity, nut quality, and tree form that the hybrids displayed." Rather than a road map, the researchers followed every potential path they could find to its logical conclusions; by making as many permutations of crosses as possible, they hoped to chance upon their desired tree.

In 1927, USDA sent one its top forest pathologists, R. Kent Beattie, to Asia to find hopeful stock for the breeding program (where he met Liu). Beattie traveled China, Korea and Japan, finding 80 to 90 varieties of the Japanese chestnut His mission, to find trees producing comparable levels of tannin to American chestnut, was driven by the need for the chemical in southern tanneries. The blight coursed through the mountains of North Carolina and Tennessee, crippling tannin production in the process.

Over the next three years, Beattie shipped more than 250 bushels of seed from the varieties he found, including the Henry chinquapin and the Seguin chestnut, two smaller plants lacking winter hardiness. These nuts produced as many as 320,000 seedlings, by some reports, which were distributed to both federal and state foresters, tannin producers, and other folks termed "cooperators." Unfortunately, planting the saplings on prairie lands, where soil proved less fertile, killed most of the trees. The extensive drought of the early 1930s undoubtedly accelerated their demise. Researchers simply lacked information about conditions necessary for growing the exotic species.

Jesse Diller, who learned much under Beattie's tutelage, established 21 plots of Asian chestnuts throughout the east. By his report, "the plots aggregated slightly less than 32 acres, and accommodated nearly 22,000 trees spaced 8 by 8 feet." Observations of these groves allowed Diller and others to determine blight resistance of the stock, the form and rates of growth, winter hardiness, and ecological conditions favorable for growth.

Working with Flippo Gravatt, a USDA forest pathologist, Clapper narrowed his approach in 1932, opting to cross American chestnut with the Japanese chestnut (*C. crenata*) and the Chinese chestnut (*C. mollissima*) and selecting favorable progeny for further crosses. In 1946, his backcross of a 50% American/50% Chinese tree with an American—FP. 555—an old stump producing sprouts that grew in the open, just 300 feet from one of the chestnut plots—produced a tree that would come to be known widely as the 'Clapper' hybrid. The Clapper and other crosses were moved to southern Illinois' US Fish and Wildlife Service-run Crab Orchard National Wildlife Refuge in 1949. Folks pinned quite a few hopes on this apparently blight-resistant tree that thrived in an area known to hold blight.

Selecting a site for the Clapper and its comrades proved a considerable challenge. Diller began the search for a likely home for hybrids, contacting Dr. Lowell Tucker at

Carbondale's Southern Illinois University. Diller had no qualms about over-specifying the type of environment he desired for the trees:

> "The University would have to furnish a suitable planting site of approximately 0.4 acres, preferably a pole-sized, fully stocked stand of the following hardwood species: yellow poplar, northern red oak, white ash, dogwood, mulberry, American elm; lesser woody species such as papaw or spicewood; and the following herbaceous species: maidenhair fern, bloodroot, Solomon's seal, May apple. Such an association of plants is usually found in a protected site, as at the head of a draw, or slight ravine, generally on a north or northeast aspect, with a slope of 5 to 15%." (Journal of TACF, Vol. XI, #1)

Once the chestnut hybrids were planted in the understory of these larger trees, workers would kill all trees taller than five feet by girdling to bring in light for the chestnuts.

Illinois' university system lacked a plot meeting Diller's exacting conditions, so the search moved to the Crab Orchard National Wildlife Refuge, where Diller found four-tenths of an acre suitable for the planting. Diller's office communicated planting instructions: "Dr. Diller's instructions left with us were to the effect that you are to plant three of our chestnuts and then one of Dr. Graves', and continue on through the planting in this way."

After seven years of growth, one tree identified as both B26 and RBC-3146, the fabled Clapper hybrid, had achieved significant growth, reaching 1.6 inches diameter at breast height and standing 13 feet tall. By 1959, ten years since planting, the tree doubled its DBH and more than doubled its height to 30 feet. In 1962, Richard Jaynes, from the Connecticut Agricultural Station, took special note of the Clapper hybrid. With remarkable foresight, Jaynes requested scion wood with which he could craft new graftings to increase the number of specimens: "Could you send me scions from three or four of the best trees in the hybrid plot? My notes indicate that B26 and B59 are two of the best trees. Four seven-inch sticks from each tree would be fine." In case of tragedy—a lightning strike or other accident—the grafts would survive.

Word began to circulate about the amazing, seemingly blight-resistant tree. The Forest Service released a press release detailing the tree:

> "The largest, blight-free, forest-type hybrid, B26:#3146 USDA, occurs in the test plot near Carterville, Illinois. It is an American x Chinese backcrossed on to an American; the cross was made by R. B. Clapper in 1946. After 17 growing seasons, this tree measured 7.3 inches d.b.h. and 45 feet in height—an increase of 0.43 d.b.h. per year, and a height of nearly 2 feet 8 inches per year. It apparently has a high degree of blight resistance, as chestnut blight is present in the plot."

By 1968, the tree stood 63 feet tall and approached one foot diameter at breast height.

Alas, that year the tree began a long, slow decline as the blight finally broke through its defenses. Watched like a dying relative who frequently shows heart-rending signs of recovery only to succumb farther, B26 struggled to withstand the blight. But in 1977, an anonymous forestry technician who obviously lacked the sensitivity accorded more skilled bearers of bad news, sent Robert Clapper, Russell's son, the sad news: "Because of your past interest in the Crab Orchard Refuge B-26 Clapper chestnut, you may be interested to learn that the tree is dead." A latent infection, present for years, had finally killed the tree in concert with unfavorable growing conditions. The individual Clapper outlived its namesake breeder; Russell Clapper had died the day before Halloween in 1973. Fortunately, Jayne's grafts of the Clapper performed well in Connecticut, keeping the promising line alive for future work.

Russell Clapper also offered early speculation of the genetics involved in blight resistance. He theorized that two genes determined blight resistance, based on an observed 103:37, or approximately 3:1, ratio of resistant to susceptible individuals resulting from a cross. These findings are still debated today.

Though no official announcement was made, the Beltsville chestnut work ended in the early 1960s when the program closed. Frederick Berry, who took over the program in 1950 after Clapper's retirement, offered no reasons for the program's closure in his writings. Other writers and enthusiasts offered various reasons for closing the program, though the most likely relates to limited understanding of genetics at that time.

Having made thousands of crosses in laboratory and field, researchers noticed that resistance never developed in the tall timber-like trees. All resistant stock had a shorter, stooped or 'orchard-like' shape, resembling orange or apple trees. From these persistent observations, the inductive conclusion that genes for resistance were invariably associated with genes for undesirable growth followed. The technical term for this connection, "linkage," means that the genes fell close together on their chromosomes; unless a strange mutation occurred, all resistant trees would be squat trees. This conclusion must have had debilitating effects on morale. Also, the old guard of Gravatt, Diller, and Clapper had not found progeny to carry on their work. Higher powers at USDA recognized an opportunity to axe a program that failed to provide the results they wanted, letting the research quietly lapse as Diller, the last of the line, cleared out his office.

An interesting article by Diller and Clapper, published after both their retirements, examined renewed interest in chestnut. In 1963, *Reader's Digest* had run an article, "They are bringing back the chestnut tree," that beseeched readers to alert USDA of any surviving American chestnuts. *Outdoor Life* had run a similar piece back in 1957. The popular articles prompted a flood of nearly 2,000 letters from throughout the US and other countries, detailing chestnut encounters.

"Of the hundreds of twigs, leaves, and fruits that were forwarded to the Forest Service's Northeastern Forest Experiment Station for verification," wrote Diller and Clapper, "fully 60 percent proved not to be pure American chestnuts." Yet hundreds of Americans surfaced, half of which were within the native range. Optimistic thoughts led the researchers to believe that these rare natives had survived the blight thanks to an inherent resistance, but tests showed that 90 percent had been "blight-escaping" rather than blight-resistant. A brief hope proved mistaken once again.

Arthur Harmount Graves had been involved in chestnut work as curator of the Brooklyn Botanic Garden, a job he assumed in 1921 after teaching at Yale and Connecticut College. He owned several acres at his childhood home in New Haven and, in 1930, began breeding chestnuts on the land. For years, he'd considered such breeding as the only realistic hope for the American chestnut. Trees obtained from Beltsville started things out.

Before working with the Botanic Garden, Graves earned his keep by tooling around New York City on a motorcycle in search of surviving chestnuts. The scientist, in his thirties, set up a range of study, defined by a circle radiating 16 miles from NYC's town hall. His opera glasses served him well except on one occasion. "I was careful not to use them when anyone was looking, for on the second day of the survey I had been arrested on the charge of being a German spy!" he wrote in the article summarizing his findings.

At the junction of the Harlem and the Hudson Rivers, Graves found a clump of 40 healthy American chestnuts, after several days of failure. Another researcher directed him to a similar clump on Long Island. Graves speculated that the trees may have developed resistant "sports"—suckers arising from the rootstock that differed genetically from other parts of the plants. Careful study revealed that blight grew on these trees at one-fourth to one-third the rate it would grow on non-resistant trees. Perhaps these initial studies motivated Arthur Graves to devote the rest of his life to the perishing chestnut.

Graves, though never an official employee of the Connecticut Agricultural Experiment Station (CAES), let staff at the station, significantly the oldest such establishment in the United States—predating land grant colleges, know of his work. In the late 1930s, chief geneticist at CAES, Donald Jones merged his growing interest in chestnut recovery with the station's mission, beginning a long effort to save the American chestnut and reestablish chestnut in Connecticut.

Graves never claimed to want to save the American chestnut. Instead, he noted, "Our main purpose is to replace our now practically extinct American chestnut with a stock at least equally good for timber purposes and for nuts, and at the same time blight-resistant." Indifferent to the heritage of that resulting tree, Graves performed numerous open-air crosses where male parentage remained unclear; no one could say for sure which tree had supplied pollen. Many a breeder would consider such sloppiness unforgivable; Graves probably considered it a way of saving valuable time. The hasty botanist hoped to produce a tall, straight-growing tree that would be able to reach the forest canopy quickly and produce the quality of timber for which the American chestnut had been famous. He also desired a good nut tree. These two might be the same cultivar or they could be completely different hybrids. The key problem was to replace American chestnut with a functionally synonymous tree or trees.

Over the years, Graves worked with a number of graduate students who maintained affiliations with the Experiment Station. Hans Niensteadt and Richard Jaynes became key figures in mid-century chestnut work. Of Graves, Jaynes maintains the utmost respect. "He and his wife would read the classics to each other before going to bed," explains Jaynes who saw in Graves a renaissance man, not just skilled in the ways of botany but in all aspects of the true scholar. The wife in question was his third, the first two having died in wedlock leaving Graves a double-widow. Everyone loved Graves who insisted on sharing his voluminous knowledge in the field, often at the expense of work completion. His daily nap, under doctor's orders after severe health problems when Graves was in his early 50s, offered a guaranteed chance for young workers like Niensteadt and Jaynes to complete their labors.

Graves employed several innovative ways of keeping his trees alive. Possibly the most intriguing method, "inarching"—still visible in plantings sixty years old, involves bridging a girdled tree with opportunistic suckers. Graves would take a shoot from below a girdled section and sharpen its end which he'd insert into a T-shaped notch above the girdling. The clever graft, a bridge from healthy to afflicted tissue, would permit the tree to maintain the flows of sap, minerals, and water, effectively short-circuiting the blight's ability to kill all growth above the point of infection. Several trees boast multiple inarchings, appearing as if the trees had placed hands on hips.

The plantings, which now compose part of Connecticut's Sleeping Giant State Park, catalog global diversity of chestnut, with representatives of the twelve species Graves recognized as well as a few hundred hybrids for which Niensteadt and Jaynes were responsible. Graves sold the family land to Connecticut in 1949 with the proviso that 8.3 acres be reserved for chestnut research. If CAES ever quits their chestnut work, the state will gain full control of the land. The aging pathologist continued his work with chestnut until his death in 1963.

Richard Jaynes, a graduate of Yale's noted Forestry School, continued much of Graves' work, overseeing the trees often referred to as "the Plantation." In the late '60s, "Project Village Smithy" drew Jaynes's talents to central Virginia. A wealthy benefactor, Anne Valk, donated a 422-acre tract in Nelson County to the Lesesne Foundation which, in turn, gave the land to Virginia. The commonwealth established the Lesesne State Forest in 1969, with several acres devoted to chestnut. As Jaynes explained,

> "Project Village Smithy provides a unique opportunity to plant a large number of chestnut trees of varied origin and pedigree in one area to determine their performance . . . . By growing these second, third, and fourth generation hybrids side by side we will have a good measure of where we are and where we can go in the future toward breeding better chestnut trees."

The trees at Lesesne came from two sources: the Connecticut Agricultural Experiment Station, and Drs. Ralph Singleton and Al Dietz who had irradiated many nuts hoping to produce beneficial mutants. 5000 hybrids took root over the course of the springs of '69, '70, and '71. When Hurricane Camille dumped 27 inches of rain on the new trees in 1969, the grove fared well while the storm destroyed bridges, roads, and buildings throughout the area.

BLIGHT STRIKES EUROPE

European plant experts watched from afar as the chestnut blight ravaged American forests, wary that they might be next on the docket. In 1938, the blight began to show up on stock in many of northern Italy's research gardens, probably brought in on ornamentals imported from Asia. The European chestnut, *C. sativa*, proved susceptible to the blight which spread slower and took much longer periods to kill individual trees than it had in the States. By 1948, one-tenth of the chestnut groves of Italy had the disease.

But Italian trees began to show signs of recovery, first observed in 1950. After the above-ground parts of original trees died, the rootstock sent up shoots that had apparent cankers that seemed to heal. Italian forester A. Biraghi noticed this healing and hypothesized that the shoots had mutated, presenting this quasi-Lamarckian idea to a conference where his explanation met with widespread skepticism. Few could believe that such incredibly adventitious mutations would appear so quickly. Yet the observations could not be doubted; somehow conditions had changed allowing these trees to form calluses and survive where other trees had succumbed.

French agricultural researcher Jean Grente, deeply concerned for the welfare of his nation's chestnut industry, sampled the fungi from large swollen cankers growing on these trees. His cultures, rather than sporting the typical yellow hue identified with chestnut blight fungus, lacked pigmentation, appearing a milky whitish. Curious about these strange variants that he didn't recognize, Grente plated out some of the spores produced by the white colonies. The result, some white cultures and others that looked like typical chestnut blight, led him to conclude that the white-pigmented variety was chestnut blight in a changed form.

Grente tested the white variant on European chestnut and found that the white fungus lacked the virulence of the yellow form, leading him to label it "hypovirulent." Indeed, it caused cankers, but the growths proved non-lethal. The trees had time to respond to the fungal invaders. Pathogenic *Cryphonectria parasitica*—the agreed upon taxonomy for the blight, easily grows through all layers of bark, effectively spreading in obvious fan-like patterns as it kills the tree. Beneath the outer layers of bark, researchers noticed that the hypovirulent strains' mycelia failed to penetrate inner layers to the heartwood.

Sandra Anagnostakis at the Connecticut Agricultural Experiment Station explains Grente's next step, "He tried putting the hypovirulent fungus into trees with killing cankers. The killing cankers stopped expanding and the cankers, instead of being sunken—killing all the bark and wood, they were swelling up because the tree was responding in the tree's natural way. The tree was callusing and trying to wall off this invader." It looked like he might have found a tool to help save France's chestnut crop.

French farmers, though, obstinately protecting their chestnut orchards, refused Grente's offers of assistance. Many would not even allow the successful scientist onto their properties to inspect trees. Grente, frustrated, needed a way to communicate the importance of stopping the blight before it decimated the trees. His solution to the problem can only be described as sheer genius.

Anagnostakis related the story of the researcher's means of convincing chestnut growers to fight the blight. Grente and his wife procured a collection of felt in white, green, and orange from which they stitched tiny vests. Descending upon the local grammar school, they drafted the kids into performing a play, knowing that every relative for miles would come to see the grand spectacle. Grente banked on the strength of rural families. In the performance, the children sporting green vests played the healthy chestnut trees, as Anagnostakis tells the story, "standing there bravely producing nuts for everyone in the community." Orange-vest wearers attacked their verdant classmates, representing the blight attacking the beloved trees. White vests then interceded, saving the chestnuts from imminent death. The morality play sent Grente's message home.

After a few days, the exceptional researcher started getting calls from farmers who'd seen the play, claiming "I've seen something orange on my chestnut trees. Do you have any of that white stuff you can come put on them?" Grente had successfully connected with the farmers; now he had to procure funding to carry out this important work.

The French government, proving as stubborn as the chestnut growers, clung greedily to their purse strings, doling out insufficient funds for Grente's work on hypovirulence. They expected the scientist to study the more lucrative relationship between oak trees and France's infamous subterranean cash cow, truffles. Like the chestnut blight, truffles belong to the kingdom of fungi. So Grente devised a way to revolutionize truffle culture in France. By surface sterilizing acorns and growing them in a sterile environment, Grente created a host upon which he could introduce the truffle spores directly. Now farmers raise huge amounts of truffles simply by planting a grove of pre-treated oaks. His patent for this technique quickly earned him enough to establish his own private laboratory to study hypovirulence.

"They had huge stainless steel vats all around the room which were the things they use in industrial microbiology to grow penicillium and stuff like that," explains Anagnostakis. "Each vat had hypovirulence strains specific for a certain region. He had maps all over the walls. His maps would show a certain region where he'd isolated the strains. There were relatively few strains coming into France." Grente would mix up a large batch of hypovirulence for an entire district. The mycelia, in pellet form—another intriguing invention of Grente's, could then be distributed to growers throughout that region. Farmers simply made holes in a tree's bark, inserted a pellet, and closed the hole up with some tape to treat their trees. Hypovirulence moved throughout the tree. France's chestnuts were saved.

Hypovirulence refused to work so simply on American chestnut, but that's a story for later chapters.

GATHERING INTELLIGENCE

Fighting the blight initially created quite a bit of confusion because researchers knew so little about the fungus perpetrating the crime. Plant pathologists began to answer some of the questions concerning the fungus that had perplexed many who had difficulty even determining a genus for the beast.

USDA pathologists lead the charge to identify and describe the fungus which had, by popular opinion, gained the name *Endothia parasitica*. The specific name remained from Murrill's early baptism, clearly descriptive of the tiny organism's impact upon chestnut. Mycologists of the day, lacking many of the methods and tools of modern experts, relied upon herbarium and collected field samples. Often, though, determining the characteristics identifying samples required employing microscopes and growing cultures. An initial diagnosis of chestnut blight had to be followed by an attempt to infect greenhouse chestnuts. If the cultured fungus appeared and acted the same way that *E. parasitica* did, scientists concluded that the organism was indeed chestnut blight. Such tests could take several months, particularly when testing the lethality on chestnut.

Cornelius Lott Shear, pathologist with the USDA, traveled to Europe for several months, consulting with mycologists, pathologists, and botanists to pin down the identity of our chestnut blight. By scouring collections and comparing samples, he became convinced that *Endothia* proved the appropriate genus for the disease agent. Yet he had to examine all available species within that genus.

Mycology is rife with terminology that sets my head swimming. Decoding common descriptions such as "Ascospores oblong fusiform to oblong ellipsoid, uniseptate when mature," becomes necessary to determine an identity. To shorten a long story, Shear and his colleagues accepted *E. parasitica* as a name. Their more important findings focus on the fungus's behavior.

Many of the early speculators of chestnut's fate prophesied that the parasitic fungus would disappear once it had exhausted the supply of chestnut. In theory, groves could be reestablished years after the last chestnut died. In practice, though, *E. parasitica* had the capacity for living on several other hosts. In 1909, J. Franklin Collins found it on black oak, *Quercus velutina*, and Haven Metcalf confirmed its identity in his Washington lab. Others found the blight fungus living on the bark of dead black oaks and white oaks, *Quercus alba*. Shear and others showed that the blight fungus could live on a variety of oaks, though only rarely killing them. Chestnut shares its family lineage, Fagaceae, with the oaks.

The researchers also inoculated a very wide variety of woody species, from oaks and maples to grapes and sassafras, to see if the fungus proved lethal. This way they would have an advanced warning about future problems. Also, they might make some observations that would give chestnut a chance. Allegedly resistant species might offer some guidance to help "fix" our native.

Other mycological work solved a related mystery. During the second half of the 1800s, numerous reports of chestnut die-off precipitated from the southern states. An 1896 report from USDA's Division of Pomology noted these problems:

> "From causes not well understood there is a marked decline in the vigor of the chestnut throughout the broad area of territory in the southern states, where the white man found this tree among the most thrifty of the original forests . . .
>
> "Observation of the native chestnut growth in Maryland and Virginia discloses the fact that many trees are dying without apparent cause. In some sections this is attributed to the ravages of insect, in others to an unknown disease resembling blight." (p.78)

In Georgia and the Carolinas, chinquapins and chestnuts started dying as early as 1824. During the heyday of Pennsylvania's Blight Commission, speculation flew linking these southern tree deaths to the new plague in the northeast.

Margaret Milburn and Flippo Gravatt, pathologists with USDA, announced that a fungal root rot held responsibility for these deaths. The agent, identified in the genus *Phytophthora*—a genus familiar to many a nursery worker, attacked the roots of plants in wetter conditions before moving to drier stock once it established itself in an area. One key difference between *Phytophthora cinnamomi*'s action and the chestnut blight fungus lies in the fact the former kills chestnut completely, from root tips to apical meristem, while the latter leaves roots structures intact to send up new shoots.

ALONG COMES BURNHAM

The 1960s and '70s were slow years for American chestnut recovery. The USDA had closed its research program in Maryland. Many of chestnut's champions like Arthur Graves and Flippo Gravatt passed away, though some of Graves' students, most notably Richard Jaynes, carried on the work the best they could. Finally, though, chestnut recovery received a kick in the pants when near-Nobel Laureate Charles Russell Burnham began considering the chestnut problem.

If the Nobel Prize were a disease, Burnham would have been biology's Typhoid Mary, never succumbing to that malady to which so many collaborators succumbed. Coincidence alone fails to explain how Laureates like Barbara McClintock, George Beadle and Norman Borlaug came to share space with Burnham throughout his career. The professor also secured a following of intriguing and enthusiastic students who thrived in his classrooms. As a tree provides shade, Burnham provided inspiration to thinkers, novices and veterans alike. A few thoughtful words from him—and, given his pervasive knowledge, almost all words proved thoughtful—could spark an avalanche of ideas.

Burnham made his name at New York's Cornell University, one of the key figures in what came to be known as "the Golden Age of Corn Genetics," from 1928 to 1935. He and his colleagues, McClintock, Beadle, Marcus Rhoades, and Professor Rollins Emerson, discovered several aspects of genetics that allowed the science to move from the chance crossing of plants to systematic chemical and cytological knowledge. At last, the unseen 'gene' stood behind the diverse traits expressed by individuals, wielding its power on structured chromosomes possessed by living organisms. The corn genetics group paved the way for modern genetics which received its next big push when Watson and Crick depicted and explained the structure of DNA.

Burnham's immersion in genetics allowed him to take a surprisingly novel look at the chestnut data amassed. In the early 1980s, an emeritus septuagenarian Burnham became aware of the USDA's abandonment of their chestnut breeding program. A Wisconsin native, Burnham did not grow up knowing American chestnut. But in 1934, stationed at his first post-doctoral teaching position at West Virginia University, Burnham witnessed the dying chestnuts. He observed several trees still putting out flowering branches, though the trees were undeniably on their last roots. The memory would surface forty-five years later when Burnham discussed the Beltsville breeding program with former director Fred Berry. He described his reaction to materials sent by Berry, "I could not believe what I was reading. Others reacted similarly. In the USDA chestnut breeding program, the backcross method had not been used in the manner required to produce American chestnuts with blight resistance."

Looking at the data from a strict genetic perspective, moreover a well-honed and practiced genetic perspective, this elder scholar could see problems not evident to serious researchers ensconced in their work. Perhaps his position as an outsider also aided Burnham's vision as he remained unhindered by the burden of too much information.

USDA's breeding program fell victim to two major mistakes, in Burnham's written analysis. First, the geneticist took issues with USDA's willingness to accept any hybrid tree that exhibited desired traits. Reasserting the importance of a distinctly American species, Burnham insisted that his comprehension of genetics would permit the breeding of such a tree. He held that as few foreign genes as possible should compose that tree's genome. We remain in the dark as to whether this view stemmed from some odd botanical nationalism Burnham held or whether he followed some unidentified scientific principle.

The second problem lies in the fact that the USDA's tree could only be bred through clones. Burnham explains, "The USDA program had been terminated about 1960, possibly because they believed that they had attained their goal." The 'Clapper' tree, in Burnham's understanding, embodied that success, but the tree produced no nuts. The key way to create more Clappers was through grafting.

Burnham's account of the closing of USDA's program conflicts with others who insist that the researchers gave up because they opted for retirement and they believed that the genes for blight resistance and timber-growth form were linked, making the breeding of a timber-type resistant tree impossible. The paper trail on these issues remains scant and most of the researchers have passed away, leaving us wondering the true reasons for USDA's decisions. Most likely, Burnham misunderstood the government's reasons for closing the program, incorrectly concluding that the Clapper had signaled their success; Richard Jaynes and other researchers do not concur with Burnham's belief.

The tool Burnham suggested to breed resistant American chestnut, the "backcross method," offered "an efficient way of adding a desired trait to a cultivar that is satisfactory in all or most other respects." Geneticists had refined the technique, having used it for breeding crops since 1922. Essentially, an original cross of American with Chinese (or another resistant) tree produces slightly-resistant progeny that can be crossed back to American stock. Each successive generation has a higher percentage of American genes with varying degrees of resistance. By selecting for key desirable traits in each generation, the ultimate tree would be fully resistant and have a high percentage of American chestnut genes.

Burnham's argument convinced others like former University of Minnesota graduate student Philip Rutter who raises chestnuts in southeastern Minnesota. In 1983, Burnham drew together the support of several geneticists, plant breeders, nursery owners, a lawyer, and other useful folks and organized what would become the American Chestnut Foundation. The ACF has since become the largest organization working to breed an American chestnut that can be restored to the tree's native range.

While Burnham's American Chestnut Foundation proved only one of numerous programs to rescue American chestnut, it has since its inception earned a lion's share of attention in the media. Its definitively genetic approach also provides the ACF with the support of a genetically-biased scientific community. Yet the eastern woodlands have harbored other chestnut zealots, eager to implement their own plans. The next several chapters examine some of these groups and individuals in depth.

CHAPTER 2

"The disappearance of great classes and orders of life from the face of the earth . . . present something enigmatic and ominous . . . a *momento mori* which both demands and eludes comprehension. Compared to those disappearances, the manmade extinctions of species seem merely disgusting sequences for which it is necessary only to sort out and fit together the links: slaughter, poison, destruction of habitat, human hunger and cold greed, imported enemies, greed, ignorance, poverty, short-sightedness, indifference, greed. In both types of disappearances however, a form of life has been condemned to die without issue. Should humanity be willing, in greed and indifference, to assign to itself nature's awesome power of condemnation?

—William Service, narrating in *The Dinosaurs: A Fantastic New View of a Lost Era*, by William Stout

"For years, we have had to struggle to explain to potential supporters just *why* working to restore the American chestnut was not foolish and quixotic, but absolutely reasonable in terms of solid science, ecology, and cold hard cash."

—Philip Rutter, 1990, *Journal of the American Chestnut Foundation*

Western Virginia's roads provided a challenge unmet by the maps I used to navigate this foreign landscape. Two dimensions on paper refused to do the three-dimensional winding of infrequently labeled roads justice. For travelers unfamiliar with the region, Virginia's panhandle, what we'd call an arrowhead back home in the Midwest, drives a sharp wedge between Kentucky and Tennessee as if separating bickering neighbors. The steel of that wedge, the Appalachians, poses a major challenge for highway designers and drivers unaccustomed to sinuous drives. Besides Interstate 81, a major east-west thoroughfare connecting DC with the bulk of Virginia, the region remains free of major highways, hiding well outside the realm of southbound snowbirds and spring breakers

These byways, built as if the engineers had followed the path of an attention deficient salamander wending its way toward a distant pond, gyrate so haphazardly, I half expected to pass myself going the other way. My plan, to head northwest after driving through the Mount Rogers National Recreational Area where I'd camped the night before, proved risky. The map faltered once the planned route fell victim to "Under Construction" signs. I chanced a left onto a road American Map neglected to include in their gazetteer and hoped for the best. Luck and a general sense of direction eventually plopped me into the tiny burg of Meadowview, home to the American Chestnut Foundation's research farms.

If not for green signage declaring its presence, Meadowview would easily be confused for a mere intersection, a slight variant on the country I'd driven for days, with slightly denser clumps of buildings surrounded by meager fields and domesticated squares of forest. Lacking a strong tourist industry, the economic leg bolstering many of the surrounding communities, Meadowview relies on the Interstate's ceaseless flow for its persistence, a metallic river allowing occasional visitors to overflow its banks for the gas up in Meadowview. Five quieter miles down the road, the town would never have endured the indelible changes it's faced the last forty years.

An old unpainted barn emblazoned with the ACF logo, dominated by the scalloped-edged leaf of their signature species, alerted me on second pass to the discreet headquarters' presence. I noticed the grade school across the street before recognizing the Wagner Farm, one of three ACF research farms within a stone's throw of Meadowview. The ACF headquarters, a modest white one-story ensconced within a split-rail chestnut fence could easily be confused for someone's home, landscaped with shrubs, a grape arbor, and one Chinese chestnut in back. It certainly wouldn't draw the attention of itinerant drivers searching for a tourist attraction. On a sunny Monday morning in June, I stepped onto the front stoop to uncover Fred Hebard and Danny Honaker preparing for a morning in the field.

Hebard, who I'd only seen in pictures now 25 years old, no longer sported the auburn collar-length locks for which he'd stood out in group pictures. His hair, gone white, quietly lodges beneath his perpetual baseball cap. A quiet, unassuming fellow, he introduced himself and others in the room, suggested I wait a few minutes, and sneaked off to ready his gear—a handful of white bags, metal tags, and other odds and ends.

Honaker, the farm's mechanic, wore a t-shirt honoring #34 and held his signature sugar-laced beverage, the probable cause for his disproportionally extensive belly. The only time I'd see him without that plastic bottle of pop he'd have a cold sweet tea in his hand. Danny, I'd learn, had an affinity for anything gas-powered. The farm's fleet of work vehicles, particularly the two cherry pickers employed for pollinating large chestnuts, made up a cast of aging characters held together with minimal funds and Honaker's raw talent.

Various other folks lurked in the house's relative darkness, most appearing college age. Bookshelves held hundreds of texts about plant physiology, identification, ecology, and pathology, with accidental literature breaking the monotony of technical works. Hebard's desk, awash in white papers, open phone book, and a copy of Barbara Kingsolver's *Prodigal Summer*, provided evidence of a mind more attuned to work in the field than organization at home, a trait with which I readily identify. The Kingsolver interested me because rumor has it that one of the novel's protagonists was modeled on Hebard himself.

In the book, Kingsolver interweaves the tale of Garnett Walker, an ancient, solitary chestnut breeder who aggravates his more modern neighbors—particularly a similarly aged grandmother figure, with seemingly disparate stories set in the same environs. Walker, a cantankerous misanthrope, complains and crafts retributions for the numerous perceived wrongs dealt him, falling into disfavor in a community experiencing the rapid modernization it had sidestepped for decades.

Fred Hebard, married to Dayle, with two daughters, lacks the social conditions necessary for breeding such crankiness. The three women would never tolerate his grouchiness for long. His work on the farm requires overseeing a sizable crew at times, not a likely profession for someone with rough edges and definitely not the environment for a hermit. Indeed, Hebard needs a high measure of social dexterity to get his crew to complete their varied projects according to schedule. I assume that Kingsolver borrowed Fred's chestnut work as a starting point for Walker and moved creatively from there, stitching the character together from experience and imagination, in part to build tension in the work that pays off in the end.

The building houses a few items rarely found in a family home. The freezer, set to -140 degrees Centigrade, keeps pollen samples and other easily damaged goods effectively inert. Other large refrigerators, the kind found in university research labs, occupy the living room's perimeter. While not exactly high-tech, the office serves the breeding program for which it has been retrofitted.

In today's world of genetic engineering, where genes twirl from one species to the next like fickle dancers changing partners with the scientists' help, the Meadowview Research Farm proves an anachronism. Indeed, plant breeding of this nature has changed little from Darwin's or Luther Burbank's day. "Burbanking," a term I'd heard bantered around among some sustainable agriculture types, involves breeding and raising thousands of plants with hope that a handful express desired traits. Genes move from parent to offspring with humans serving only as possible pollen transferers. The whole process occurs naturally, but traits are selected by humans, giving the practice the alternate name, artificial selection. While neither Darwin nor Burbank knew the nature of genes or of the existence of DNA, they could understand Hebard's basic mission with a little training. In short, Fred works to breed out undesirable traits and to maintain desirable traits, evident by looking at an individual plant or testing it. His key tool involves moving pollen from one specimen to a receptive flower on another select tree.

In a former bedroom off the living room, a stuffy little space without fans or open windows despite summer's heat, a brown table serves as site for one of the breeding program's more menial tasks, removing pollen from male flowers. This job, reserved for younger staff, begins with a careful cleansing of the table and hands with high-proof Everclear, a fabled alcohol—merely a rumor in my college years—responsible for more than a few traffic fatalities in those rare states where one could legally purchase it. The table's surface needs to be sterilized so that any dawdling pollen from earlier shake-downs cannot taint the new sample. Workers sit around the table and methodically tease pollen from male catkins collected that day, running the flower stalks between thumb and forefinger repetitively. A yellowish dust with short hairs, along with aphids, tiny spiders and dirt, builds beneath each worker's hands. Once all catkins are processed, one person scrapes up all the dust and processes it with wire strainers, their screens sterilized with burning Everclear. The practice produces high grade pollen which can then be shipped or kept in cold storage.

Once Hebard pulled his gear together, we exited the house in a drove, heading for the fleet where we paired off in some randomly determined division of labor, me taking shotgun in a 1978 white Ford truck with its gas-powered cherry picker in the bed. Lou, running shorts and shoes under a flat-top grey head of hair and straw hat with one of these strings that rides under the chin, climbed in behind the wheel. Honaker directed us up and over the hill to a single chestnut sporting fifty or so of the same white paper bags Hebard had grabbed. The tree stood twenty feet high, its trunk branching a few feet off the ground. Underneath, out of mower's range, grew healthy black raspberry canes covered with ripe fruit.

Lou fell right into the procedure once Honaker directed him to the right tree. Firing up the cherry picker, he hoisted himself to the tree's crown where he systematically exposed the female flowers secreted beneath each paper bag. Twelve days earlier, a crew sacked the tree's immature female flowers, preventing the orchard's wind-borne pollen from reaching these petal-less greenish blossoms. The American chestnut cannot self-pollinate, relying on the wind for the bulk of its pollination; errant birds and insects account for a small fraction of the tree's successful procreations. A sack of specially selected anther-covered catkins at his waist, Lou rubbed the pollen source over each receptive stigma, sliding the catkin from end to end twice to ensure pollination. From above, he showered me with information about the farm and minuscule grains of pollen, too small for the eye to see unless collected in mass against a neutral colored object like the thumb.

Every tenth female flower receives a metal tag identifying the cross being made. That flower, a control, remains unpollinated in the bag. In the fall when the crew collects fruit, any nuts in the control bag reveal the unfortunate fact that the particular tree had been pollinated by unknown and, hence, undesirable pollen. Perhaps a careless beetle introduced pollen on its legs or the flower in question became receptive before being bagged. More likely, the flower had received wind-borne pollen before the crew could affix a bag to cover it or the bag wore out. When a control produces nuts, all the tree's production for that season needs to be removed from the breeding program since any or all might be the product of accidental wind or insect pollination. The cross will need to wait another year when reliable nuts may be produced.

Since 1991, Lou has traveled from Memphis to volunteer his services a few days each spring. Manager for a chemical giant, he's established certain expectations of rigor which the Meadowview Farm clearly violates. The fleet, particularly the truck we'd adopted, might be overqualified for the term 'ragtag,' but, according to Lou, it sure beats the days a decade earlier when adjustable three-legged ladders offered the only access to treetops. Lou recalled the delicate balance and constant repositioning needed to navigate tripods to deliver pollen to target flowers.

Raising his voice to cover the intermittent barrage of noise emanating from the cherry picker's droning engine, Lou explained that he'd like to expand his managerial role to include this farm's activities, foreseeing uniforms for its numerous staff members and an army of clean, new vehicles akin to what one would see at a competitive business or the Forest Service. Chomping on raspberries, I watched his technique, hoping I'd get my shot soon. The work looked dull and repetitive but I drove 900 miles for this experience and I intended to get my hands dirty.

Minutes later, I levitated high atop another tree, carefully unfolding the twisted paperclip holding bag to branch and rubbing the catkin along the female flower. The catkin, anywhere from two to nine inches long, suggests an octopus tentacle, with small male flowers in place of suckers surrounding the central stalk. Some people prefer slightly browning catkins as the pollen releases more effectively. The female flower, a green sphere with a collar of protruding spikes, has several cream-colored stigmas emerging from its summit. I swept the catkin over the stigmas, hopefully dropping pollen onto the receptive surface where it could begin growing its pollen tube toward the ovary to fertilize the flower. The ultimate burr would hold three closely packed nuts if my work succeeded.

Hand controls allowed me to move my bucket through the tree to reach all 57 bags. It was a tricky navigation as I didn't want to break branches or knock off bags. The bucket moves either horizontally or vertically from a central pivot point, so maneuvering requires constant three-dimensional awareness. To arrive at a nearby bag, I might need to move up, over, down, and over to reach it through a series of stutter steps. The controls tended to overshoot my target. When I found a sizable branch in my way, Hebard below yelled, "Don't worry—the tree can take it."

Earwigs, those pesky little beasts with apparent pincers at both ends, liked to congregate in the thin sleeve where bag and branch convene, raining on my wrists as I opened the bag. And the picker's motor kicked up quite a din. Otherwise, pollination proved a relatively quiet, contemplative activity, akin to berry picking or weeding.

Below I saw a new person enter the scene. Fred was telling her that the wet spring had pushed the whole Meadowview breeding program back a few months. Later, I'd learn that she was Susan Freinkel, a San Francisco-based writer researching a book on chestnuts. She'd written on sudden oak death for *Discover*, an article I had read a while back.

Hebard explained the farm's dynamics to her. In a forest green t-shirt, a cap advertising *Big M Farm Service, Inc.*, and straight-leg blue jeans, Hebard fit in visually with local tobacco farmers. His hair was cut short and pretty much covered by the cap. Elsewhere, I'd heard him described as a hippy, a young upstart who caught many a critical eye at Virginia Polytechnic in Blacksburg, Virginia, by tromping around campus barefoot. I could still see a bit of that alleged rebel in the late-fifties agrarian though I doubted the locals at Meadowview's only diner would recognize youthful rebellion in the chestnut farmer. Fred works to fit in. He'd traded his beads for hill country camouflage.

If Fred Hebard were typecast in a western, he'd play the stoic gentleman, older than most but wiser than all, who quietly watches the greenhorns surrounding him mess up. He delivers terse verbal quips that shame the hapless fool, levering guffaws from everyone else. He suffers fools with minor annoyance—and fortune does send more than a few his way—yet Fred finds just the right turn of phrase, like the shock you get from carpeting in the winter, to jolt his quarry's confidence, to coerce them into holding their tongues.

Preparing for my trip at home in Wisconsin, a state fully removed from the American chestnut's natural range, I had noticed a proliferation of Chestnut Ridges, Chestnut Hills, and simple Chestnut Streets littering the topography of cities, towns, villages and ruralities from Ohio on south and east. Affluent areas included Pennsylvania's Chestnut Hill, in Philadelphia's northwest quarter. It surprised me to find out that Fred Hebard grew up in this up-scale neighborhood. While my favored tree may have nearly vanished from the woodlots it once occupied, it still maintains a dominant position in the pages of my eastern atlas.

The youngest of six kids—a mix of full and half siblings, Fred lost his lawyer father as he entered adolescence. Family wealth paved the way for young Fred who, fighting wanderlust, wound up at Columbia University to nurse his budding interest in botany. Fred's northern accent still makes guest appearances in conversations, becoming more or less pronounced as befits the occasion and the company. Long gangly arms combined with his slight stoop at the shoulders—a slouch that reveals a burden of worries bearing down on him—suggest that Fred could have easily portrayed a teen-aged gear-head, probing beneath the hood of his GTO, in Hollywood. Outsiders assure me that Fred, a plant man, lacks the affinity for engines commonly expected of Appalachia's males. One fellow laughed about Hebard getting his pickup stuck in mud way back on National Forest land, noting they needed a tow truck to extricate the besieged vehicle.

Hence, the farm's need for Danny Honaker, bearded, in his late 30s, able to maintain the wide range of equipment deployed in daily operations. Honaker wields the gift of gab as effectively as he controls a torque wrench. He'll detail the long process of purchasing the farm's champion cherry picker, a red International truck complete with out-riggers to keep it from tipping on hill sides, following up with a dozen tales of that vehicle's finer moments. Danny prefers a pre-emptive strike on fools, tending to knock them out of action before they can foul up his day. I relished the fact that I sat shotgun when another worker dropped the white truck into an undetected ditch. I eagerly ran to fetch Honaker who'd driven ahead, knowing I'd be the first to hear any barbs slung the unfortunate driver's way.

Upon finishing my tree and descending, Hebard offered me a tour of the Wagner Research farm with Freinkel. We traveled through time, passing the various years' chestnuts in reverse chronological order. Shaped vaguely like a westbound comet, the farm packs all of its buildings into its coma, the head, while a string of sequential fields trail behind. The easternmost plot, once home to second backcrosses of the legendary Clapper tree that fell to the chainsaw, included a new planting of later backcrosses planted just that spring. Thin aluminum tubes protected the developing seedlings from the litany of calamities awaiting young chestnut. Black fibered plastic sheets kept weeds at bay and warmed up the soil. One field sported only a few apple tree-sized chestnuts, the rest culled according to Hebard's plan. With three farms spread throughout the area, Fred still needs to scrimp on space, removing trees that served their purpose years earlier, though chunks of the acreage still stand vacant.

Blight, evident in most of the trees, could be native or introduced through plugs of fungus-rich agar inserted into drilled holes. Hebard once believed that hitting young trees with near-lethal doses of blight would allow him to select resistant trees earlier, speeding up the breeding program. He admitted his error. Apparently, trees need to reach a certain size or age to express their resistance. Certainly a good number of resistant specimens succumbed to early infection. The seedlings, arrayed in beds holding 200 a piece, would probably be inoculated with blight fungus when they reached four years, the figure Hebard believed safe for testing trees.

Climbing a slight hill, the pickup slid laterally, Hebard plying the steering wheel in an attempt to right the tires. Mud flew from the driver's side tires, remnants from the spring's drenching rains. Rivulets left sand and soil deltas in the gentle slope of the field.

When asked a question, Hebard chews on it, fixing his inquisitor with an expression of loss or simply staring out the windshield. At first, I thought his hearing failed him. Sitting in the cab of his pickup, he'd surprise me with a novel answer addressing the details of my question. He makes no effort to offer stock answers, the kind folks distribute like business cards in planned public relations ploys. He also avoids changing the question asked to allow for a quicker response. Hebard's clearly a thinker insistent on such philosophical oddities as truth and consistency. Sometimes a sharpness in his eyes or a slight laugh reveals the fact that Hebard values his answer as much as his inquisitor; it might help him direct the breeding program in some slight way.

I had first noticed Hebard's detachment on that tour. Over the next few days, I'd realize that his mind was juggling more information and problems than he wished. But there he sat, entertaining two writers stealing some of his valuable time. The weather that season had already tempered his ambitious plans for the breeding program. That day he had to show us the ropes, a task he did well, answering a plethora of questions he'd answered countless times before, yet somehow with an awareness of losing valuable time. Later, he related an anecdote concerning a magazine article. The author appeared with photographer in tow. Fred sacrificed one-and-a-half hours of valuable work time posing for that nitpicky shutterbug who needed perfect light to get the precise shot he wanted. It's a sacrifice Fred makes in the name of public relations, a pairing of words that Hebard would probably expel from the English language if he could.

Fred ushered us toward a relative jungle of chestnuts flooded with a waist-high network of briars, raspberries and other invaders. His trademark tree, the one he saved to show all visitors, still earned his respect despite its declining health. Besides blight, the farm's trees are susceptible to numerous other maladies and pests. Oriental chestnut gall wasps (*Dryocosmus kuriphilus*) attacked this dense grove of 1991 intercrosses, decimating the leafy canopy and allowing light into the understory where weedy species took off. Introduced in 1974 by a grower who illegally evaded plant quarantine, the insect makes galls that produce larvae which consume chestnut leaves rapaciously. Fred just shook his head and shrugged shoulders when I asked him how the wasps might affect eventual restorations.

He pointed out select cankers among the trees. Ironically, the ones he termed "big uglies" earn his greatest respect. In these cankers, heartwood—the deep dead wood protected by the cambium and other bark layers—lies exposed to the elements, surrounded by a thick callous of bark. It's like a coffee cup-sized scab, usually on the tree's trunk. Hebard likes these cankers because they signal a success. Trees boasting big uglies will likely live ten or eleven years because they have minor resistance. That callous signifies a few more years of potential nut production, pushing Hebard nearer to his goal.

TACF only began leasing the Meadowview property in 1989. Before that, they had located their trees on select sites throughout the east—the campuses of Ohio's Oberlin College, Virginia Tech in Blacksburg (then known as Virginia Polytechnic Institute), and West Virginia University in Morgantown, and in Great Smoky Mountains National Park in Tennessee. While many trees grew in Minnesota—TACF's original home, the region, free of blight, failed to offer the stressful conditions necessary to determine resistance. The eastern locations all featured rampant populations of the blight-causing fungus.

The organization's president through most of the 1980s, Phillip Rutter, had searched for six years to locate land appropriate for TACF's breeding program. Traveling the country, giving talks to raise money for the research, Rutter happened upon Anna Belle Wagner and her two daughters, Jennifer and Cheri, at one such talk in Scientists Cliff, Maryland (a retreat coincidentally founded by early chestnut breeder Flippo Gravatt and his wife Annie, also a forest pathologist). Anna Belle offered to lease twenty acres of prime pastureland in Meadowview, an offer TACF couldn't refuse. The site proved excellent—smack dab in the traditional home of the American chestnut, within range of trees growing at various altitudes, and within earshot of our nation's capitol where USDA and other governmental bodies resided. TACF hired Fred Hebard to supervise the research farm, and the breeding program was off and running.

Early TACF crosses came from isolated trees in Minnesota and Iowa arboretums, as well as grafts of various trees at Connecticut's Agricultural Experiment Station in New Haven.

April 15, 1989, proved the ultimate groundbreaking for the Meadowview farm with Phillip Rutter delivering a station wagon full of young chestnuts he'd gathered on his drive from Minnesota. Charles Burnham supplied 30 of his 75% American trees from the University of Minnesota, while Dr. Mark Widriechner, then TACF's vice president who lived in Ames, Iowa, relinquished his entire crop of potted chestnuts. Rutter had to unload all the young trees into his tiny Iowa hotel room his first night on the road under threat of frost.

Rutter consistently refers to the organization's Superintendent as Dr. Fred, to whom he turned over his car-load of trees before sitting down to a dinner with the Wagners. The following day, Rutter and Hebard addressed Meadowview's elementary school student body, spoke to Emory and Henry University's biology classes in nearby Emory, met with folks from the Chamber of Commerce and the Rotary Club, and provided a slide show to the public. The next day, the grand opening of the Wagner Research Farm, would complete the festivities.

Rutter remembers the dismal weather forecast for April 15th. A 70% chance of showers threatened to wreck opening day activities. Apparently downpours are not uncommon events in Meadowview's spring weather calendar. "While it never quite stopped raining, it did slow to just a slight misting drizzle. Not the weather that first comes to mind for a celebration, but in fact it turned out well. Perfect weather for planting trees, which is what counts," writes Rutter of that auspicious day. Eighty people showed up that morning, with shovels in hand: "Dr. Fred had the spots for the holes marked, with trees laid out in the mist waiting to be planted. We said a few appropriate words, and our great crew dug in with gusto."

These rather flowery words, worthy of repetition, lay out the mission of the Meadowview Research Farm:

> "We are gathered here today, on the sight of the rain and the wind, the mountains and the trees, to join with each other and with this land in a bond of holy determination.
>
> "We are determined that these trees we plant will survive, and grow, and flower. We are determined that this farm shall succeed in its goal, which is: to grow chestnut trees, in the face of wind and sun, flood and drought, lack of funds, and blight; until chestnut trees are found which can once again grow free on these hills.
>
> "Why are we so determined? We could talk about economics, and ecological necessities, but the future of all life on the Earth is in our hands. We must care for it and nurture it. The chestnut especially deserving, because we caused its current plight, it is only fair for us to restore its health."

These sentences, ringing with a religious intensity, ground chestnut's restoration upon righting human error. An honorable goal, indeed, but one wonders if such thoughts verge on hubris, as if it just might prove too optimistic to believe that such a wrong could be turned around without causing still more problems.

Notable in attendance at the event were the American Chestnut Cooperators' Foundation's backbone of John Elkins and Gary Griffin, and M. Ford Cochran, who penned a February 1990 article for the *National Geographic* about chestnut revival.

The trees planted had been donated by various nurseries across the United States. The participants planted a border of hybrids—what Rutter termed "grafted nut-type trees that are known to be resistant"—along the road so that visitors and passers-by would have healthy trees to look at. Though these specimens would serve a mostly ornamental purpose, they could play minor roles in the research as well. The research trees, planted by Hebard and his workers on a more secure, isolated part of the farm, went in later. The two main strains of interest to the breeding program were both first backcrosses—roughly 75% American trees. The 'Clapper' and the 'Graves' trees, their names honoring those earlier breeders, would provide the stock for several more generations grown at the farm.

After all these trees went in, someone remarked that they needed some water to lessen the transplant shock and get the new trees ready for success. It had been a long day and the thought of watering all those trees held little charm to the herd of workers. Fortunately, one of the volunteers, also a volunteer firefighter, summoned the Meadowview Fire Department to the rescue. As Rutter recalls, "Five minutes after his phone call the Fire Department's huge tank truck, carrying thousands of gallons, was slowly making its way up our slippery, muddy hill, deep soaking each tree."

The Wagners then hosted the picnic lunch they'd prepared but, due to the soggy conditions, it moved inside, muddy feet and all. The Meadowview research site officially opened for business.

A year later, Dr. Frederick Hebard began what has become a tradition of annual reports from Meadowview, published in TACF's journal. The Hebard family, including two pre-school aged daughters, Kyla and Paige, lived on the farm itself in the house now serving as office, library, and laboratory. The first report, brief at a mere three paragraphs, noted quite a bit of work: fence building, planting 300 trees in hand-dug holes, constructing a base for the pollination ladder because the cherry-pickers were just a dream in those days, and participating in various public relations events, such as Earth Day 1990 in Washington, DC. That year also included harvesting the first nuts and being inundated with mail after the article ran in *National Geographic.* Fred Hebard found himself exactly where he wanted to be, in the middle of a storm of interest and activity over the tree he loved. His wife, Dayle, though not enthused to be stuck in rural western Virginia and unable to find work involving her plant pathology degree, understood how much this work meant to her husband. She opted to make the best of a questionable situation and pursued work as a nurse.

Over the years, these annual reports to TACF's supporters detailed the successes and failures of the Meadowview breeding program, with Hebard revealing the abundance of knowledge gained in the process. In 1993, he noted that new trees flowered in only their second year, an unprecedented benefit that helped shorten the time needed to develop resistant chestnuts. Fred credited substantial rainfall over three years combined with regular shots of Mir-Acid for prompting this "precocious flowering." He also fashioned this rapid flowering into a plea for funds for an irrigation and fertilization system that would speed up the program. The Price farm, a few miles from the Wagner site, now has such a system.

At the same time flowering occurred quickly, pollination of wild trees was dealt a blow. "Not only did it cause early flowering of most trees," writes Hebard, of the rains, "it also compressed the length of the flowering period. Trees at high elevations in the Virginia mountains flowered at about the same times as trees at lower elevations, and trees in Connecticut flowered at similar times to trees in the Virginia mountains." Running a tight schedule, the Meadowview team lacked time, equipment, and laborers to perform that year's controlled pollinations. Hebard's frequent calls for volunteers in future reports reflect those early years where too few hands performed too much work.

After joining the rest of the crew, Fred announced lunch at the diner. Contrary to dining experiences I was accustomed to, seating at the diner brings all attendees into one communal conversation. Introductions, offered to an inquiring gaze, are quick and easy. "I'm the electrician." "He used to grow tobacco before subsidies chased him from his fields." Taciturn Hebard becomes quick-witted and jocular, mixing with the regulars who've taught him a lot about farming.

Bill, the electrician, relates tales of old Meadowview, the town he grew up in, where Saturday nights jammed the sidewalks so full that many had to walk in the streets. The downtown boasted three gas stations, restaurants, places to play and listen to music. Folks came together socially rather than park themselves in front of 128 channels of diversion.

Today's Meadowview boasts a line of concrete-faced brick buildings painted varied pastels, an inexpensive shot at invigorating the social significance of this near-ghost town. While these buildings might have stood in place a hundred years ago, their new tint breathes a bit of life into what was once a town square. A close look, though, reveals relative disrepair, with one of the buildings' second floors collapsed into its first. No one occupies these claptrap Easter eggs as almost all have drifted out to the country. The jobs that kept someone Meadowview-bound disappeared decades ago as the automobile offered cheap transport away from town. But the springtime colors draw a few spectators. Big M, around the corner from the diner, looked like it might fight off the big boxes a few more years if the local population maintained loyalty to its implements.

Seven miles down the road—by back ways or by Interstate 81, if one can tolerate breakneck speeds in the sea of semi-haulers flowing in and out of DC—lies Abingdon, home to Wal-Mart, the six-screen Cineplex, bars, restaurants, grocery stores, strip malls, and nearly everything else a person might be convinced they need. Abingdon serves as a giant sponge for Meadowview earnings, providing the new necessities at a fraction of their cost in those disappeared small town general stores—the Ben Franklins and Woolworth's. But it's a scenic town, a bit touristy with its galleries and shoppes, the WPA-era Barter Theatre, and restored mansions now housing insurance agencies and the tourist information center.

All this hustle and bustle rests in deep western Virginia, that obtuse triangle of land earning its own quadrangle in my gazetteer. A few miles to the south lie both Tennessee and North Carolina. The three states converge near the small town of Damascus, a mecca for family bicyclists who pedal an asphalt trail snaking through the Mount Rogers National Recreational Area. Hebard's younger crew members like to hit the bars there, sometimes jeopardizing their work habits the next day.

While many would consider Meadowview's residents to be, for the most part, economically challenged, talk at the diner revealed a hidden economy built around age-old practices. Electric Bill manages a few beehives. Everyone stalks the woods with varied weaponry during hunting seasons. Benji Cornett, the farm's young manager, raises all kinds of vegetables and is respected for his canned hot peppers and chow chow. In more gentrified areas, the folks of Meadowview might be considered 'hobby farmers,' but such an appellation fails here. Resourcefulness flows in the citizenry's veins. These hunting and gathering practices are more than diversions sought by otherwise gainfully employed dabblers in agriculture. If most northern hunters are weekend warriors, burning a few vacation days at the plant to trade Milwaukee's confines for the Nicolet National Forest, these Virginians compose the regular army—serious soldiers fighting the way their daddies and their daddies' daddies did, in a recursive line going back hundreds of years, to put food on the family table.

Turkey hunting, a mainstay for mountain families, died back with population declines echoing chestnut's demise; now it's on the rise again. The birds who'd grow fat on the prodigal chestnut's excessive mast have only recently found alternative food sources, though they'll probably never match the size they once attained.

Folks in the diner also talked about deer hunting. Poaching, an activity they avoided, nonetheless drew defense from these farmers fed up with an oversized herd of the animals John Muir should have called "hoofed locusts." While Muir's famous phrasing referred to sheep, a critter famous for devouring all fauna indiscriminately, deer prove more than qualified for the criticism. They browse rare understory plants, pushing some species toward extinction. Indeed, Hebard's young chestnuts stand as good a chance of winding up in a deer's gut as they do of dying from blight.

The common currency here is land. A farmer needs acreage to grow the crops or draw the subsidies for not growing tobacco. Much of the land stays in families for centuries. Land speculators probably learned long ago to leave the locals alone, understanding why rock salt serves such a good deterrent when it flies from the business end of a shotgun. Public lands serve as hunting grounds as well as depositories for less-legal crops. A few of Fred's employees assure me that parts of the woods should be avoided lest one irritates the illicit farmers and their cash crop, high-grade marijuana grown tax-free right under the Fed's collective nose.

The rural region, like many throughout the country, also has its share of methamphetamine labs, where the chemically-minded churn out a lethal stockpile of the stimulant known locally as 'crank.' Perpetrators of such illegal activities often support the anti-government attitude said to pervade this part of the United States. Folks tend to believe that Washington, only a few hundred miles away, would like to control this region much more closely than the locals find acceptable. Thus, they turn to a range of anarchic, libertarian ideals pervading our culture. Presidential candidates win votes by suggesting their opponent wishes to take away the guns, firing off a volley of grassroots support out of blatant fear.

But communal values underlie the local economy. Folks share knowledge freely, unaware of potential competition. Folks take care of one another. Hebard dryly explained the cigarettes in his sagging t-shirt pocket as "supporting local tobacco growers," though the few he lit up in my presence couldn't account for more than a few packs of support a week.

Long swaths of green—federally-owned forest land—sandwiches Meadowview and Abingdon. The Iron Mountains, which include Mount Rogers—Virginia's highest spot at 5,729 feet, parallel I-81 to the south, while the long finger of the Appalachians winds north and east, hugging the Virginia/West Virginia border.

The Appalachian Trail climbs through these aged mountains. In fact, 550 miles, more than one-fourth, of the trail lies within Virginia. Hikers claim the Commonwealth's southwest section of trail, a cordon that grew substantially when trail keepers decided to extend the Maine-to-Georgia trail, to be the most pleasing part of the 2160-mile whole. On a quick 5-mile jaunt in the Iron Mountains, I ran into 75-year-old Tom Cannon, owner and operator of Cannon Air-conditioning-Refrigeration Company of Bristol, Tennessee. A tall willowy man, Cannon sported shins built from years of traipsing up and down these hills. "There're sixteen switchbacks up this mountain," he told me, pointing to the trail south of us. "I can get up there in 67 minutes."

Cannon beamed to hear of my interest in chestnut. "We had a tree when I grew up in Carolina. That tree was still producing nuts in '38 when my family moved up here." He knew a particular tree hidden back in the woods, near an old farmstead and gave me detailed instructions along with a gallon and a half of water and the location of a good camping spot. He insisted I take the water so I did, despite five gallons lurking in my car's back seat. At my asking, he admitted a fondness for honey so I gave him a jar from my own hive in thanks. Later, I found the chestnut, the Chinese species, a disappointment in comparison to a native tree though my interest remained piqued.

Anyone older than sixty seems to have fond memories of chestnut, perhaps contributing to the American Chestnut Foundation's popularity throughout the region. Cannon asked if he'd be able to visit the farm. Other folks I ran across held onto similar stories of family trees, though many had only imagined chestnuts from stories told by older relatives. J.D. and Gladys White, campground hosts at Cave Lake National Forest Campground, both in their 70s, listened rapt to my limited tales of the American chestnut, J.D. sharing his memories from childhood.

The crew in the diner apparently shared this love of chestnut. Several of them attended the opening ceremonies years back. Some had relatives working on the farms. Most have a deeper understanding of the ecological and economic fallout from chestnut's exodus. The recent resurgence in turkey populations catches their interest, but they know only widespread American chestnut will maintain populations as big as those a century ago. They know the value of chestnut's incredible mast for fattening wild and domesticated animals, as well as putting green in the pockets of young entrepreneurs willing to harvest the nuts.

In the afternoon, Hebard had duties in the office so he dispatched a crew to check out some trees in the National Forest. We drove an hour or so only to find that the trees, growing back in some clearcuts, had already passed the point of bagging. Ideally, bags go on as soon as the female flower appears. The female remains unreceptive to pollen for five days after the male catkins start shedding pollen. The trees are best bagged as soon as pollen is shed; then, twelve days later, Hebard sends his crew to pollinate the tree. Fred keeps an internal clock that tells him when and where to prepare trees. Honaker figured that the higher elevations escaped the cold temperatures delaying chestnut flowering at Meadowview, reasoning that colder air, denser than warmer air, pools in the valleys while upslope trees develop normally. Hebard simply miscalculated.

The ACF has quite a few trees out in the sticks, roughly within an hour's drive of Meadowview. After the US Forest Service goes in and clearcuts an area, newly available light hits the former understory. Chestnut sprouts that may be one inch thick and more than twenty years old take off. Size rather than age proves the key factor determining blight susceptibility, so these small diameter shoots stand a statistically high chance of producing fruit before dying back to the root stock.

Before arriving at Hebard's farm, I spent a few days exploring the woods in the Mount Rogers area. I'd climbed a stretch of trail and was resting at the summit when I caught my first glimpse of a real American chestnut. On the hike up, I'd marveled at the irony of traveling 900 miles to see a tree that, according to most popular records, no longer existed. What was I hoping to find? A sign proclaiming, "This used to be a chestnut"? But sitting, relaxed, I recognized the tell-tale teething of a chestnut leaf in a clump of twigs and greenery just a foot off the trail. The plant stood barely a foot tall, its foliage splayed out in a small canopy plane, a photosynthetic umbrella, each leaf positioned to get maximal sunlight. But the much larger forest trees overhead prevented 95% of the available light from reaching the forest floor. This tiny survivor subsisted on a diet of minimal light, adjusting its growth accordingly to survive rather than die in a futile attempt to reproduce.

As I marveled at my solitary specimen, other minuscule American chestnuts intruded upon my field of vision. In moments, I realized I was surrounded by stunted versions of the once ubiquitous giant.

The chestnuts surrounding me brought to mind the Silver Age comic book hero, the Atom, "the World's Smallest Hero." A normal-sized physicist, Ray Palmer developed a shrinking ray that allowed him to manipulate his size, shrinking down at first to six inches but, with technical improvements, to subatomic size. Imagine the Mighty Mite, as he was known, stuck at the size of a paper clip, forced to go through daily life at such a miniature scale, ignored by Batman and Wonder Woman. The trees around me suffered that very fate. Less evident than shrubs, their pencil-wide trunks possibly decades old, these survivors held on, indifferent to their fate. Simple botanical processes kept this species clinging to these mountainside homes. A few relative giants grew to ten feet. No signs of blight disfigured this lot.

Unlike the ACF's backwoods trees, this forest along the Appalachian Trail was unlikely to ever get the clearcut that would release these trapped Atoms from attaining their full potential.

Few of the hikers passing through are likely to notice the trees, indistinguishable from the other shrubby plants trying to survive at the dark forest floor. The scalloped leaves, not that different from alder—the plant I would have assumed these shrubs to be if not for the dry understory attributes of this site—prove the only factors that would alert a wary hiker to the chestnut's presence. But most of these travelers, younger than the sixty and seventy-year-olds that remember bigger trees, probably know nothing about American chestnut. As time passes, fewer folks that experienced real chestnut can pass their tales to younger generations.

Honaker explained our troop's failure to Hebard upon our return to the office. Tension mounted as the two faced off but Hebard recovered calm, accepting Honaker's reasons for not bagging trees. Nonetheless, he frowned in disappointment with another setback.

The following day, Fred led another expedition to pollinate trees an hour's drive from Meadowview. The weather changed to sunny high pressure, offering views of the majestic countryside as we climbed in elevation. Most of the wild chestnuts occur at higher elevations, partly because these areas are more isolated from human interference, partly because these areas can be clearcut. Hebard and Honaker both wield keys to the Forest Service's gates, allowing us vehicular access to spots others reach on foot.

Hebard had told me that the moniker, "Redwood of the East," affixed to American chestnut like a brand name, really didn't make much sense unless the phrase referred to the tree's resistance to rot. Both redwood and chestnut stay intact, making them excellent woods for outdoor use; redwood favored for decking, siding, and roofing while chestnut found deployment in railroad ties, telephone poles, and barns and sheds. But a size comparison between redwood, a true giant, and American chestnut, a large forest tree, made little sense.

One management tool favored by Lou the Volunteer involves eliminating most of the competition for the few forest chestnuts. Hebard has reserved a special appellation for the volunteer everyone knows as "Chainsaw Lou." Over the course of a few hours, Lou ripped through a stand of tulip, or yellow, poplar, striped maple, oak and other species, to provide more light to a relatively small number of trees. From high atop the bucket of the ACF's bigger cherry picker, Edmund Brown, a knowledgeable college student from Philadelphia, and I watched Chainsaw Lou denude the forest with a ferocity unknown to mellower types like us. Once we descended after pollinating a few trees, I heard a "Doug, Doug," emanating from the woods. Checking it out, I found Lou with the chainsaw's bar stuck at a weird angle into a 5-cm wide tulip poplar. I pushed on the top of the trunk, allowing Lou to extricate his toothy weapon.

Hebard summoned Susan Freinkel, Ed Brown, and me to a quiet stand of trees far enough from Lou's chainsaw to allow for discussion. On the way, he quizzed Ed on the identity of a tall, skinny tree with sizable catalpa-like leaves that I'd never seen before. "Pollonia," replied the sharp young scientist-in-training. Later Ed would give me a treatise on the odd Chinese tree that made its way to the US as a fluffy packing material, amazing me with his encyclopedic understanding of the plant. Hebard continued to explicate the dynamics of blight, showing us some hidden stumps with ascending shoots.

Fred seems utterly in his element talking about and observing the natural world. His passion for the plants, infectious and refreshing, reminds me of elder botanists who made livelihoods out of wandering and cataloguing the varied greenery in their paths. When reading Hebard's reports, I'd find little gems. Every once in a while he throws out an observation, such as his suggestion that volunteers might be lucky enough to see hummingbirds working chestnut flowers as he did one year. He possesses an impressive knowledge of the region's species that he imparts to his receptive workers. I picture him more at home in the age of Linnaeus, a time when a generalist could thrive as a scientist. Today, specialization rules the roost with few generalists able to scrape together livings as scientists. I find generalists more interesting, though, as they inevitably have a greater understanding of the interconnections between organisms and between organisms and their physical environments. Hebard's ecological awareness, though, holds little value for his higher-ups in the ACF.

Hebard claimed that blight strikes trees of a certain size. It's common for the fungus to kill trees narrower than a thin wrist, the spores responsible dispersing themselves radially from an infected tree. Statistically-speaking, those spores have significantly less opportunity to find purchase on a smaller tree's bark in the same way that the bull's eye gets harder to hit as you move away from the dartboard. Individual smaller trees also have a statistical advantage because they are usually more densely packed than larger chestnuts and farther away from big trees.

Twenty minutes later, as Hebard rounded us all up to leave, we discovered Lou in a much more precarious position. The chainsaw, stuck about three feet up the trunk of a 10-cm wide striped maple, hung by its bar, vibrating, while Lou pushed and pulled at the immovable tree. Edmund and I joined the fray, yet the tree failed to relinquish its hold on the hated chainsaw. Fred, shaking his head and rolling his eyes in the most subtle of ways, pulled out a chain and affixed it to the cherry picker on the smaller truck. Lou, who scampered up and down the tree like Curious George several times, asked Fred to throw the chain. Fred shook his head once again and walked the chain to Lou who bounced up the trunk once more to swing it around a Y-branch 15 feet up.

After convincing Lou to climb down, Fred fired up the cherry picker and slowly, surely, pulled the tree clear. I grabbed the chainsaw, seemingly undamaged though the bar might have been bent. Lou, in a fit of passion, launched into the tree, pushing it downhill where it collapsed a few others, leaving a wide opening for a sole chestnut. We cleaned up the roadway and pulled out of there, Lou visibly seething from adrenaline overkill.

In 1992, the American Chestnut Foundation received the "Award for the Protection of Biodiversity" from the Italy-based Slow Food organization. After a few malt beverages, Hebard seemed ready to talk about the award and his resulting trip to Italy for the ceremony. Fred and Dayle had opened their house to the crew, Susan Freinkel, and me, a chance to dine at the family home north of Emory, just a few miles east of Meadowview. Dayle and a crowd of high school-aged females, one being their elder daughter, filled the kitchen. The young women perked up every time one of Fred's workers showed up.

Gathered around a picnic table on the porch overlooking a wide valley, our crowd finished eating as Fred began telling stories. "When I hear 'slow foods,' I think sloe gin fizz," he commented, while his wife, Dayle confessed that she thinks of slow cookers. The term actually began as a counter to the ubiquitous fast food that critics claim not only ruins our health but also destroys cultural, particularly culinary, diversity the world over. The Slow Food movement started in Bra, a small Italian town not far from the French border, in the late 1980s when local food activists realized they had to begin "safeguarding our gastronomic resources." Like environmentalists arguing for the protection of natural resources, they argued that regional flavors, unique tastes developed over centuries, would vanish unless we acted to preserve them. The organization, growing like a dish of bacteria, has expanded to near-global proportions with more than 60,000 members.

To give a sense of the breadth of Slow Food's project, other award recipients included a Colorado rancher who reverted to feeding his cattle only grass grown on a grasslands wildlife preserve, a Guatemalan women's association that raises chickens, and an organization in Malaysia that assists communities in improving their food supplies by managing local forests.

Fred told how he and Dayle flew to Torino, Italy, along with the ACF's Executive Director Marshal Case, expenses paid, to participate in the annual event. Fred, seldom seen in any shirt of the non-tee variety, had to don coat and tie to remain respectable. Both he and Dayle described the fete as "hoidy-toidy," a term not thrown around superfluously in rural Virginia. Titles such as 'Duke' and 'Duchess' seemed commonplace among the attendees, keeping Fred on his toes lest he use the wrong fork or word. Dayle recalled the banquet where her vegetarian ways pushed her to grab some lettuce cloaked with dead octopi. Fred focused on the pair of Malaysian award recipients who just wanted a few bowls of rice; they tried to communicate their hunger for the staple unsuccessfully.

Overall, the affair proved quite nerve-wracking for Hebard who rarely takes a day off from managing Meadowview. But public relations requires major sacrifices, including the suit and tie combo so uncharacteristic of Fred. His return home could not happen soon enough.

Fred Griffith, who heads up the Cleveland convivium for Slow Food with his wife Linda, originally nominated TACF for the award while researching recipes for a cookbook appropriately titled *Nuts*. The couple wanted to include a recipe using chestnuts. In searching for samples, their contact, Greg Miller of the Empire Chestnut Company, supplied the couple with hybrids of European and Asian varieties, not the American chestnut they so desired. Like many people today, they only discovered the tragic tale of chestnut's ecological collapse through Miller who introduced them to the story and the folks at TACF. Not only did Fred, a Cleveland radio and television personality, nominate TACF for the Slow Food award; he and Linda also joined the organization, becoming fast fans and supporters of American chestnut.

Fred Griffith, who just happens to claim a world record "for most time on live TV—nearly 14-thousand hours," has learned a lot about food while penning a string of six cookbooks with Linda, one which earned a James Beard Award. After learning about American chestnuts, Griffith contacted Hebard concerning his plans to nominate the chestnut breeder for Slow Food's award. "When I first talked to Fred about this, he seemed incredulous, wondering why anyone in Europe (where chestnuts continued to thrive) would be interested in what he was doing," explained Griffith, who found Hebard's modesty refreshing.

The Griffiths also attended the event in Torino, running into the Hebards from time to time. Fred Griffith mentioned that Fred Hebard seemed to have a wonderful time, apparently enjoying the attention of an international crowd. But the ultimate reason for the Griffiths' nomination, getting attention for a significant American effort, helped Hebard realize the importance of TACF's mission. Fred Griffith believes, "If he had any doubts about the value of what he had been doing, I think this event got him past them. My hope was that he could use this international recognition to gain more support here for his foundation."

If nothing else, the Hebards' trip to Italy did succeed in bringing international attention to the American chestnut's legacy. It also brought renewed interest in native nuts among culinarists across the United States.

Hebard has also become a key supporter of the local economy by offering reliable employment to his band of local workers. Honaker and George Sykes, a soft-spoken gentleman who prefers to listen rather than share his views, compose the older core—reliable men who grew up in the region. Sykes started out as a part-timer when Hebard assumed the reigns at Meadowview in 1989. Around 1995, he moved up to full-time farm hand, a job he enjoys well enough. Medically, George has had his share of troubles. He had a spot of cancer removed from his nose. His former teeth, yanked to the last, will be replaced by dentures as soon as George has the money. At 36, he's seen co-workers come and go, but he stays, a quiet rail of a man contributing his share.

After a long string of odd jobs, many of them relating to agriculture or mechanics, Honaker finally chose a career on Hebard's farm. Honaker's skilled at scraping an income from the strangest activities. He recounted a story of his teen years when a big chemical spill meant income for all his friends. Due to someone's negligence or corporate malfeasance, tons of mercury found its way into a local river. Ignorant to any health risks, Danny and his friends would meet at the river with pop bottles. They patrolled the shallows, looking for chrome bubbles, the pooled quicksilver, and submerged their bottles, letting the toxic metal flow in the neck, replacing the water. The company paid them cash based on the weight of recovered mercury. Such opportunities never amounted to much in the way of regular employment but they did keep Danny alive. Though he might gripe a bit, he understands the value of his current position and will stay as long as he can.

The younger crew, a mix of local college students, interns from farther away, and locals who've found their way to TACF, practice varied work habits. Some show up when they need the money. Leon had started four years earlier, a nineteen-year-old trouble maker who opted to perform community service on the farm in repentance for some transgression. Drawn into the unfolding drama of the American chestnut, he told me that he wanted to plant his own trees, possibly on federal land. He also would like to drive or fix trucks if the opportunity presented itself.

Hebard had also landed a couple of sharp interns from northeastern schools this summer. Jason Corwin, from Cornell, performed research on the potential for genetically engineering chestnut. He was piecing together the final research he needed to earn his Master's degree. Edmund Brown, the undergraduate from Philadelphia with the remarkable ability to explicate the whole story of *Pollonia*, allows his future to unfold as he goes. Young and idealistic, Brown did not foresee a future in chestnut. He hoped to build environmentally responsible housing, perhaps running a bed and breakfast in buildings he constructed himself. Both young men had outsider perspectives to which Hebard pays careful attention. A critical thinker himself, Fred realizes that the fresh knowledge these youthful biologists bring to his farm might prove of use in restoring the tree.

Other members of the crew came and went as they saw fit. Even on slow days, Fred tries to find work for these guys who need the money for rent or other pressing necessities. Late spring and early summer, busy times at the farm, require a larger work force for pollinating, collecting catkins and removing the pollen, planting, and maintaining the farms. Fred has his farm manager, Benji Cornett, round up the troops necessary.

Benji, a 2002 biology graduate of Emory and Henry College, faced the daunting challenge of overseeing workers his age and a bit older, some of whom he'd known most of his life. Not always receiving the respect he deserved, Benji struggled to learn how to wield authority without losing the friendship of his crew members. He'd been known to yell at times, creating rancor but getting work completed. Crew members knew Benji as a stickler for doing a job correctly. Oftentimes, sharing music, which he loves, or homegrown concoctions from his own garden helps grease the social rails. But Benji faced the classic problem: folks simply detest taking orders from someone their age or younger.

The core crew of workers I had the pleasure to work with included Tim Lowe, Leon Porter, TR Odum and Ryan Smith. Tim and Ryan attended nearby colleges, earning spending money during summer break.

Hebard's an easy-going boss, putting up with problems he could nip in the bud if he chose. Over the years, he's lost employees, one to suicide and another to the penitentiary. But the fact that these guys show up when he needs them plays a vital part in TACF's ultimate success. If they would rather not devote their lives to chestnut the way Fred has, they still work their butts off on tasks that are often repetitive and tiresome. Hebard feels no need to bust them over the head with some imagined work ethic because, deep down, he probably felt the same way as they did when he was young, before he found his mission. I picture a young, prodigal Fred, traveling the country, if not the world, a reflection of Kerouac, searching for some meaning in the overt senselessness visible daily. He's never lost connection to that former self, providing him a fair share of compassion for working with the young people of Meadowview.

Fred drove me out Highway 11 to a second research farm. Rain pelted the truck as we traveled through a June wet enough to keep pushing the breeding program back. Hebard looked at the rain the way one looks at a pregnant rabbit eating one's garden lettuce. Pointing out a collection of 6-foot high chestnuts, he noted, "Those ones don't like it growing out on the flat." We'd been talking ecology, a topic near and dear to Hebard who, constrained by the breeding protocol, finds himself having to compromise the program in ways he finds damaging to the trees. Those particular specimens should not have been planted on that even plain. The soil held more moisture, keeping the chestnut roots damp at all times and inviting problems.

"Those up there," he explained, pointing to a hill crop, "They're doing well." Sandy soil drains well and the sandstone hidden beneath the hill's crest dissolves in rainwater and filters downhill to alter the local soil conditions. "That's as successful a planting as we have in here, best conditions for reintroduction." Meanwhile, he fought the steering wheel, keeping the tires from sliding in the water-logged earth, preventing us from taking a sudden swim in the pond to our port side. The trees above us seemed a healthier green. Younger than the trees growing on the flat, these beauties grew just as tall and might have been a bit fuller in foliage.

That acreage, the Price Farm, boasts the fancy irrigation equipment speeding along the breeding program. Drip hoses form an extensive grid, shaped like a giant many-pronged pitchfork, throughout the land ushering water, fertilizer, herbicides, and other aids to growth to the individual trees. Fred slung a bunch of bags full of greenish crystals over to the tank where he dumped them and added some water. A series of pumps move the liquid supplement through the fields.

As an employee of the American Chestnut Foundation, Hebard reports to several bosses. Al Ellingboe, retired plant geneticist at the University of Wisconsin, oversees the strict genetics of the breeding program. From time to time, some fiery e-mails flit between Hebard and Ellingboe, though the two have nothing but respect for one another. Hebard's frustration stems from needing to breed the specific third backcross tree on a schedule that might make Hercules flinch. The breeder has consistently amazed folks within the organization and without by exploiting new ways of reducing the lengthy period between generations. Usually one would raise a generation of trees and wait for them to express their phenotypes before selecting successes and culling unwanted trees. Hebard has reduced that time to four or six years. Every time he communicates with Ellingboe, he gains a fuller sense of the breeding program's greater complexity.

Ellingboe understands that plant genetics has similarities to chess. A youngster can learn the basic moves and occasionally win against a slightly better player, but both endeavors involve an ever-deepening understanding, with layers of complexity incomprehensible to novices. It takes a lot of practice to become a grand master at either pursuit.

Taking genetics to the next level, Ellingboe examines the interactions between hosts and disease organism genomes rather than focusing on individual organisms. The fungus, *Cryphonectria parasitica*, has distinct genetic traits as does the American chestnut. When the two combine, the genetic story becomes very convoluted. Variations in both organisms' genomes create a panoply of possibilities, resulting in a wide range of partial resistances to the blight. Ellingboe himself refuses to buy into the relatively simplistic breeding program developed by Burnham and Rutter. Hence, he tends to complicate Hebard's life as well. If Hebard failed to understand or appreciate these complications, he'd be a happier man. But, then, his program might ultimately fail out of ignorance.

Complicating Hebard's work even further was the loss of staff geneticist Paul Sisco who left the research farm in 2002. Now Fred has to assume all those genetic responsibilities until another geneticist can be hired.

Hebard's doctoral work also complicates the picture. He studied under Gary Griffin at Virginia Polytechnic Institute, in Blacksburg, Virginia. Griffin's keen awareness of environmental conditions and their effects on chestnut growth and survival definitely impacted Hebard's scientific views. In the field, Fred points out ecological aspects that play little or no role in the ACF's published mission. As example, Fred's job duties do not include responding to the gall wasp, despite the insect's threat to reintroduced trees.

Hebard's other bosses, most notably Executive Director Marshal Case, might not understand the pressure Hebard faces. Like the space race of the 1960s when the United States pushed to send a few humans to the moon, TACF is driven to accomplish a goal, though sometimes the precise goal becomes a bit ambiguous. The organization peppers their publications with the tagline "Toward the restoration of an American classic." This goal, predominantly ecological in several respects, involves returning the tree to its native range.

Often, though, another goal seems to eclipse the restoration goal. In the fall of 2002 edition of the organization's journal, Fred succinctly captured this other goal in words: "At The American Chestnut Foundation, we are trying to transfer the blight resistance of the Chinese chestnut tree to its American cousin, but otherwise restore the traits of the American chestnut." This honorable goal, distinctly genetic in its aims, drives the breeding program. If NASA had struggled to create an astronaut that could survive on the moon, that mission would correspond to the breeding program.

Hebard remains aware that restoring a species and breeding a blight-resistant tree are two different projects, intimately related but still separate. Nonetheless, his worries about the restoration cloud his mind as he works to breed the resistant tree. Once the resistant tree exists and survives various trials on the farm and in the wild, the restoration project will begin. At that point, though, TACF will need to address quite a few political, ecological, and economic questions. While the breeding program itself requires a certain amount of funding, a small allotment of farmland, and the brainpower and labor to design and realize the program, restoration to the native range proves incredibly more complex.

First, the homeland for those restored trees has yet to be determined. TACF will need to deal with USDA, the Forest Service, the Sierra Club, and a litany of other governmental and non-governmental organizations overseeing the uses of federal and private lands. One cannot simply plant thousands of trees where one wishes. A potential labyrinth of Environmental Impact Statements (EIS), hearings, and permit applications awaits TACF once they reach that stage.

Those EISs will require analysis of how chestnut reintroduction will impact other species, animal, plant and otherwise. American chestnut will likely require clear-cutting of some areas. Herbicide use might be suggested to improve the trees' chances. These ecological issues involve much study to determine potential outcomes of reintroduction. TACF might spend years working to figure out the ecological impact of their project.

All this additional research and presenting of findings will tax TACF's limited funding, posing economic challenges to the organization. If restoration ever gets the green light from overseeing government agencies, labor may prove the next huge expense, particularly if the group hopes to really bring the tree back to its entire range. If only 1% of the original estimated 4 billion trees will be planted, TACF will need to find enough people to set those 40 million trees in the ground. Assuming that

Boy and Girl Scouts could perform a fraction of the labor, with private landowners and volunteers doing the rest, TACF still needs to supervise the whole procedure to guarantee a job done well.

Modern genetic theory—the theory informing TACF's breeding protocol—dictates that an individual's observable traits, its phenotype, arise from its genetic constitution, its genotype. Thus, all the desirable and undesirable qualities of American chestnut can be linked to specific genes which work individually or in combination. The Chinese and Japanese species have a number of traits Hebard wishes to avoid, such as "orchard" growth form, the common apple tree-shaped growth pattern. TACF wants "timber" form, the tall, canopy-dominating straight-boled trees favored in historical publicity stills of the trees. But Asian trees express the resistance that just might save our American species. The trick for Hebard involves incorporating resistance while eliminating all the other Asian traits. It's like trying to get three "Jackpot" signs on a slot machine. You can either play one machine long enough or work several machines at once to earn, eventually, the big prize. By growing thousands of specific crosses at once, Hebard banks on the probability that a few will express the desired traits.

The breeding program's initial step happened decades before Fred Hebard entered the world. In the early 1900s, insightful souls bred pure American trees with Chinese stock, creating 50% American/50% Chinese hybrids. All resulting progeny of this cross gained half their genes from each parent. For decades, up until the early 1960s, the US Department of Agriculture (USDA) worked with these trees and their progeny, developing new crosses to serve as potential stepping stones toward a new resistant American species. They failed, due in part to poor planning and a lack of understanding of genetics. While they knew their destination, they lacked the maps, intuition, and simple luck to get there.

As detailed in Chapter 1, Burnham and Rutter looked at the USDA work nearly twenty years later and drew conclusions contradictory to those of the agency. They devised a way to employ backcrossing with pure American stock to produce, at least in theory, a fully resistant American chestnut. This specimen would have at least 93.75% American genes along with the Chinese genes for blight resistance.

Backcrossing works a little like a washing machine. To clean clothes, the machine uses a dose of detergent which is removed through repeated freshwater rinses, taking soil with it. Hybrid crosses introduce a wide range of foreign genes which are then systematically removed through a series of backcrosses, hopefully leaving the genes for resistance behind. In both cases an unwanted residue of soap or genes remains which we learn to minimize and accept. Diminishing returns prevent breeders from continuing backcrosses past a certain point, particularly when one cross can eat up 8 years of labor.

Consider a 50/50 American/Chinese tree. When that tree gets crossed with a pure American, a wide range of progeny result in the first backcross, or BC_1, generation. Through a random process, like the slot machine, each parent places 50% of its genes into each pollen granule or embryo sac in the ovary, so the 50/50 tree's pollen can contain anywhere from 0 to 100% American genes. The BC_1s can then contain anywhere from 50 to 100% American genes with a bell curve distribution within that range, 75% being the statistical average. Unfortunately, present technology will not allow Hebard to examine a given specimen and determine where it fits on that spectrum of purity. He needs to make educated guesses in assessing his young trees, once again employing a greater sample size to increase his chances at success.

The fact that no one knows precisely how many genes code for resistance clouds this backcross process. Hebard summarizes, "In 1993, the data suggested that two or three incompletely dominant genes control blight resistance. Seven years later, we still cannot pin the number down." Evidence suggests, though, that three genes code for resistance. If three genes prove necessary for resistance, then an estimated 87.5% of the BC1s will have little or no blight resistance, while 12.5% will have intermediate resistance. None of the progeny will have full resistance to blight. The situation proves a bit simpler if only two genes code for resistance.

To recall a bit of genetics, genes come in matched pairs in the genome. In a homozygote, the alleles—the various forms the genes can take—are identical, whether dominant, recessive, or otherwise. A heterozygote has non-matching alleles, meaning its paired genes vary in type, analogous to a pair of shoes composed of a left-footed sneaker and a right-footed hiking boot. Partial resistance occurs when a heterozygote codes for a third condition other than what either homozygous genotypes code. The classic case in genetics textbooks involves four o'clocks, a flower, where the RR genotype, the homozygous dominant, codes for red, the homozygous recessive rr codes for white, and the heterozygote, Rr, codes for pink. (Technically speaking, the terms 'dominant' and 'recessive' fail to apply in this case as neither allele precludes the other's expression. Instead, the R-allele codes for a functional pigmenting protein, while the r-allele codes for a non-functional protein.)

If three genes code for blight resistance in chestnut, then a given tree could have any one of 27 different combinations of genes for resistance. Depending upon whether or not the three genes for resistance are dominant or recessive (and it is possible that one might be recessive while the other two are dominant or vice versa), these 27 combinations assign various levels of resistance to their trees. Only one combination, though, offers complete blight resistance. If only two genes code for resistance then, of the 9 possible combinations of alleles, one profers full resistance.

Surprisingly, these percentages for resistance remain the same for the second and third backcross trees, the BC_2s and BC_3s, though the latter will possess an average of 93.75% American genes. BC_3s are intercrossed (BC_3 x BC_3) to produce a second generation third backcross, BC_3F_2, with 1.6% of the resulting trees fully resistant to blight. Roughly two-thirds will have intermediate resistance while one-third will possess little or no resistance. When two BC_3F_2s are intercrossed, the organization believes they'll obtain 100% fully resistant trees, though a footnote in their journal notes: "This percentage of highly resistance (sic) trees is a hope of The American Chestnut Foundation. It is based upon certain scientific assumptions and cannot be proven at this time."

One assumption TACF makes is that the genes for resistance assort themselves independently of other genes. USDA breeders believed genes for resistance sat on the same chromosomes for growth form and other key traits. Resistance and orchard form were assumed, probably faltingly, to be linked on the same chromosomes. Researchers based this conclusion on never finding a tree that combined timber growth with resistance. According to this assumption, when the chromosomes segregate during meiosis, any carrying a gene for resistance will also have the gene for orchard-growth form. Looking at the data, Burnham and Rutter determined the USDA assumption to be in error,

While the scientific establishment—with ample financing—has managed to map a substantial range of genomes for humans and varied laboratory creatures, similar monies have not surfaced for detailing the genomes of chestnut species. Hebard's labors prove similar to those of the noted monk Mendel who fiddled with pea plants back in the 19th Century. By making crosses and tabulating observations of observable traits in the progeny, Mendel and Hebard posit educated guesses of the hidden genetic story underlying the percentages. Mendel came up with remarkable findings, courtesy of likely cooked books offering better numbers than statistically likely, that helped 20th Century geneticists connect their formulations of dominance and recessiveness with developing theory of genes and understanding of DNA's structure. Hebard has access to a wealth of information Mendel could only dream of, yet in many ways Meadowview has become just another monastery crafting much larger progeny with a fraction of the understanding available to an outfit with much greater funding.

Mendel lucked out by choosing traits in peas coded by one pair of genes where only three different genetic combinations were possible. He arrived at simple ratios of 1:1, 3:1, 1:2:1. Hebard's three-gene resistance could produce a much wider range of potentialities, but what makes resistance such a sticky beast is the fact that years must pass before it can be tested. Trees injected with blight respond in several ways. Some quickly become girdled and die. Others resist by building large eyesore cankers that buy the tree a few years of health before ultimately succumbing. Others produce smaller sub-lethal cankers, though the compromised tree may still die from some other scourge. Others fall prey to other calamities, never providing data useful to Hebard's mission.

Another complication with resistance lies in measuring it. Hebard has resorted to measuring the size and severity of individual lesions as well as the rate of growth of lesions and speculating from there. He's also examined development of cankers on other species, most notably scarlet oak and Chinese chestnut, to gain perspective on how resistant trees respond. By compiling statistical data, he has developed a rough ordering of resistance that allows him to quickly categorize individual trees, though the visual inspection leaves room for error.

The unfortunate truth behind all this genetic talk is that TACF still might fail. The real causal story behind blight resistance remains highly speculative. No one can identify the particular genes responsible for resistance or even show that genes impart resistance rather than susceptibility. Inside the individual cell, where genes code for particular proteins that control the actions of the organism, a whole host of strange operations may occur that complicate the whole blight resistance phenomenon.

Similarly, since blight involves several species interacting, a focus on the chestnut's genotype will do little to change *Cryphonectria parasitica*'s behavior. Fungi have special adaptations to allow them to infect various hosts. Since the fungus pervades the eastern woodlands, we cannot know how it will react to restoration of an allegedly blight resistant tree. Perhaps it will find new ways to destroy chestnut to benefit its own survival. Given the rapacity with which this fungus destroyed the American chestnut in the 20th Century, only a fool would discount its ability to decimate a new generation of trees.

Examining the genetic constitution of American chestnut in isolation proves a key problem in TACF's plan. Once two species come together in a parasite/host, pathogen/host, or other relationship, the genetic story becomes even more complicated. Each organism responds to the other's actions. If a parasite begins secreting a toxin, the host might respond by secreting a poison for the parasite. The parasite then might respond accordingly by whipping up an internal antidote to beat the toxin, and so on. The point is that two organisms in a relationship express themselves in unpredictable, complex ways, not unlike two lovers in the heat of argument. If these relationships persist over evolutionary time periods, species interactions become even more amazing, often with the organisms finding ways to co-exist to their mutual benefit or with minimal harm to one another.

Resistant chestnuts throughout Asia and in Europe have had time to co-exist with *C. parasitica*, which still pervades their environment. Many of these trees still develop unsightly cankers, but the fungus proves sub-lethal. We do not refer to these trees as immune to blight because the fungus still hampers their growth. The term 'resistant' refers to the trees' ability to survive an attack of blight. As the fungus develops new strains with new capacities for lethality, these trees might ultimately succumb. In the larger evolutionary picture, such interactions between species where one pushes another to near extinction, prove rather commonplace. According to pollen records, which go back thousands of years, the American hemlock declined for a period of 1000 years before repopulating its native range. Unlike the chestnut, though, hemlock still occupied 5% of its native range. American chestnut has a slight chance of doing the same without human interference, though scientists lack the ability to determine its ultimate fate.

In 2004, the buzz over TACF's progress seemed to have reached a crescendo. The Wagner Farm grew the Graves B_3-F_2s, the offspring of third backcross trees, the tree which the breeding program had set as its goal for the previous two decades. The media had publicized this tree's existence, creating a stir of interest and expanding the ranks of American chestnut aficionados. The trees, only sticks protruding from the soil, would grow a few years before being tested for blight. TACF bigwigs predicted that this particular line should have 100% of the genes for resistance, though several unproven assumptions underlie this speculation. It's still too early to expect seeds from this tree to be available to the general public. Playing it safe, TACF may release the seeds in 2010, after they have had ample opportunity to test the larger trees.

Perhaps the most challenging aspect of Hebard's job, determining which trees to cull and which to keep, requires careful attention to details and a willingness to kill most of the trees to which he's devoted his time. Simply looking at a seedling climbing out of its protective aluminum sleeve tells little about that tree, its resistance to blight, or any of the other characteristics that determine whether or not a specific tree meets TACF's harsh criteria for survival. Hebard has needed to develop a series of tests for assessing his stock. The earlier he can test reliably, the quicker the breeding program progresses and the closer we draw to the über chestnut so desired.

Consider the major differences between American chestnut and Asian species. The American had a straight bole, growing up in a competitive forest where a quick race for the canopy produced tall, straight trees—"timber type" growth. Chinese has "orchard type" growth; it reaches a relatively short height and bushes out. Nut size varies between species, with the American generally having smaller nuts. Most significantly, the Chinese and Japanese species show relatively high levels of blight resistance while the American has lower levels or no resistance whatsoever.

Growth form and nut size require quite a few years before they can be detected, ruling out their utility for the rapid breeding program. This leaves blight susceptibility which Hebard employs regularly. In the past, his plan involved infecting trees as quickly as feasible to remove less desirable trees. A hole drilled into a two-year-old tree allowed insertion of an agar plug rich with spores causing blight. Unfortunately, this technique failed. Hebard discovered that blight resistance took longer to express itself. Hundreds, if not thousands, of potentially blight-resistant trees had been culled from the breeding program.

Within the genome, certain genes determine when other genes express themselves. Apparently, American chestnut's genes prevent the tree from expressing blight resistance in the first few years of growth. Such a finding concurs with observations that wild shoots often survive in blight-ridden environments for nine or ten years before succumbing. The species saves energy by only producing blight resistance when needed.

Minor differences also help differentiate between species. Besides selecting for blight resistance, Hebard selects for general 'American' traits, a list including such technical fine points as "progeny without simple hairs on the interveinal regions of abaxial leaf surfaces and with 1) sparse, long, simple hairs on abaxial midribs and secondary veins; 2) hairless twigs; 3) red stem color; 4) small stipules; 5) small, dense lenticels; and 6) cylindrical, pointed buds. We select against dwarf progeny, progeny that form thick bark layers early, and male-sterile progeny. We select for progeny which do not break bud before the first frost-free date (about May 15-17 in Meadowview)." [The Journal of the American Chestnut Foundation, Vol. XII, Autumn 1998, pp.8-11.] Suffice it to say that Hebard and his colleagues pay close attention to fine physiological details. For simplicity's sake I'll stick with a tool I've grown accustomed to, the Tongue Test.

The Tongue Test's effectiveness relies upon detecting small hairs on the underside of leaves. If you find hairs, then the tree probably has more Asian genes in it, while lack of hairs suggests American. But such a test loses its utility when examining hybrids. Consider the original cross between an American and a Chinese tree done back in the 1930s. The resulting hybrid, a 50/50 tree, might or might not have hairs, depending upon the genes inherited from parents. One needs to look beyond the Tongue Test to learn more about the genome of this tree.

Chemical analysis allows greater accuracy in separating American chestnut from other species. Genes code for proteins, so different species will necessarily have different proteins in their cells. Enzymes, the most commonly used proteins for this work, exist in a variety of forms, known as iso-enzymes, shortened to isozymes. By analyzing a sample's isozymes, a tree's analogue to a fingerprint, we can determine more accurately its composition. Unfortunately, such analysis proves expensive and requires access to a laboratory. Hebard has to ship select samples out for analysis.

Isozyme analysis provides some important data Hebard employs, though a larger scale use of the practice proves too costly for his budget. Once again, lack of finances limits the use of a powerful tool in Hebard's pursuit of a pure American. He reverts to simple visual inspection of his trees, hoping to pick the right specimens for further work.

Hebard knows that decades of work at Meadowview might result in an ultimate failure. Like Sisyphus, he might plant his burden at the top of the hill only to watch it descend to its same bleak beginnings. In the *Journal*, discussing TACF's long-term goal, developing an American chestnut that can co-exist and co-evolve with its nemesis, the chestnut blight fungus, Hebard waxes optimistic, "We don't know whether . . . the chestnut blight fungus will evolve means of overcoming the genes for blight resistance that we are breeding into American chestnut. In fact, we currently *have no evidence* that the chestnut blight fungus will overcome our resistance. (italics added)" A sentence later, he retreats a bit and admits, "However, we also have no evidence that the chestnut blight fungus will *not* evolve means of overcoming our resistance; it could happen, and we need to take all the steps we can to avoid it."

Indeed, what happens once a 15/16th American chestnut leaves the relative safety of the research farm for the wilds of New Hampshire or North Carolina remains a mystery. The behavior of biological systems simply cannot be determined in the way we understand purely physical systems, like the motion of planets around the Sun. Harvard biologist Richard Lewontin, who writes frequently on the complexity of natural systems, challenges several of the tenets of modern biological thought. Concerning adaptive fitness of plants, he argues that engineered plant species, upon reintroduction, change the ecosystems of which they are parts. As breeders alter plants in even small ways, according to Lewontin, "The plant engineers are chasing not only a moving target but a target whose motion is impelled by their own activities." (*Triple Helix*, p. 57)

When the restored chestnut re-enters its traditional forests, those forests will change in unforeseen ways, in effect "moving the target" at which the breeding program aims. *C. parasitica* will be affected by the reintroduction but so will every other species in the forest, plant, animal, fungus and protozoan alike. Even if the blight fungus loses its lethality, other pathogens, parasites and pests stand excellent chances of capitalizing upon chestnut's return. Recall the gall wasp infestation plaguing Hebard's Meadowview trees? That's just one possibility haunting Hebard's thoughts at night.

To help stack their deck, the American Chestnut Foundation's planners have worked to expand the genetic variation in their breeding program. First and foremost, they strive to introduce multiple sources of blight resistance from different lines. The 'Clapper' tree's genetic constitution may be different from that in the 'Graves' line, so both varieties, along with some Asian varieties with yet different genes for resistance, enter the breeding program. In theory, the fungus developing strains to defeat the Clapper-type resistance will be stymied by trees with resistance inherited through the Graves or other lines. At present, though, no one really knows if Clapper's resistance varies from Grave's. Hebard may be creating a one-trick pony that *C. parasitica* consumes as an appetizer.

TACF has also started breeding lines at a range of locations through state chapters in Maine, Massachusetts, Kentucky, Pennsylvania, Tennessee and North and South Carolina. Judy Dorsey, vice-president of the Maine chapter, reported that in 2002, their number of mother trees, wild trees that could play roles in the breeding program had swelled to nearly 20, aiding them in meeting TACF's goal of 20 different lines for pollination. The organization also collected more than 8,000 seeds to sell and store in a gene-bank. Other chapters achieved similar successes, ultimately contributing diversity to TACF's breeding program.

One of the key reasons for state chapters involves rescuing local genetic diversity that might ultimately aid restoration efforts. Hugh Irwin, recent addition to TACF's staff as Vice President for Science, explains how a "bottleneck," a narrowing of chestnut's ability to adapt to novel environmental situations, can develop if breeding involves too little diversity. (*TACF* Journal, Vol XVI, 2, p. 11) Such a bottleneck will likely evict rare genes from the gene pool and reduce variability for specific traits. The rare genes may prove vital to the species in the face of future problems. Indeed, blight resistance itself may have required a specific rare gene one-hundred years ago, leading to the survival of lone individuals possessing that special gene throughout their range.

Determinining how many breeding locations will be needed to rescue genetic variation proves a vexing problem for TACF researchers. Forest geneticists Thomas Kubisiak and James Roberds undertook a study to determine the degree of genetic diversity in American chestnut, analyzing samples from 22 different locations. The samples, studied at the USDA Forest Service's Southern Institute of Forest Genetics in Saucier, Mississippi, revealed that localized populations had almost as high degrees of genetic variation as the entire population. The researchers concluded that "extensive gene flow, probably via long distance pollen movement, was possible prior to the blight." Therefore, Hebard and crew wouldn't need to concern themselves with bringing in stock from throughout the native range to insure genetic variability.

Complicating matters, though, was a common phenomenon known as "clinal variation of allele frequencies." As one moved northward or southward, certain alleles of genes became more common, showing a small, yet statistically significant, genetic variation between populations.

Recent ecological research emphasizes the importance of retaining local genetics. Ecologist Denise Seliskar and others described research that showed local populations of a common salt-marsh plant, *Spartina alterniflora*, had genetic adaptations particular to their local ecology; these adaptations are called 'ecotypes.' The team of researchers took three samples of the abundant plant from coastal locations off Georgia, Delaware, and Maryland. They prepared the samples and then planted them in a special environment on Delaware's coast. When the plants grew, they expressed distinct phenotypes particular to their original environment. One particular result showed that the Georgia strain "produced significantly greater above-ground biomass" than the most-northern strain from Massachusetts. Though all plants represent the same species, they are particularly adapted to their particular ecosystems. Their genetic constitution reflects the specific nature of their immediate environments.

It makes sense to assume that American chestnuts also exhibit ecotypic variation. Maine's trees evolved in conditions significantly different from more southern trees; they probably have specific traits that allow them to survive the extremes of winter and a shorter growing season. Likewise, a North Carolina tree has special adaptations for day length and other conditions. If trees from both environments did not vary according to a trait such as bud release, the date that the tree's buds start growing, it would be likely that either the Maine trees would bud out before a late frost, potentially restricting growth to more bush-like patterns, or the Carolina trees would not be able to out-compete other tree species in their region. Kubisiak and Roberds concluded by suggesting that the breeding program include "a MINIMUM of at least three regions, representing northern, central, and southern portions of the species range" to assure that genetic variations be accounted for (emphasis in original article).

Suffice it to say that adding genetic variation to the breeding program requires a lot of work. Fred Hebard claims that he needs ten acres of land to grow 20 lines of chestnut, with one hundred trees of each line. Those 2,000 trees need a lot of love and attention, not to mention water, fertilizer, and pest control. That's one reason the original farm at Meadowview grew into three properties over the years. Hebard simply didn't have enough room to achieve his mission. The need for space also fueled his urge to test trees for resistance early. He could remove less-resistant plants prematurely to make room for further projects.

Restoration, TACF's ultimate goal, remains sketchy for Fred Hebard. He explained his thoughts concerning reintroduction:

> "First of all, you probably need a disturbed site without an overstory of trees to get it in. You'll probably have to break some eggs if you want to get into the natural forest. By breaking eggs, I mean cutting trees. I expect we'll have to organize some planning program with the National Forest that will require quite a bit of work to do that. We've already started research on silviculture, how to do it, how to get trees back in the woods. But we still don't know what the best methods are to do it. If you plant nuts they tend to get eaten by critters. The nuts are probably the best way to propagate chestnut. If you plant seedlings, then you need to dig a big hole which can limit the number of acres you can do.
>
> "In open lands, it's easy. They plant seedlings on CRP [Conservation Reserve Program] land all the time. You can use a drag setter, just plump them right in the ground, squirt them with herbicide a few years and they're off and running. For getting into mountainous terrain, natural areas, we'll probably require some cutting. Hopefully, we'll have some people test closed canopy although I've done some and—well you've seen how they grow under closed canopy—they just sit there for a hell of a long time. I'm sure there'll be some enthusiasm from mountain landowners to plant on their own. And we'll have to have a whole planting extension service built up to answer people's questions about how to plant, seed distribution, seedling production and nurseries. That whole network has to be worked out. I'm just concerned about producing the seed myself."

Hebard downplays the political poker game TACF faces once they wish to plant chestnut on public lands. From sites I've witnessed, the open conditions needed by chestnut require clearcutting or, in rare cases, seedtree cutting, where lone trees remain to disperse their seed. Once the land's cleared, competitive growers like tulip poplar and striped maple take off as effectively as American chestnut, necessitating an army of Chainsaw Lous patrolling the hillsides. It's likely that the organization will need to micromanage plots to keep these species at bay. Or else, TACF will need permits to apply species-specific herbicides, a situation certain to be opposed by every environmental group in the country. If only a few acres were in question, these problems would probably not pop up. But Hebard wants more:

> "I'd like to see us get 200,000 acres out over the next fifty to a hundred years, which may sound like a lot—and it is a lot in terms of actually getting that much planted—but it's one-hundredth of the acreage that had chestnut

> on it—not that all that acreage was pure chestnut. I wouldn't want to see it go more than that. That's sort of an upper limit, in my mind, until we see how these trees do. Certainly, if someone wants to plant commercially, they plant a mixture, there's nothing wrong with going over 200,000 acres but I don't really see it until we're pretty certain it's going to work."

This acreage will be divided between the various state chapters and other constituents of TACF's mission. But the labor considerations alone for managing that many acres prove astonishing. A volunteer force can perform much of the original planting work, but assessment of growth and examination for blight resistance will require a flotilla of trained individuals. The federal government, even if it is solvent, won't be likely to foot the bill.

Virginia and West Virginia's wealth of strip coal mines, where miners literally removed the tops of mountains to get at the fuel beneath, offer Hebard another opportunity. "Minelands are another thing, too, which are planted. There's a shitload of removed mountain tops that are in grass all over West Virginia, Kentucky, and Virginia. A lot of those could be re-planted. That'll be tough," noted Hebard, who recognizes problems with this option. "One thing there is just getting mycorrhizae on them. Just a standard PT or something will work but no one's really tried to optimize mycorrhizae for chestnut."

When asked about his worries about reintroduction, Hebard shot straight with his biggest concern, "They won't grow." He laughed with that tension signaling a shred of truth to the humor. But his other fears seem more realistic: "Deer browse is probably your number one enemy. Nut theft from rodents and such is a problem with nuts but with other seedlings deer browse is the major problem. And bear can be a problem but there just aren't enough of them to be a big problem." Clearly, Hebard experiences moments where his rose-colored glasses come off and he takes a realistic look at chestnut's future as he wipes the sweat from the bridge of his nose.

Hebard's mission at the Meadowview farms becomes more complex as I consider the many perspectives that need to be considered to craft a blight-resistant tree that will fit into the ecosystems of Appalachia, ecosystems that have changed during the last one-hundred years. He's juggling information from a plethora of scientific disciplines while working with human beings in an ever-growing network peopled by experts, dilettantes, fans, critics, and the curious. On a daily basis, he needs to please a few dozen folks, many he knows but others who drift in on a whim to see the Wagner Farm. He needs to work within the confines of the equipment he's accumulated while keeping an eye on up-dating his arsenal of tools. A severely finite budget prevents him from taking reasonable steps that might speed up the program in favor of public relations maneuvers that satisfy his higher-ups. I hope that TACF finds ways to aid Fred without undercutting his control of the farm.

I worry about Fred Hebard. He doesn't have a mean gene in his genome. He carries the world, or at least this breeding program, on his shoulders. Every little error, whether caused by the weather or by hasty humans, adds mass to his burden. This early summer of 2004 seemed particularly strenuous for Fred who occasionally glimpses the troubling big picture. But he reminds himself, healthfully, that this is his job; he needs to do this to feed his family and keep his sanity.

My greatest concerns involve human changes of these natural systems. Despite volumes of work explaining the problems with non-native species combined with strong laws restricting import of foreign stock, we still get invasive species changing our landscape—zebra mussels, garlic mustard, reed canary grass all make their long march across our country, decimating native species populations. Even our attempts to manage species like the white-tailed deer culminate in loss of species—the rare orchids which indiscriminant bucks and does eat like candy. What chance does American chestnut have in an environment we have already squandered with our short-sighted approaches to conservation?

The most pressing human change, the one we pay the least attention to, is global warming. Already scientists expound on species quietly succumbing to new pests and pathogens. The misnamed "sudden oak death" threatens to snuff California's tanoaks, oaks, and, eventually, redwoods. Wooly adelgid, an insect, erases hemlocks from the southeastern forests. Though it's been in the US since 1924, only recently did adelgid kill most of Virginia's hemlocks. Witnessing the white greasy fuzz coating the undersides of hemlock's needles, I cower at the realization that another intriguing tree species makes its way to the dustbin of environmental history. Hemlock approaches the head of the extinction line, a morbid parade of tree species frighteningly longer than the queue of geeks formed to see the latest Star Wars film or to save these embattled species.

The World Conservation Monitoring Centre predicts that 8,750 tree species face potential extinction. That's one out of ten species known to science! We think that global warming might be the hidden hand behind these problems.

I look out at the lush green hills and I see a future bereft of the familiar species. I imagine forests of two-foot high garlic mustard rising from the rotted hulks of maples, oaks, chestnuts. Snags dot the landscape with streamers of kudzu and other tropical vines hanging from their barren boughs. The shrill drones of abundant insects replace the chattering of squirrels, croakings of frogs, and the warbles, whistles and tweets of varied songbirds.

I tend toward the pessimistic. But, immersed in nature most of my life, I have reason to be. As stewards, we've proven quite unsuitable when we measure our negative impact upon the multitude of species populating the planet. Now as we enter the great Age of Extinctions, a time of ecological catastrophe unimaginable in the not-too-distant past, the scrambling of a few hundred folks to rescue a species from the brink of non-existence, a tree beloved by millions yet unknown to new generations, seems to border on the futile. Perhaps TACF is just fiddling while New Rome burns. On the other hand, I'm quietly glad they fight on. To give up the battle before it's ultimately lost would prove too cynical even for me. I look out the window and enjoy the scenery, forgetting for a moment the ominous fate hanging over all of us. I marvel at the work of Fred Hebard, Philip Rutter, and unnumbered others who take a stake in the American chestnut's resurgence.

My time in Meadowview prompted more questions than answers as I consider the size of their task. A dis-ease seizes me as I examine humanity's current state. We've reached the point where we not only recognize the errors of our ways but also propose solutions to those grand mistakes. But, like kids trying to hide the broken vase from adult eyes by gluing its fragments together, our responses seem to be half-baked attempts to stop the problem without addressing its root causes. Yes, I believe that geneticists can breed a tree with all the desirable genes of American chestnut intact and just enough Chinese genes to bring about resistance. Once we've accomplished this feat, though, what have we really done to prevent the next major extirpation or extinction?

Chapter 3

"In an attempt to increase the productivity of crops, plant engineers make detailed measurements of microclimate around the plant and then redesign the pattern of leaves to increase the light falling on the photosynthetic surfaces and the available carbon dioxide. But when these redesigned plants, produced by selective breeding, are tested it turns out that the microclimatic conditions for which they were designed have now changed as a consequence of the new design. So the process must be carried out again, and again the redesign changes the conditions. The plant engineers are chasing not only a moving target but a target whose motion is impelled by their own activities."

—Richard Lewontin, *The Triple Helix: Gene, Organism, and Environment*, p. 61

Some 100 miles east of Meadowview sits the home and headquarters for the American Chestnut Cooperators' Foundation, my destination upon leaving Fred Hebard and his crew. On the Interstate, I could have covered the distance separating the organizations in little more than an hour, but then I would have seen nothing but billboards, SUVs, cars, and the amazingly long triple-bottom trucks that make me hold breath inside as they flash by. I opted for the back roads, a slower way to unwind and put more distance between me and TACF. I wanted to switch gears to open my mind to the ACCF's program.

If the commonwealth of Virginia were the giant crawdad it resembles in outline, the lengthy border shared with West Virginia would form the peak of its carapace. Driving parallel to that border, I came across few people on a Saturday morning. All the license plates declared one of the Virginias as home. The few folks out congregated on porch swings, in garages, or at flea markets. The two-lane twisted and turned, though not as sharply as the mountainous roads I had driven in western Virginia. In the foothills to the Appalachians, I found myself mentally humming Aaron Copland's "Appalachian Spring" as I crested the minor peaks, passing through tiny towns with common names—Broadford, Ceres, Bland, Crandon, Mechanicsburg. Occasionally, a younger driver tailgated me, waiting for the most dangerous spot to boast the vehicle's power as he or she rocketed past.

As my thoughts drifted, I returned to one common theme: Everything I'd read about the ACCF confused me. While TACF's breeding program seems pretty straight forward with its series of backcrosses, the Cooperators' literature, mostly appearing as professional articles in journals like the *Southern Journal of Applied Forestry* and the *European Journal of Forest Pathology*, approaches chestnut blight from several apparently non-related angles. One piece will offer detailed analysis of the vegetative compatibility groups of fungi attacking chestnut while another will examine the ecological conditions favorable to chestnut reintroduction. As of then, I had been unable to find a quick, encapsulated formulation of the ACCF mission.

Success can pivot upon a brief mission statement, a pithy encapsulation of one's goals that excites potential contributors. The Cooperators, as they're known by nickname, violated nearly all the rules of public relations, creating an approach to rescuing American chestnut all but opaque to anyone not already versed in the gospel according to chestnut. Their website lacked the flash sported by larger organizations. And those articles, always penned by Gary Griffin and less popular figures, proved difficult to find and nearly impossible to comprehend without a few hours of concentrated study and a solid background in botany, genetics, and mycology. After several fruitless hours of research, I'd determined that my only way of grasping the ACCF's program was to get myself to Blacksburg, Virginia and meet the directors face-to-face.

If TACF is the New York City of chestnut restoration programs, then the ACCF ranks alongside an Akron or Muskogee or Oshkosh in popular opinion. Folks hear the calls of TACF's pitchmen hawking their cure for blight in just about every article written about American chestnut. Even our most respected publications have failed to give the ACCF much coverage while lauding TACF's work. While the citizens of Oshkosh, like the ACCF, know at heart they're key players in our national drama, outsiders still slight them as if a few key epicenters accounted for our nation's *zeitgeist*.

The 1992 *National Geographic* article opened with a godlike image of Philip Rutter, an amber glow highlighting his omniscient visage peering down on the reader. A few pages later, a less-becoming shot of Gary Griffin examining a canker gave visual evidence of the ACCF's existence, while below, fellow Cooperator John Elkins' fingertips made the frame of a picture showing chestnut grafting. The caption read: "Close inspection of a blight-resistant American chestnut by plant pathologist Gary Griffin finds a small number of spore-producing bodies on a swollen canker, signifying a non-lethal infection. Griffin's research is shared with chemist John Elkins of Concord College in Athens, West Virginia." Author M. Ford Cochran failed to credit even the existence of the ACCF, leading the reader to assume that Elkins and Griffin were just a couple of loose researchers, not part of a larger collective with a coherent plan to restore American chestnut. I wonder if the writer was so taken with Philip Rutter's charismatic spiel or simply confounded by the ACCF's complex approach to restoration when he offered such an unbalanced take on chestnut restoration in the United States. Nonetheless, the article contributes to the false idea that TACF offers the only show in town.

Familiar with TACF's hierarchical system of Executive Director down to laborer and volunteer, with state chapters and a national office, I failed to discern the overall structure of the ACCF. A few names came up repetitively, the most common being Gary and Lucille Griffin toward whom I made headway. Lucille maintains the organization's web page and had been my key contact via e-mail. She had helped answer questions and, the fall earlier, welcomed my self-invitation to volunteer my services to the ACCF while learning more of their mission. John Elkins' name also popped up from time to time. He once served as President of the organization and was rumored to live in the wilds of West Virginia.

The terrain changed gently on my move eastward. While farms dotted the landscape, some of them quite large, national forest land began to dominate. Unlike the National Park model, where the native inhabitants were chased off at inception, the National Forest model incorporates residents within the public lands, often blurring the distinction between public and private. While the region I navigated stood out a vivid lime green in my atlas, the obvious code for federal forest property, the eye made little distinction between National Forest and farm out the windshield. A sign stretched over one dirt road proclaimed my trespass upon a private hunting preserve that stretched for a mile or so before another sign let me off the hook.

I spent the better part of my weekend wandering the woods north of Blacksburg. On Monday morning, I'd call on the Griffins. Until then, I had plenty of time to explore an area noted as Mountain Lake Scenic Area. My first stop, a place called Cascades—recommended by Tim Lowe of Hebard's crew, required a two-mile trek up a steep river valley to one impressive hundred-foot waterfall. Tourists lined up to take the same picture that folks had taken for decades, simply changing the family members in the frame. Everyone makes the long haul uphill to see the display—little kids who need to be carried on the hike down, Indian women in saris with their families, an older man leaning on his hiking staff. On exit, I spoke with a crew of young Forest Service workers operating the attraction's information station. While all three—recent graduates in forestry—had heard about American chestnut, none knew anything about the Cooperators. They knew their way around Virginia Tech, the university where Gary Griffin taught, though they'd never heard of him. I asked if they had ever seen chestnut around there and they confessed to only knowing the Chinese trees growing along roadsides.

Taking to the side roads, I followed an asphalt way, 713, that quickly reverted to the gravel surface common throughout these mountains. Twisting and turning, climbing and dropping, I drove for what seemed an hour, looking for chestnut and a place to camp. The Forest Service workers assured me that this stretch of National Forest received minimal supervision, allowing me to camp just about anywhere I could park the Civic. The feds lack the money to patrol the lands they oversee, effectively creating a refuge for all kinds of activities—legal and illegal—within their jurisdiction. Eventually the road ended at a downed tree, or at least my forward progress ended. I backtracked, hoping to follow the route I'd taken in, but enough forks made that near impossible. Instead, I discovered the White Rocks campground, a veritable deal at $4 a night, without any of the electrical hook-ups that send camping rates and noise levels soaring. The obligatory nature trail wound one-and-a-half miles through lower, wetter areas, giving me opportunity to catch up on my salamander search. Lifting rocks, I found that in the rare cases where I failed to find one salamander, I'd often find two.

The Appalachians have the greatest diversity of salamanders in the world, suggesting that the mountains offered shelter to today's varied species during the ice ages. Localized environments in these mountains served as refugia, offering safe places for species otherwise unfit to survive the harsh arctic conditions brought about with progressing and retreating glaciers. The Appalachian mountains offer a wide selection of environments within a relatively small area because changes in elevation mimic changes in latitude. With latitude, one might drift a thousand miles north before experiencing substantial changes in climate. In the mountains, that same thousand mile change can occur within a mile as one climbs a few thousand feet in elevation. Thus, northern and southern species can exist in close proximity, ensconced in very different microclimates. Northern species, accustomed to colder conditions, like the Allegheny Mountain dusky salamander, with a range across Pennsylvania and New York, can be found concentrated at high altitudes in Tennessee, Kentucky, and Virginia while southern species live within walking distance at lower elevations.

Salamanders would be only one such creature surviving those harsh icy conditions. The American chestnut itself probably disappeared in northern states 13,000 years ago, as the Wisconsin glacier crept across the land. Species followed the retreating ice, establishing populations in traditional homes or invading new spaces, ready for repopulation. The American chestnut, which researcher Fred Paillet identifies as an effective invader species itself, probably expanded its range after the ice age, moving north through Maine into parts of Canada. Paillet, studying the almost-forgotten grove near La Crosse, Wisconsin, documents how an initial planting of a dozen or so American chestnuts ballooned into 2500 trees ranging over 70 acres in just 70 or 80 years. Apparently, the species has the capacity to supplant well-adapted native trees effectively, transforming into a dominant species in the woody plants' version of a heartbeat. After glaciation, the chestnut would have moved even faster, facing fewer competitors to impede its progress. Given 10,000 years, the species might move hundreds of miles.

I didn't find a lot of signs of chestnut in the White Rocks area of the Jefferson National Forest. Hiking along another spur of the Appalachian Trail, I gathered some panoramic views of the countryside, with wide valleys brimming with greenery. The trees may be fifty years old on average, not impressive in size, but as a collection of individuals stretching as far as I could see, they reminded me of our American urge to save some of the wilds. The AT hiker needs to step away from the trail to find the overlooks and open spaces that reveal the larger picture; otherwise, they remain under the canopy, in a darkened tunnel defined by white blazes on the trees and the bare dirt left in the wake of thousands of feet.

On Sunday afternoon, I began advanced scouting of the American Chestnut Cooperators' Foundation. The address I had, my only apparent guide to their headquarters, detailed Forest Road 708 in Newport, Virginia. The folks at Newport's grocery and gasoline stop suggested I try back in the morning when the local staff worked.

Monday morning, the local convenience store clerks, with no awareness of such a road but guessing it could be that road at the top of the mountain, directed me to Newport's hardware store. "Talk to Eddie across the highway at the hardware." Eddie stroked his beard and pledged his disdain for the fools who went and renumbered all the roads. He'd never heard of FR 708. So I flew down the mountain—a two hump camel's back—into Blacksburg, where Eddie said I'd find the Forest Service. On the way, I checked the "road at the top of the hill" which did not have any sign declaring it FR708.

From the barrage of foliage blanketing the hills, I had no sense of plummeting into an urban area. Only the traffic, dead set on bettering land-speed records, reminded me of urbanity's roar into oblivion. A Forest Service sign declared Pandanas Pond Recreational Area within a mile of Blacksburg. The city itself begins gently, with a smooth transition from forest to country club forest to suburbia. Before I knew it, small businesses began to pop up amid a growing density of houses. Soon I advanced upon Virginia Tech where road construction, combined with a series of one-ways, created the type of snarl annoying local drivers to no end. Elsewhere, the situation would be business-as-usual, but Blacksburg's a small town in many regards, its citizens safe from the heavier traffic issues they might experience in downtown Roanoke half-an-hour away. I caught quick glimpses of falafel restaurants and record stores, the staff of campus life even there. The city's deepest reaches retain a healthy forested feel, with plenty of trees offering earthen seats for readers to congregate. Green lawns spoke of plenty of rainfall combined with homeowner pride and costly chemical applications. Only on its southern end does the city become denser with fast food and strip malls. (A few years later, I'd be shocked to learn that this quiet campus became the stage for a sadistic drama. The serene setting seemed completely antagonistic to violent gun crime.)

Upon reaching Blacksburg's municipal boundary, I performed a statistical analysis on the density of pastel green trucks bearing the chocolate seal of the US Forest Service and honed in on the southside headquarters, keeping an eye peeled for tell-tale brown signage. The receptionist, new to the area, asked a slew of folks behind a partition where to find this "chestnut organization." I began to worry that the ACCF was simply a dreamed-up fiction or, worse yet, a defunct mom-and-pop chased out of business by gargantuan TACF. Even in their hometown, they remained a virtual unknown entity. A uniformed gent, verifying the name "Griffin" rather than his assumed "Griffith," directed the receptionist to the Rolodex where she unearthed an address. "Go past Pandanas Pond," the guy noted, clearing up my confusion over the recreational area's correct pronunciation, "and continue up the mountain." Accordingly, the house sits on the very road referenced by the grocer an hour and one gallon of gas earlier.

No one bothered to post a number on Forest Road 708. Apparently, the Griffins, who boast their proud name right on the mailbox not fifty feet from the highway, and the mail carrier know, and that proves sufficient. I guess the organization did not expect many visitors. I straightened my hair, wiped crumbs off my shirt, and knocked on the door to find Lucille Griffin absolutely unprepared for my visit. She had never received my confirmation e-mail of a week earlier due to a short-circuit with husband Gary's e-mail at Virginia Tech.

Lucille Griffin stands roughly five foot seven, with charcoal grey hair fading to white around her ears. She's got the short haircut conducive to field work and her key recreation, swimming. In fact, she was then the current national long course masters champion in her age class for the 200 meter butterfly—a taxing stroke that seemed incongruous with her claims of joint pain—beating her closest competitor by 0.41 seconds. She failed to mention that she also took second in the 200 and 400 meter independent medleys, and third in the 100 meter backstroke. A thin athletic woman in her mid-60s, Lucille quickly adapted to my intrusion upon her Monday morning. Gary was at work at Virginia Tech and she was getting ready to work at her site downhill from the house.

I perused the cottage—from the outside, this building actually meets that one-word description, unlike so many claiming cottage-hood. Nestled in a bounty of wild flowers and a few American chestnuts, the aged wood structure features a rock chimney and wild gardens stretching below the deck walkway on the downhill south-facing side of the house. A few outbuildings and a long row of trees and flowers on the hilltop hide the house from the road. Groundcovers of various kinds climb the flagstone walls of the garden where tiny praying mantids congregated among ripe raspberries. It's an idyllic building helped along by the Griffins' architect offspring.

Lucille emerged with work implements and a couple bottles of a green tea/grape juice concoction she swears by for its antioxidant properties and we descended the hill to her closest plot. The slope approached 45 degrees as we meandered a couple of switchbacks. At her request, I grabbed a roll of the wire fencing she uses to make tree shelters and followed her the 100 meters down to a clear-cut area, partly terraced to provide a home to Lucille's chestnuts. The Griffins, desiring a site close to home, petitioned the Forest Service—curators of this property—to allow them a site to grow American chestnuts. A small half-acre or so would need to be clearcut. Before long, the Sierra Club, a local bikers' organization, and the Environmental Protection Agency joined the Forest Service in determining if the land could be used as the Griffins and the American Chestnut Cooperators' Foundation desired. After a battle, chestnuts won and the land was shorn of trees by folks in the Blacksburg Ranger District. Lucille then began the meticulous work of moving downed logs and branches, and crafting small four-foot diameter landing pads for her saplings.

Given the substantial slope, she needed to shovel a flat area, often shoring it up with pieces of wood to keep the sandy soil in place. For each site, she made a metal cage that would protect growing trees from deer and other irritants. A pink ribbon waving in the wind lets deer know they shouldn't run into the cages. With thirteen trees to a row, and probably room for 13 rows descending the opening, she could raise 169 trees. But she had a lot of work to do yet, with only five or six rows already completed.

Micromanagement proves the key to Lucille's success. While she carefully began weeding existent rows, pulling the one-inch high tulip poplars growing in the hundreds per square foot, I set off to clear more area for trees. The dried ghosts of rivulets made apparent the high erosion potential for the slope. I worked to set up flat places where the trees would grow well. With a southern exposure, the trees would receive excellent sun year round. I scrounged the piles of debris for arm-thick branches that would keep soil from trickling downhill in the next rain. The work, slow and tiring with Sol beating down on me, required both creativity and flexibility. The sandy ground, offering excellent conditions for the chestnuts which prefer drained soils, would also erode more quickly given any surface runoff. If the soil could stay in place just long enough for Lucille's trees to become established, the roots would help hold the loose soil.

Once level spots were available, Lucille would craft round cages from the fencing I'd toted down the hill. I thought of all the wear and tear Lucille would put on her wrists when she used the wire cutters to cut fencing for her cages.

Planting the actual seed involves a whole new protocol, detailed and time consuming. For each seed, after weeding and removing all roots from the site, Lucille digs an 18-inch deep hole. She mixes a tablespoon of Diazinon into the soil and replaces it in the hole, adding an 8 to 10 inch tube pushed 3 inches deep into the center of the planting. A special weed-retarding tree mat goes down, and then the 5-foot high wire protection cage is installed. If I failed to mention the seed itself, that's because it only enters the equation once it's ready in the fall. Lucille builds all her seed sites well in advance of planting so the actual process of sticking chestnut into dirt goes smoothly.

A few hours of labor go into each individual tree before its roots even taste earth. Unlike TACF's Meadowview farm, though, these trees already occupy the land they are destined to restore. Lucille's laboratory, the actual environment in which chestnuts once grew and where they hopefully will thrive again, serves as a seed orchard. The Griffins will harvest a share of the nuts but squirrels, jays, and other local residents will abscond with their share of the booty, ideally expanding the grove's range.

Sweaty and covered with dust, I joined Lucille in pinching off the young tulip poplars. She explained that she visits each one of her sites weekly, working mornings before the temperature rises too drastically. The little trees need a lot of attention that she showers upon them, like a veteran mother nursing hundreds of babies.

Unlike Hebard, Lucille lacks even an assistant. Gary spends the bulk of his working hours in his lab on campus. Volunteer workers are few and far between. I discerned a flash in Lucille's eye when she realized she had my hands and back at her disposal for the week. Simply transporting wire for cages down the hillside would save her a lot of pain and frustration. She has occasional help but the ACCF cannot afford to pay a regular staff. As I later learned, much of the organization's funding comes out of their own pockets, with little left for luxuries such as labor.

As I would see over the course of the week, Lucille has an intimacy with the trees on her various plots evident as soon as she starts pointing out some of the problems her saplings face. On one site, fairly overgrown and in need of trimming, she spotted dead trees before I could even make out their cages. She maintains a mental map of all the plantings, knowing her way through the plots so that every tree receives attention. She also knows the identity of each individual tree. On larger plots, like the one in Lesesne State Forest, the trees go in alphabetically so that the fourth tree in row 6 earns the name 6-D. But at smaller plots, she'll point to a tree and label it a 'Floyd' or a 'Craig,' much like one would introduce a well-known cousin.

At first, the names befuddled me. I saw no recognizable difference between these trees that I assumed were varieties common to chestnut breeders. I'd heard of 'Paragon and other varieties, though Lucille's naming structure seemed completely strange. After she picked up on my confusion, she explained that the names refer to the counties where surviving chestnuts were found. Floyd County sits due south from Blacksburg while Craig County is northeast, abutting West Virginia.

The American Chestnut Cooperators rely on pure American chestnut stock for their breeding program. Long before the organization existed, a few researchers, Bruce Given and Al Dietz, carried out their own work on chestnut. Given USDA's abandonment of its breeding program in 1960, chestnut work became a vocation for a few isolated individuals. While many assumed that all the chestnuts had died, a few old timers survived in the backcountry. The average wanderer would be unlikely to recognize a standing chestnut. But Given and Dietz knew what they were looking for and when to look.

In the summer, American chestnut appeared much like its neighbors—a trunk with branches and leaves—a distinct trunk, branches, and leaves but only if you examined each individual tree. The dynamic duo of researchers relied on shortcuts for detecting chestnut easily. Each spring, Given and Dietz patrolled the Blue Ridge Highway keeping an eye out for flowering chestnuts. Given the tree's height, the dreadlocked flower clusters appeared like bits of snow in the canopy, making the isolated chestnuts stand out like new cars in a junkyard. One of the fellows would record the tree's relative location on a map and they'd move on, mapping out huge sections of the Appalachians, finding long, lost survivors. In the fall, they would hike back to the approximate location searching for the revealing burs. Chestnut litters the soil for meters with its spiky seed-carrying burs. Once Given and Dietz found the tree, they'd collect a supply of nuts for their breeding program. Many of these strains—identified by county or perhaps another location or person—remain in the ACCF breeding program.

When the Griffins first moved to Blacksburg in the 1970s, Lucille immediately scoured neighborhoods for potential swimming spots before agreeing on the small apartment they occupied with their young children, just a few blocks away from the pool she selected. She's stayed at the same club ever since, though the family moved uphill to their current house once the property entered their economic means. Uprooted from Morehead, Kentucky, where Gary had started his professorial career post-doctorate, the family had failed to sell their Kentucky home due to strange circumstances involving vengeful bureaucrats and politicians, including a governor who prevented the sale of property within their area. So, despite already owning a home, the family found itself strapped for cash, making enough for a tiny apartment from which Lucille and the kids would walk everywhere.

Gary left Morehead State as soon as the opportunity to research American chestnut presented itself. While the Bluegrass State had its share of the trees, his department chair saw little importance in researching the lost species and kept Gary busy in the classroom with a menacing teaching load. When Virginia Polytechnic Institute announced an opening, Gary convinced the search committee that his work on American chestnut would put the school on the map. The institution, which changed its name to Virginia Tech to offer a more up-to-date, cutting-edge facade to the world, still struggles to become the Top 30 research facility the administration desires. Driving to build its programs in cellular biology, where the big money lurks, VT still remains in the second tier of US universities. Griffin's work with chestnut simply fails to impress the big dogs focused on genetic engineering and other perceived modern miracles. No one will ever make a fortune off chestnut restoration so companies like Monsanto look elsewhere for lucrative breakthroughs.

Griffin's lab, hidden at the end of a long hallway on the first floor, stands out for its lack of fancy equipment. A few graduate researchers, in white lab coats, make the rounds. Petri dishes, a few incubators, maybe a centrifuge, compose the main tools of their work. Some of the more technical work is shipped to other labs where researchers do it for a fee. Gary lacks the facilities and money to buy the fancy electrophoresis equipment his graduate students could use. Chestnut work, not relying on the manipulation of genes in test tubes, can be done cheaply, so the university expects Gary to work cheaply.

After she had her noontime swim, Lucille took me out to a stand of chestnuts hidden in the campus arboretum. Virginia Tech has a picturesque campus, mostly built out of hewn white stone. She and Gary maintain a small plot near a field where the veterinary program keeps horses. The trees, perhaps 15 feet tall, occupy an oval island in a sea of manicured grass.

The ACCF makes use of small spaces throughout Blacksburg for their crosses. These trees are various crosses, all known by name to Lucille, who regrets the planting as a few healthy little trees fall under the shade of larger chestnuts.

Lucille pulled her supplies out of the bed of the truck—a 6 foot ladder, a plastic carry-all with the varied supplies for pollinating, and a squirt bottle. Removing a silky bag through which air and light pass readily, she examined the female flower which she sprayed with a fine mist of water from the bottle. In the time it would take any ACF worker to pollinate three or four flowers, Lucille does one, paying keen attention to the work. The water helps the pollen grains adhere to the stigma on the female flower, increasing the chances of successful pollination. She applied her selected pollen with a paint brush, drenching the white stigmas with the dust. Then she tied a small stick around the branch to prove that the flower was treated. She knows that repetitive tasks tend to induce error so she uses every means of avoiding mistakes that might set the breeding program back. She'd return within the next few days to re-pollinate, a task that eats up time but improves her rate of success.

Lucille, who doesn't particularly care for the fruit but eats it for health reasons, almost always totes a banana along on her trips to the field. After devouring the inside, she carefully inspects her chestnuts, selecting a deserving candidate. With a green plastic trowel, she digs an indentation in the soil at the lucky tree's base and deposits the nutrient-rich peel. "I give them every possible help, you know," she admitted matter-of-factly.

Lucille's attention to detail makes her vital to the ACCF's work. She not only oversees most of the Virginia plots, but she maintains the organization's mailing lists and distributes seednuts to members. The cooperators, of which there are currently around a thousand scattered throughout the United States, pay membership fees—$20 annually. In order to get seednuts or seedlings, they agree to submit an annual report each August detailing the health of their trees. The form they fill out asks for height of the tallest tree, number of survivors, number of nut producers, and asks for the number of trees bearing sunken, flat, or swollen cankers. Cooperators also describe the topography of their site and offer any other details they think might be interesting.

Tennesseean Ed Greenwell, formerly one of the more active Cooperators, obtained a clutch of chestnuts as soon as he became a member of the ACCF. One grew to have a notable rust-colored canker encircling its slight one-quarter inch stem. Greenwell kept an eye on that little tree and observed something relatively amazing. Instead of losing its leaves and keeling over, the tree healed, covering the canker with tough tissue, all within one season. Ed named the tree after his son, Nathan. The so-called Nathan Pease tree, surname taken from its genetic parent, has managed to fight off similar cankers over the years, exhibiting a significant degree of blight resistance. Ed crafted a web page, detailing the tree's development with a series of photographs showing the healing process. Greenwell's careful work has allowed the Foundation to start grafts of Nathan Pease in their Virginia Tech plots with hopes of incorporating its capacity for recovering from cankers into their breeding lines.

While she admits that deadwood members—folks who never submit their reports—exist, Lucille notes that she's fairly vicious in culling them from the organization's roles. "We're not a charity and we're not here to see how many members we can get," she reminds me, adding that the whole reason for the cooperators is to produce essential data so chestnut restoration can proceed. Her reference to membership numbers provided a slight jab at TACF which she considers to be driven primarily to become a bigger organization, a criticism shared by some of TACF's people as well.

Ultimately, Lucille maintains databases and spreadsheets tabulating the information submitted by the cooperators. She knows all the various trees out there and can follow growth trends looking at her data. She can figure out which strains fare well at higher altitudes or which prove less susceptible to blight. Some of the cooperators will call or e-mail more regularly, especially those involved in special projects. Preferred cooperators might grow particularly important trees or test out different growing conditions according to the ACCF's needs. Potential financers donate more freely when they see the scope of the ACCF's breeding program, with some 88,643 seedlings and 41,480 seednuts planted by April of 2003.

Lucille manipulated the ladder to reach some of the higher branches, though she's seriously constrained to lower branches on some trees. Lucille's not comfortable bending branches from above with hooks because she fears damaging the tree and inviting blight into the cambium directly through the wounds. While some of the trees have cankers, they seemed much less severe than the "big uglies" Hebard exhibited. Some of the cankers appeared as simply shrunken bark. Surprisingly, the branches and leaves above these cankers looked unaffected by the blight.

Later that day, I met Gary Griffin back at the Griffin home. A pair of work shoes in his hand, already abandoned for the comfortable sneakers on his feet, he stepped out of his car to find me quietly watching a bobwhite quail trolling the yard for bugs. The bird drew a smile from Gary who had released three of the creatures a few weeks earlier. This lone quail remained of the triumvirate, its two peers taken down by feral cats or hawks. Gary found the wreckage of one, a pile of loose feathers, down the road. As Griffin tried to capture the elusive survivor, the bobwhite rejected his half-hearted attempts to imprison it, coolly meandering around the property consuming grass seed.

I introduced myself as the bird continued its patrol. Gary, an avid grouse hunter, hoped the quail would help train his newest bird dog, a mellow beast that sat in its kennel oblivious of the quail within feet of the cage. Griffin has the looks of an older Robert Redford, emphasized by his failure to color his hair as Redford, his contemporary, allegedly has. His work with chestnut has grown out of abundant hours spent bushwhacking the hills of West Virginia in search of ruffed grouse or fly fishing streams rich with native brook trout. His athleticism is of the lean, coordinated type. While Lucille claims the climb from her plot below the house winds her, she notes that Gary skips up grades that might euthanize men twenty years younger. He's evidently no desk jockey, luxuriating beneath fluorescents while interfacing an electron-fed screen. He's an outdoorsman, loyal to the flora and fauna of the Appalachians.

Once Gary changed into clothes more amenable to walking in the woods, the three of us took off for Mountain Lakes. In his pith helmet, Gary assumed the wheel and began to tell me his tales of American chestnut. Retired as a plant pathology professor at Blacksburg's Virginia Tech, Gary maintains his lab, stocked with a crew of capable graduate students. Gary didn't exactly stroll into retirement willingly; his hand was forced by higher-ups who fail to see the importance of his work. Perhaps economic factors forced their own hands as they realized a younger professor would operate with a smaller salary. Or else they simply didn't see a need for plant pathology. No matter the reasons, the powers-that-be started foisting new classes on Gary, requiring more preparation time and stealing time from his chestnut work. While protocol suggested a particular way of assigning courses, the Dean followed his own plan, not so gently pushing Griffin to retaliate. Fed up with a system that, instead of making its senior members comfortably respected, made him constantly agitated, he chose retirement with a few provisos. Keeping the lab was one such proviso.

According to our discussion in the vehicle, I gathered that Gary's major influence is one E. Lucy Braun, who published her *Deciduous Forests of Eastern North America* in 1950. A keen observer, Braun tromped through these woods examining the relationships between tree species and keeping track of variables such as slope, orientation, height, and other factors that affected the forest communities. While Lucille waited in the vehicle, Gary and I exited and climbed up a steep rise near the south end of Mountain Lake. We were close to a renowned hotel hewn of stone, the site for the film *Dirty Dancing*. E. Lucy Braun stayed in that same hotel and walked these very hills, writing about a plot perhaps within a hundred yards or so of our position.

Over the course of an afternoon, the plant path professor demonstrated a broad and profound understanding of the wood and its inhabitants. The type of scientist who can recognize a stand of mixed hardwoods last visited more than twelve years ago, Gary pays close attention to plant associations and other environmental markers that differentiate one spot from another one hundred yards away. He has a way of looking at the forest and understanding it the way teachers remember their students, holding a multi-perspective view where certain traits stand out and individuate the setting. Though the trees had obviously grown, which Gary remarked upon, the mixture retained some of its unique characteristics—a red oak stood perilously close to a hemlock, the latter tragically dying from woolly adelgid; a certain pattern of chestnut sprouts followed a path he remembered.

Momentary panic struck when his prized compass disappeared. Gary pulls out the tool as frequently as a restless school boy checks the classroom clock. He dug through overpopulated pockets looking for the compass, breathing a sigh of relief as it surfaced. Griffin wanted to show me how mesic sites vary from those classified as dry, or xeric, and others described as wet, or hydric. His compass helped align us with the topography and prevailing weather patterns that determine rainfall, which ultimately helps determine American chestnut's presence and density.

Gary explained, "The chestnut is most often found on northeast and northwest slopes, fairly shallow coves." Gary talked about coves. The maritime term seemed to have little use up there hundreds of miles from the ocean and thousands of feet above sea level. His coves are merely three-dimensional land forms that would be more evident if the trees disappeared from the land. Topographically speaking, a cove in the mountains is the same as one in the sea—a slope curved inward with two arms reaching out to form a bay, perhaps looking like the hand's palm holding a few pebbles. Given a similar slope, the depth of the cove depends on how close the arms sit to one another. At the center of the cove lies a focal point where the cove's run-off drains. Gary explained that chestnuts will populate shallow coves most readily because they can out-compete other species effectively. Deeper coves will also house chestnut but the trees will not grow as large or as quickly as in shallow coves; water proves a limiting factor as deeper coves become xeric from rapid run-off.

E. Lucy Braun's work continued to pop up in conversation. It was clear that Gary Griffin recognizes the importance of ecological conditions for a future chestnut restoration. A life of climbing through the hills has instilled in him a strong ecological perspective. One aspect of the ACCF's approach involves determining the best conditions for chestnut growth and then situating trees in those environments. Griffin disagrees with TACF's practice of developing trees on a farm. The agricultural setting simply lacks key elements for chestnut's long-term survival. By growing trees in the actual environments they once populated, the Griffins witness problems that will pop up and update their research program accordingly.

An American chestnut growing in the woods behaves much differently than one on a farm. The woods, populated with chestnut's competitors and the environmental factors which shape and restrict the development of the species, stresses individual trees in the many ways they require to adapt and survive. As Lewontin's observations opening this chapter argue, chestnut's environment is a dynamic system with all interactors, physical and biological, shaping the living beings there. The ACCF's trees, occupying mature forest sites, shape and are shaped by interactions with their surroundings, adapting to those specific conditions. Gary Griffin knows that he aims at the "moving target" that may offer American chestnut a niche considerably different from the one it left in a century ago.

Chestnut faces a long list of competitors. Other tree species vie for the canopy where greater access to light offers a greater chance at survival. Pests like the chestnut gall wasp will challenge chestnut, as will fungi, bacteria, and viruses. Humans will also prove a challenge, some favoring cleared agricultural land to chestnut-filled forests.

Chestnut will also face competition with other chestnuts. If a generation of chestnuts makes it to take up a fair percentage of the canopy, they will likely shade out the next generation of saplings who will huddle in the dark like the dwarfed trees in the woods nowadays.

Griffin's view that American chestnut will have its best shot at recovery if it grows in its eventual home, the forest, agrees with held views in ecology and evolution science. Any survivors will already be exposed to the many factors that affect their long-term survival. TACF's farm trees, on the other hand, will face many of these restrictions for the first time once recovery planting takes place. Removing a tree from the forest, altering it, and eventually returning it to its home may fail because that home environment changes over time. TACF's ultimate blight-resistant tree will not fit like a key in a lock into the forest's ecological systems. The long period in which the species adjusts to living conditions may greatly reduce the success of the overall program.

Back in the truck, Gary related our findings to Lucille who asked specific questions, recalling some details from earlier investigations. The two share a keen interest in individual trees, developing their own language to discuss features of both environments and certain specimens. To an outsider, their talk may sound like gibberish, though one would certainly detect the passionate undertones to their deciduous dialect.

The most renowned individual—a tree that Lucille and Gary speak about with hushed reverence—the Amherst tree, survives on private land in Amherst County, Virginia, between Lynchburg and Lexington. A few years back, Gary studied a downed-limb from the Amherst, counting one-hundred annual rings; the tree itself must be substantially older—at least 120 years old. Lucille, who had taken another writer to see it a week earlier, regretted that we could not go visit that week. The property owner prefers his privacy so she strategically limits her intrusions upon the legendary tree, hoping to keep the owner appeased enough to work with the Cooperators. Seeing the reverence she has for this rare survivor, I had a feeling that she'd build a shrine around the tree if she could.

These isolated survivors needed some advantage over their neighbors to withstand decades of blight. Gary Griffin, following Given and Dietz, attributes this survival to inherent resistance to blight. The entire ACCF mission builds upon this naturally, natively occurring resistance. On our hike, Gary pointed out a few more of the apparent chestnuts hiding under the light-limiting canopy, trees he claimed are at least 60 years old. Their craggy bark, or rhytidome, characteristic of only older trees, gives their age away the way lines on an actor's face betray his years despite a well-colored head of hair. Gary doubts that these little trees have resistance, though he admits that they might.

Gary and Lucille also talked about a trio of larger trees planted in the 1960s surviving in their plot in the Lesesne State Forest. *Phytophthora*, a ubiquitous root rot, had recently taken one of the prized trees out, causing Gary quite a bit of grief. He's not used to losing his champions to such common problems. This death was analogous to a child dying from diarrhea; it happens often in the world but speaks volumes when occurring in societies with quality medical care. Griffin clearly felt responsible for this special tree's death. In response, Gary flooded the soil surrounding the trees with a fungicide, working to kill any *Phytophthora* remaining in the soil.

The importance of those few older trees should not be underestimated. From a public relations perspective alone, the very existence of older pure American trees makes a strong case for the ACCF approach to conquering chestnut blight. But for Gary and Lucille, these trees provide impetus to continue their labors. When one becomes accustomed to small sapling-sized trees, a larger specimen proves very inspirational. One begins to glimpse the potential that this troubled species contains. Most importantly for the ACCF's mission, though, these survivors show that we don't need to import Chinese genes to maintain the trees.

When Charles Burnham, Philip Rutter, and others started TACF, they never banked on any survivors, despite awareness of some trees far outside their native range that had never experienced blight. For all they knew, American chestnut had been extirpated—completely wiped out—through its range. Yet, when TACF members heard word of survivors, they quickly jumped aboard as the organization incorporated them into its breeding program. Cooperators emote more than a bit of disappointment with TACF's alleged hijacking of their approach to breeding. But TACF's managers, without the underdog's perspective, seem to see nothing wrong with borrowing ideas or techniques from the smaller organization. Perhaps the problem lies in a failure to credit the Griffins with masterminding these novel approaches.

I believed that John Rush Elkins was a giant of a man from pictures I'd seen. Upon meeting him, though, I was surprised to find him shorter than me. In a floppy white fishing hat that he sometimes traded for a maroon one of the same make, Elkins looked like he'd be at home lazily fishing from shore. The organic chemist, though, spends the bulk of his time working on chemistry-related problems with American chestnut.

Lucille Griffin, upon learning of my urge to meet John, promptly set up a meeting. On the phone, John gave me the kind of directions that not only helped me find him but which also detailed much of the countryside between Blacksburg and Beckley, West Virginia. A two-hour drive later, I found John in a fast food restaurant's parking lot. Once I shifted my gaze down a foot from the six-and-a-half foot height I expected, I found him searching the lot for me. We connected with his wife Joyce Foster, a government biochemist, and drove cross-town to a residential neighborhood.

Though I knew we were headed to the laboratory John and Joyce had set up to study American chestnut and blight, I assumed that he needed to run to his house to pick something up. We parked in front of a modest suburban home, flanked by a pair of similar dwellings, and approached the building where John tapped out a complicated code on a keyboard. I entered to find the living room occupied by a desk with some equipment, and a row or two of chairs facing the desk. John fiddled with the alarm as I noted a few signs detailing safety procedures. Stepping into another room with a water bath and various dial-covered devices, I realized this little suburban house was the laboratory.

Upon his recent retirement from Concord College, south of Beckley, Elkins decided to take the money he'd collected and invest it in a not-quite-state-of-the-art laboratory facility where he could continue to study chemical markers for blight resistance in American chestnut. A teaching college, Concord allowed John little time to perform original research. So John opted for retirement. The house itself, a two-story plus basement, needed to be rewired with the type of electrical system a modern Dr. Frankenstein would find quite useful. Firewalls and other essential structural protections appease the local fire marshal who's examined the building several times. The neighbors have little awareness of the scientific venture taking place within these walls.

On a tour, John and Joyce showed me the second-hand equipment they'd rescued from various chemical-related companies up-dating their stock. A variety of gas chromatographs, photospectrometers, centrifuges, and other salvaged tools lined the counters and shelves of the house. Though some of the equipment, untested, may falter or require major or minor repairs, Elkins believed he would be able to start designing a laboratory test to measure blight resistance in various stock. Such a chemical screen for resistance could save years if not decades of labor.

The backyard of the facility featured several rows of stunted chestnuts and an outbuilding where more dangerous procedures would occur. While John and Joyce had not yet begun their research, they had crafted a home for their work. The neighbors remain in the dark as John prefers to keep a low profile to deter vandals and thieves. While none of his equipment cost him dearly, one destructive invader might set his work back years. The alarm system, installed for safety as much as keeping out burglars, will warn him and the police well in advance of any damages.

John and Joyce treated me to lunch at Tamarack, West Virginia's center for regional arts. Walking Tamarack's halls, I took in the wealth of cultural offerings in music, art, photography, furniture, and crafts. For a small state, West Virginia had an intriguing history and an inspiring display of arts and crafts. I soon gained access to John Elkins' encyclopedic knowledge of home state, facts and anecdotes he was more than willing to share. He pointed out a book piled in a display, giving me a quick plot synopsis. Some woman, kidnapped nearby, escapes from her captors after they've dragged her several hundred miles away. She makes the trek back home on foot. The author, paying heed to the details, actually re-enacted the heroine's journey, keeping meticulous notes of the sites, sounds and smells she would have experienced more than one hundred years ago. John smiled wryly, noting: "Nowhere in the book did she stop to eat chestnuts." The author, roaming a chestnut-free world, never realized that the popular nut tree would have been a mainstay of the woman's survival. After a few such stories involving chestnut's mysterious non-existence in pre-blight scenarios, or worse, its ubiquity long after blight removed it, stories appearing on film as well as in books, I understood that John Elkins knows far more than chemistry. If I were on a game show and needed to answer a question pertaining to any aspect of West Virginia—its history, literature, geography, or other matters some might call "trivia"—John Rush Elkins would be my most promising resource.

He's an avid proponent of his state. Having grown up in these hills that dared to secede from the state of Virginia at the same time Virginia sought to secede from the United States, Elkins proudly noted that two-thirds of the most wondrous spots noted in a popular book about Virginia fall within the boundaries of West Virginia, "which has the only spot where the Mason-Dixon line runs north." As I polished off a plate of fried green tomato sandwiches, he rattled off a litany of facts about West Virginia. Joyce grinned, accustomed to John's enthusiasm.

John and Joyce insisted on directing some of my ultimate journey homeward. First, identifying a common interest in photographic genius O. Winston Link, we discussed the new Link Museum in downtown Roanoke, Virginia, a remarkable site I made time for the following day. He also insisted that I visit a small museum in Dover, Ohio—even if it was off my path of travel. He informed me that I had to go there—to witness the carvings of one Ernest "Mooney" Warther. The couple had visited there recently. Joyce showed me the wooden pliers she'd garnered, carved on-site by Warther's grandson using only nine cuts with a specially-designed knife. While John took me on a tour of Beckley, Joyce copied pertinent materials that she'd share later. (Eventually, my visit to the museum offered a restful break from a full-day's drive. Presenting the Warthers with a chunk of native American chestnut Lucille Griffin had volunteered, I enjoyed the museum's intricate carvings as a guest and earned my own wooden pliers.)

A few hours into my visit with the pair, I remembered that I came to learn how to graft chestnut trees and mentioned this fact to John. John looked up at the rapidly descending sun and realized we needed to move on so we gathered his materials and headed off to a tiny, triangular plot of chestnuts interspersed with a few dwarf fruit trees and berry bushes. Unlocking the gate to the plot, he told me that he grew up in a house across the street. But when he was a child, that house sat half a block over on a different street. In all, I believe that house, a regular house—not a mobile home, had moved three times. I imagine a young John Elkins coming home from school, searching the neighborhood to find the latest spot for the errant building.

The chestnut plot had once been his mother's garden. The raspberries growing there, descendants of her plants, produced a delectable large fruit that helped invigorate the next few hours of work. The chestnuts, once again all-American stock, stood from ten to twenty feet tall. Limited signs of blight showed, though for a site located immediately next to a busy highway, behind a wall, the trees looked remarkably healthy. Most of them were grafts.

As plants grow, they require a careful balance between above-ground and below-ground growth. A tall tree with many branches needs an equally extensive root network to pump water to the leaves, deliver necessary minerals, and serve as an anchor. If we could somehow take existing root networks, cut off the parts of the plant above ground, and then tap into that root network we would save a lot of time growing plants, particularly larger trees. Grafting allows us to do this.

Grafting, an age-old technique for combining two different stocks of plants, primarily woody though the technique works with some herbs, requires matching the vascular cambiums of two plants so that they grow together. Oftentimes, nursery keepers will graft a branch of a desirable apple variety that might not brave local conditions onto other hardier stock, potentially growing rare types in new climates. Scion wood, the wood being introduced to the established tree—the stock, will more rapidly grow to produce chestnuts. Often a graft will need only three seasons to produce nuts while a planted seed will only produce nuts after seven to ten years. Thus, grafting saves years in the restoration effort.

Grafting allows us to establish difficult stock that might not grow well from seed. It also allows us to introduce branches from wild trees. For example, instead of driving 50 miles to pollinate a given tree in the National Forest, we can bring scions of those trees into nearby plots and establish closer populations.

The key tool for the work, the grafting knife, requires a frequently sharpened squared blade. A hand lens helps the grafter see their stock, while various materials such as bees' wax or tar seal the wounds in plant tissue. John pulled a slim suitcase-sized package that we unfolded into a working four-seat picnic table—the perfect place to teach grafting.

Grafting, for John Elkins, requires the utmost preparation and precision, not unlike brain surgery or bomb defusal. One false move, one imprecise cut, one lapse in concentration may prevent the graft from taking. Near-sterile conditions reduce the opportunity for infection from blight fungus which poses a serious threat as the pieces of wood are sliced open to the air. John informed me that 10-20% success of grafts once constituted success. When he learned the craft at the hands of earlier chestnut hero Bruce Given, Given touted a success rate of 25-33%. Elkins, paying careful attention to the stock as he's performed hundreds, if not thousands, of grafts, claims his observations account for an increase in successes to 50-70%. He taught Lucille his tricks and she claims a slightly lower rate. Both examine their unsuccessful attempts, positing reasons for the failure and composing solutions to improve future work.

Given the substantial investment in scouting a site, gathering scion wood, preparing root stock, performing the graft which can take as long as an hour, and housing each graft inside a metal cage, any increase in success rates translates into hours, days, and, potentially, years saved for other work. Elkins hoped to raise his success rates even higher.

We' were pushing the season, claimed John, who rarely grafts past the middle of June. This second last day of the month, a week past the solstice, proved experimental. Elkins wanted to see if the grafts would succeed, allowing him to extend his season a bit. Grafters maintain an arsenal of varying grafts, each suited for particular times of the year. The whip graft, employed for just a few days in early spring by Lucille Griffin, combines similar sized branches of stock and scion with Z incisions cut into each piece and fitted together. This day, John would show me a modified bark graft, or stump graft, where a tiny twig of scion from a young branch will join a stump cut one-inch above the ground through a slice in the latter's bark.

John began by selecting a six-inch long twig from a collection he had harvested earlier. Using the grafting knife, he clipped a section containing one bud and handed it to me to examine under the magnifying glass. Woody plants feature xylem and phloem, narrow straw-like tubes running vertically that carry water and sap. These tubes are grouped together to form phloem fiber bundles, visible in the cross section of the twig with magnification. I examined them as Elkins explained the importance of lining up cuts so that one of those phloem bundles would be exposed on the surface, ultimately connecting with similar tissue on the stock stump. In cross-section, each segment of a branch has woody pith at its center, the toughest wood to cut, with a four or five lobed amoeboid surrounding it. The bundles of phloem and xylem appear as darker areas at the tips of the lobes.

John then showed me a series of careful cuts he made on the one-inch twig, first shaping it into a wedge and then shaving down one side of that wedge to reach the phloem fiber bundle. The grafting knife, sharp and dangerous, remained in his firm grasp, moved deliberately and precisely. The veins and muscles on the backs of John's hands—the very hands featured in that famous *National Geographic* article that neglected the rest of Elkin's person—stood at attention as he worked blade against wood. With 24 years of practice behind him, his minute motions remain deliberate, removing the optimal measure of bark, wood, and cambium.

He placed his prepared scion into a plastic bag with water in it and selected another for my attempt. I examined the fiber bundles and determined my cut. Wielding the blade, I sliced through bark and cambium easily but the denser heart wood wanted to turn the knife's edge away. I knew how sharp the knife was and displayed a bit of trepidation that Elkins picked up on immediately. He reminded me that cuts need to be firm and deliberate. I lined up my wood, keeping thumbs out of the mix, and made a strong cut, removing a chunk of the scion. He examined it under the lens and suggested I shave away even more to reach the fiber bundle.

Muscle memory plays a key role in grafting. Elkins, after years of experience performing grafts and leading Bruce Given Memorial Grafting Clinics, feels the wood and sees his cuts the way a sculptor views stone, recognizing the pieces that need removal to create a work of art. One needs to remove exactly the extraneous material leaving only the core stone, or wood in Elkins' case.

Our scions snuggly hidden in John's pocket, we prepared the stock—a short two-inch diameter stump at the base of a larger clump of trees. John's devised a way of finding phloem bundles on the larger stock. Unlike a twig, one cannot look at a cross-section of a larger diameter piece of wood and pick out the bundles. Instead, Elkin's learned to inspect the bark where tiny lenticels, pores in the bark that allow the free exchange of gases between the cambium and the air, appear in greater density where phloem bundles occur. He showed me that the chestnut actually twists as it grows, evident on older snags with their helical growth, so he needed to take that rotation into account as he made the graft. The prepared scion twig rested in its ultimate position as John positioned his knife perpendicular to the line tangent to the bark's surface, set it off kilter five degrees toward the scion, and sank the blade's tip into the bark to the heartwood. Driving the sharp edge the rest of the way in, he held bark on one side of the knife's steel and twisted the tool to open a flap of bark on the opposite side. Scion wood fit perfectly into this woody pocket as foreign cambial layers met. John wrapped tape around the stock, keeping the scion in place. All wounds were sealed with a special pitch tar, keeping the bud free to develop. A raincoat constructed from a sandwich bag, to keep water out of the black emulsion, was slipped over the tar and Elkins finished by labeling the graft.

Once John let me take a shot at grafting, I realized that his dexterity came from years of practice. As a beginner, my moves were less precise and ultimately less likely to produce a successful graft. But I got a feel for the basics, seeing that I'd improve quickly with practice.

A graft can fail anywhere in its first few years. The tender union between plants can succumb to disturbance by deer or cattle, excessive precipitation and flooding, or even the gnawing teeth of rodents and other small critters. On a visit to her Rocky

Mountain Road site, Lucille groaned in alarm. Her prize graft that had performed well for a year had withered and died. Meticulously, she inspected the graft, explaining aloud to herself the possible causes of the loss: "Leaf damage here and on this one, too." She speculated a hail storm responsible for damage throughout the stand but considered that bugs might have chewed the foliage. She bounced back from her initial disappointment, taking it all in stride as she has to if she wants to succeed. At the end of the season, her analysis of the year's grafts measured a surprisingly low 30% overall success which she attributed to a new problem, "tiny ants colonizing the new grafts inside their shelters" that ate the buds. Some sites boasted greater than 60% success while a few had less than 20%.

By the time we'd finished two grafts a piece, my stomach needed sustenance. We found Joyce in town, grabbed a few sub sandwiches, and headed out to New River Gorge, a national riverway northeast of Beckley. Folks amassed at an amphitheatre to see the Hatfields and McCoys reenact their noted feud while herds of deer browsed the park, oblivious to our approach. The sun, on its descent to the horizon, offered adequate light to climb stairs up a bluff from where we could see the New River twisting its way through forested hills, deep green with the vitality of June. Signs of humanity proved few—a railroad bridge down below, flat top mountains where greenery has replaced the stripped mining land. We sat down to eat and I thought back over the afternoon. At one point, I'd asked John how chestnut came to play such a central role in his life. He took a thoughtful pause and replied:

> "My grandmother cried when the American chestnut was killed out by the blight. My aunt told me that about a year ago. In those days, everybody went home—the whole family of nine, ten kids, however many it was—they all went back to grandpa's place to visit every Sunday. It's what you did. All the cousins would play out in the yard, and every now and then, I'd wander through where all the adults were talking, and they were talking about chestnut more often than not. Quite often about chestnut there, as well as all the people in the family and in the neighborhood. And so it was a subject matter and I was just interested in it.
>
> "When I got into chemistry, and did my Ph.D. in organic chemistry, one of the requirements was that they wanted me to do a research proposal on something I thought I could apply my chemistry to, and I thought about chestnut. And so I did some chemical literature research on what had been done with the chestnut and, uh, wrote a little proposal. I've certainly expanded on that now to get into the host-parasite interaction, looking specifically for physiological, chemical, biochemical differences in a blight-resistant and a blight-susceptible American chestnut.
>
> "My grandmother . . . saved in her family scrapbook, saved an article that was written in 1942 during the second World War by a local editor of the *Beckley Post Herald.* It was an article in his "Waking them up" column . . .

> on American chestnut. It was very evocative. I found it in my grandmother's scrapbook after she died. And even after my mom died, because it became my mom's after that. So you can go on and see what people thought and what a role the American chestnut played in their lives as they grew up. That's the environment I grew up in."

The one-thousand plus Cooperators comprise the bulk of the American Chestnut Cooperators' Foundation. A disparate collection of individuals pursuing a common goal of chestnut restoration, the Cooperators maintain varying connections to Lucille's Blacksburg mothership, some just growing a few trees ornamentally in their yards, others evangelically spreading the word to potential converts. Ed Greenwell, at 40 years old, falls toward the left side of a Bell curve sorting Cooperators by age.

Greenwell's far too young to remember chestnut's decline personally. Instead, a string of events stirred in him an interest in the species, eventually helping him stumble into the Griffins' organization. In pre-adolescence, that age where kids still dare to find solace in nature, Ed and his father helped "Granddad Greenwell" replace a light pole, a naked piece of wood feeding power lines to their milk house. An inquisitive youth, Ed asked his grandfather about the pole's nature. Grandad, a former school teacher and agricultural extension agent, told him that pole which had endured 30 years of the elements and decomposing powers of the soil came from an American chestnut. The species, the grandfather maintained, had quite a story behind it that he shared with his grandson.

A few years later, Ed happened upon chestnut again, in a *Boys' Life* story about some rare survivors up in Michigan. The seed his grandfather planted began to send out a shoot and roots. Ed's mind had been colonized by the long, lost tree, though decades would pass before the thoughts produced viable fruit. Ed progressed through life, earning an MBA, claiming a position as an electrical engineer, while building his connections to the natural world through gardening and escapes to the woods when time permitted.

Eight years ago, circumstances found Ed browsing the Internet in search of information on American chestnut. His first find, the American Chestnut Foundation's website, offered promise, though Ed shied away, wary of their risky use of foreign stock. Greenwell had developed an awareness of threats imposed by non-native plants, undoubtedly from seeing the many invader species re-tooling the forests he hiked.

A more exhaustive Internet search uncovered the ACCF's less evident web presence. "After reading through their entire website at least 20 times, I decided that I wanted to be involved with the trees and also to be involved with spreading the word about their fantastic work through the Internet," Greenwell told me. Greenwell started growing a few pure American chestnuts provided by Lucille, but his fascination developed almost as quickly as those trees. Today, he teaches nutgrafting clinics for the ACCF, maintains his own website featuring pictures of the Nathan Pease tree, networks with fellow growers, and leads scouting groups in chestnut restoration activities. Lucille considers Ed a tremendous asset to the organization, a homegrown champion who's helped spread the word in Tennessee and elsewhere. Greenwell simply enjoys helping embattled tree species get a shot at survival.

The American Chestnut Cooperators' Foundation assumes a tri-pronged approach to re-establishing American chestnut throughout its native range. First, they scour the backwoods for surviving chestnuts of appreciable size. These relics may have partial resistance to blight. Second, they exploit this naturally-occurring blight resistance in their breeding program, working to produce more resistant trees. The third prong, undoubtedly the most difficult for any but a trained mycologist to understand, involves hypovirulence, the virally weakened strain of blight, introduced to the stock to increase resistance.

Hypovirulence first became a topic for chestnut researchers in 1951, when plant pathologist Biraghi, working in Italy's Genoa region, noticed that cankers on sprouting chestnuts exhibited seemingly spontaneous healing. As noted earlier, Italy had experienced its own chestnut massacre during the 1920s and 1930s. After three or four generations of sprouting in which the blight would quickly kill the emerging sprout, Biraghi noted healing of cankers. The blight fungus while still populous failed to destroy the cambium, essential to the tree's survival. Biraghi hypothesized that the trees gained a measure of resistance after repeated cuttings, an odd, quasi-Lamarckian explanation that had little grounding; he did not explain how the trees might acquire new traits through repeated coppicing.

French researchers began isolating varying forms of the *Cryphonectria* fungus, then known as a member of the genus *Endothia*. Their "B" strain, the fungus associated with non-lethal cankers, the cankers Biraghi viewed as healing spontaneously, had a profoundly different impact upon chestnut: "When a tree is inoculated with a B strain, a small canker develops over a limited area. The fungus produces a red band, about 1 cm in diameter, around the inoculation site before ceasing to spread. Callus then forms at the inoculation site. When a cross-section is cut through the canker it becomes apparent that under the diseased bark there is a new bark, formed by a suberophellodermal generative layer in reaction to the infection." In other words, the canker failed to destroy the cambium, proving less lethal or "hypovirulent." It had taken decades for hypovirulent strains of fungus to spread throughout Italy, but when they had, chestnut made a serious come-back.

Naturally, researchers in the States seized upon hypovirulent fungi as a new potential cure for our chestnut blight. Ideally, hypovirulent strains would work analogously as immunizations work against human disease. Once the strain is introduced to the population, those trees would become immune, or at least less susceptible, to blight. Unfortunately, despite the best of efforts, simple release of hypovirulent strains in the wild had negligible effects on the trees; they still succumbed to regular virulent forms of the fungus. Somehow the biology and ecology of hypovirulence proved beyond the ken of many of the researchers. While hypovirulent strains moved among populations of

Italian chestnuts, such motility has not occurred to date in American trees. The ACCF continues to study the possible use of hypovirulence in saving American chestnut.

Virginia Tech graduate student Eric Hogan stakes a future career on intra-species inheritance of resistance. Soft-spoken, with brown wavy hair and wire rims, Hogan, working under Griffin, studies the ecological factors involved in virulent and hypovirulent strains of *Cryphonectria parasitica*. In a series of articles co-written with Griffin and others, and one of which he claims sole authorship, Eric shows that the virus that decreases the pathogenic fungus's powers moves throughout the tree effectively despite vegetative compatibility groups. In other words, hypovirulence does spread on a single tree fairly well. It does not move from tree to tree very effectively, though.

Fungi, composing their own kingdom of organisms, opposed to animals, plants, protozoans and bacteria, have their own bizarre ways of accomplishing life's varied tasks. When growing in Petri dishes, two fungi with different vegetative compatibilities build a barrier when their cells come into contact, theoretically to protect the colony. Vegetatively compatible fungal colonies mix when making contact, with varied results. Some form a heterokaryon, a hybrid of the two forms that may have traits of either or both forms.

Eric Hogan has studied the large Thompson tree at Lesesne. Armed with surgical scalpel, he obtains small samples of fungus from multiple colonies on the tree, flagging the sampled sites with pink forester's ribbon. After culturing his samples on agar, Eric can test them for virulence, identify vegetative compatibility which is organized into groups, and determine how hypovirulence spreads among fungi populations.

While blight resistance determined by the chestnut's genome offers one way of potentially overcoming blight, hypovirulence may allow researchers to strike at the blight fungus itself. If hypovirulent strains could be released to spread throughout a stand of chestnuts, then trees would be more likely to survive even if they had reduced blight resistance. While hypovirulent fungus still causes cankers, the fungal hyphae-analogous to plant roots—fail to penetrate through the bark far enough to damage the tree's systems for transporting water, food, and minerals. In effect, the fungus and the tree achieve a symbiosis where neither dies from their mutual connections.

Back in Blacksburg, I returned to helping Lucille in her plots. One stand, behind a locked fence, sits right at the end of the city's airport. While the rest of the country endures high security at airports, Lucille calmly keyed the lock, opened the gate facing a small elbow in a suburban street where we parked, and entered the airport's grounds. She had pollinations to perform while I wielded the clippers and hand saw, clearing the trees and vines invading her babies. The security force, patrolling the grounds on four-wheelers, left us alone in our labors.

Across the board, cooperators praise Lucille's work. John Elkins puts it simply: "She's the key to our program. She's really doing tremendous work." Her husband also lauds her commitment, bemoaning the fact she was chased out of science so quickly: "She was in biology, a mix of botany and zoology—animals and plants. Anyway, she learned she faints at the site of blood and that was it." Lucille stayed in college, majoring in French, a language her mother spoke and which afforded her a year abroad. Gary insists she would have made a fine botanist and believes she would have earned a Ph. D. "When we go to Canada on vacation, she has a third of the passion for talking French that she has for chestnuts," he observes. Even if she missed her calling back then, Lucille Griffin has found it today that her kids are all grown up.

The next day we traveled less than ten miles to her Rocky Mountain Road site where we found the failed graft. With saw in hand, I removed a huge swath of undergrowth shielding her trees from the sun. As I began cutting, I realized the overhanging mass sat precariously upon a few questionable trees. The grapevine snaking through the trees above counted for a hundred pounds itself. Past cuttings had allowed a build-up of branches, trunks and miscellaneous parts that could rain upon me tragically, so I did my best to be careful, listening for the threatening groans of the shifting weight. After a half hour of hard work, the entire woody mess began shifting and collapsed to the ground as I moved deftly away.

If a wanderer were to tromp randomly through the deep woods of Virginia—a remarkable expanse for anyone accustomed to Arlington and the greater DC area northeast—an extremely slight chance exists that they'd uncover one of Lucille Griffin's research plots. The distance from the Lesesne, due east of Lexington and the Appalachian Trail hiker's favored Montebello, to Mountain Lake, northwest of Blacksburg, exceeds one-hundred miles, according to the airborne crow, translating into nearly double that distance on road and highway. The rows of wire cages flying their pink flags to discourage deer and increase their profile house chestnuts varying from a few inches tall to fifteen feet. A host of weeds—sassafras, locust, poison ivy, poke, pipevine, wild grape, blackberries, grasses, and other nuisances—invade the cages, prompting Lucille to remove them by hand. In her soiled white t-shirt and slacks, sun hat and goggle-like sunglasses, she comes off as quite the control freak, eliminating each and every hindrance to her trees' growth.

"You have to go in there every week and weed. Otherwise, gazzing!, the weeds take over and you lose your tree," she explained in a vestigial Long Island accent tinged with an Appalachian lilt. She's essentially decreasing competition for her spoiled specimens while making light available and preventing rot.

On Thursday, I awoke with the sun's first light, fortunately re-scheduled by an intervening rain shower. Lucille was waiting in her driveway, performing a series of calisthenics and stretches to help her remain limber. We had a long drive to the Lesesne stand, snugged into the George Washington National Forest east of Lexington. On the way, conversation took its natural course. We discussed competitive swimming, a pursuit we had in common. Lucille described the camaraderie that pervades the racing events. She enjoys getting together with the crowd of swimmers, some familiar and some new. Every once in a while a ringer—a former Olympian or college swimmer—steals the show but most of the time the swimmers practice their own form of compassionate competition. She told me of the book she wrote and self-published, teaching other adults how to swim the competitive strokes. Swim coaches use the book at various high schools and some colleges, but Lucille's never made much money on the book which she sees as a labor of love.

We crossed railroad tracks in a small burg. She mentioned railroad photographer O. Winston Link's famed print of the crossing where a young couple fills their gas tank while eyeing one another lovingly. As we passed beneath a bridge, she pointed it out as the Blue Ridge Parkway, the same highway frequented by Bruce Given and Albert Dietz decades ago in search of long, lost surviving chestnuts.

The Lesesne State Forest stand, first planted by Richard Jaynes, Dietz, Given and others starting in the late 1960s, contained an interesting mixture of trees. Of the 10,000 trees planted between 1969 and 1975, selections from the Connecticut breeding program, eight had the traits desired when examined in 1981. The stand also featured Al Dietz' trees grown from irradiated seed.

Two of those original 10,000 trees remain, a third the afore-mentioned victim of *Phytophthora*. Gary had stopped additional plantings until the root fungus treatment proved effective. Unless *Phytophthora* is eliminated in the stand, it could spread to all the trees, effectively wiping out the ACCF's largest and most successful plot.

Lucille unlocked a gate and we drove down an overgrown two-track trail to the stand. A small creek sang among scrub trees on our right. The several acres unfolding before us seemed huge compared to the ACCF's other plots. Row upon row of five-foot American chestnuts covered the gentle east-facing slope, the sun positioned halfway between horizon and high noon. Pink ribbon fenced off the zone treated for *Phytophthora*, the dead skeleton of an apple tree-sized chestnut flanked by a lively pair of relative giants. One-hundred years ago, the trees wouldn't have garnered a second look, but today I examine them respectfully, noting the many small ribbons spaced on the bark, marking Eric Hogan's sample points.

The Virginia Department of Forestry clear-cut this swath through the larger 421-acre state forest, originally a philanthropic gift donated with the express purpose of re-establishing American chestnut. The National Wild Turkey Federation, seeking habitats in which their favored birds can roost and find nourishment, has contributed $4,320 to the ACCF's project at Lesesne, with the National Fish and Wildlife Foundation adding $2,880. While $7,000 might not seem like much, the Griffins can extend those dollars farther than one would expect. Old enough to have parents and grandparents talking about the Great Depression, Gary and Lucille pay strict attention not only to dollars, but to nickels and pennies as well. They abhor waste, thus prompting methodical planning and careful implementation of those plans.

I'm continually amazed at the number of people tangentially involved in chestnut restoration. Lesesne offers living proof that we need social networks to accomplish significant goals in this day and age. If not for all these outside contributions, Lucille's 5-hour round-trip drive, performed weekly, simply wouldn't be worth it.

Once again, the division of labor found Lucille weeding individual cages while I ranged over the plot, excising larger growth such as the precocious sassafras competing with the young chestnuts. Every once in a while, I overheard Lucille sharing her observations. Hunkered down near the soil, she would reach in and yank out stems and root clusters, finding the lone chestnut lurking in its metal cage, muttering oaths beyond my range of hearing. When something dreadful happened, when a tree was missing due to gnawing rodents or other natural disasters, her voice rose in volume. I understand the depth of suffering of both Lucille and her trees. With such time, energy and care invested in each tree, Lucille deserves a moment of mourning for each lost seedling.

I patrolled the field, removing the larger invaders with a venomous energy. Lucille's zeal proved contagious as I carefully cursed the weeds ruthless enough to invade Brother Chestnut's turf. At times, it was difficult to find the chestnut leader within all the other stems protruding from the ground; I had to be careful not to cut the prized trees. The hills surrounding us, lush with greenery, offered a distraction as I clipped the endless ocean of weeds, painfully aware that the copious rainfall would bring them back with a vengeance in a week or two.

The drive back to Blacksburg offered contemplation as Lucille and I were both rather tired from the morning's labors. I examined the small towns along the way, their cemeteries, small stores, showy sideyards bedecked with pre-Independence Day gaudiness—blue, white, and red ribbons and banners—hearkening back to days before my birth. Away from the Interstate, we found small towns dozing in their rural somnolence, free of the franchises for fast food and home goods polluting the more traveled routes of America. The smiling lawn mower waved a hand our way. The tip of the finger on top of the steering wheel announced oncoming drivers. The pace recalled a time when nature called the shots rather than the bosses. I wonder if chestnut could belong anywhere but here. For me, chestnut represents all things slow. Certainly, trees stood as giants throughout these woodlots but they had taken half a millennium to reach that size. Lucille and I avoided political confrontations, knowing we diverge in core beliefs, but I think we share an awareness that these communities may disappear soon, that this way of life, correct and good, simply fails to fit into the larger schema of modern life for which we both blame different parties. I wanted to ask her how we could save this world but I lacked the heart, fearing that her answer would simply reject my world view, as I knew my response will injure her.

The cultural and political divide between us seemed unbridgeable, her truck a microcosm of our society. The disparate parties here quibble over minutia while ignoring the larger picture we all treasure. While on the same side, we try to convince ourselves that we need enemies which we devise out of family and neighbor The banality of it all left me despondent on the long drive.

Gary maintains few illusions concerning chestnut restoration. He talked about the historic disappearance of hemlock roughly a millennium ago. The species, driven to a mere five percent of its original numbers, repopulated its range in a few hundred years. Human intervention proved unnecessary in recovering the species. American chestnut might do the same given 500 years or perhaps a millennium. The ACCF hopes to speed along the process, though, maybe reducing the time to 100 or 200 years. Unfortunately, the ACCF faces extinction long before their mission can be completed.

Unlike the many-armed TACF, the ACCF relies on the work of three key people. Gary and Lucille, in the latter half of their sixties, and John Elkins, recently turned 60, form the heart of the organization. While younger people—possibly Gary's graduate students or some of the Cooperators—might step into the footsteps of the Dynamic Trio, the amount of information lost in such a transition would be substantial.

Philip Rutter defends his initial plan to include state chapters in TACF's long-range program by arguing that, given a collapse of the national organization, one of the stronger state organizations might step in to resume activities. Beehives exhibit the same behavior. When a queen gets old, the workers feed royal jelly to larvae to produce new queens. One emerges to replace the dying elder. Rutter, tracing the history of the Audubon Society, notes times when state groups needed to take over, keeping the larger organization alive. Without state groups, we might not have an Audubon Society today.

The ACCF could fade given one tragic accident, not an unlikely possibility given that two of the key elements live together and spend a lot of time driving dangerous roadways. Almost all of their data and vital information sits on a few computers in the house and at the lab. And Gary Griffin's brain carries even more of the information vital to the Cooperators' work. Without Lucille to maintain her databases and communicate with the individual cooperators, the organization would grind to a sudden halt, not unlike a derailed train.

Gary Griffin seems to have suffered the most from TACF's overshadowing his work. Though he never favored conferences where oodles of self-serving academicians offered their two cents in pursuit of tenured comfort, instead finding ways to sneak off to the woods or the waters, he has completely cut such activities from his calendar. I guess that the cacophony of viewpoints, where no one's work stands out, contributed to his disdain for such events. Gary has a concrete belief in his work and will not stand to see it pushed to the side or diluted by all the lackluster research performed by relative novices. Griffin's pride has alienated him from the bulk of workers in chestnut, particularly the folks at TACF whom he considers minor criminals for taking his ideas and implementing them without affording him the credit he's due. An intellectual iconoclast, Griffin knows his program will disappear unless he prepares the next generation of researchers himself. He'll fight to maintain his lab space at Virginia Tech, knowing that the lab's closing would mark the end of the ACCF.

Over the course of the week spent talking with John Elkins and the Griffins, and working up a sweat in the field with Lucille, I'd come to a deeper understanding of Gary Griffin's master plan. From a personal bias steeped in years of environmental research and writing, I gravitate toward the ACCF approach since it assumes a much more complex understanding of nature.

From a childhood love of the natural that, like most consuming passions, appeared out of the blue, or perhaps out of the green in this case, I derived an academicized understanding of non-human life where the fauna and flora fail to meet our anthropocentric expectations for them. We make theories that they continually refuse to respect, finding novel ways of violating our supposed limits. Rather than accord the scientist complete knowledge of their realms, the denizens of our alleged kingdoms of life—a division of kingdoms that continually changes and which scientists cannot even agree upon—remain aloof, intractable, anarchic. The key lesson I've learned from my sojourns as a scientist and a philosopher leads me to respect the natural world for its complexity that reveals itself like fractals as we aim our tools—electron microscopes to radio telescopes—at its various levels of organization. Once the riddle of nuclear DNA appeared solved by Watson and Crick, up popped mitochondrial DNA to muddy the picture. With the mapping of several species' genomes, we still find that the simple causal story we desire between codons and behavior fails. The nature/nurture conflict refuses to collapse or prompt some dialectic deterministic understanding of the natural world. When we think we have chestnut blight beat, as TACF spokespersons claim from time to time, we learn of mutations in *Cryphonectria* or new diseases and pests threatening to destroy the trees we place in the clear-cut forest.

Griffin and his allies refuse to accept a simple mechanistic view of nature where the retraining of a few cogs or the tightening of a spring might set the whole apparatus working like the created clockwork assumed by many an agnostic scientist. A few introduced genes carefully parked into the chestnut genome will not make all right once again. Elkins and Griffin understand that the relationship between chestnut blight and the American chestnut is a bizarre tango between organisms wrestling for the limelight as they seek to do what all organisms do, survive and reproduce. Gary explains his role in chestnut's history as simply giving it a hand through its current crisis, a mere moment in geological and evolutionary time from which he believes the tree would recover fully in half a millennium or so without human aid. Griffin gains my respect because he refuses to paint *Castanea dentata* as a victim. Instead, the species is simply a favorite that he wishes to benefit with his time on Earth.

Elkins, likewise, offers his aid to chestnut to recover a human way of life mourned by his grandmother and relatives. A proud promoter of the Appalachian ways of life, John understands the complex interplay between essential species and the folks inhabiting this sea of hills. Appalachian identity, built and maintained by the American chestnut, has diminished as the tree disappeared from the reefs and ridges of the Virginias. The vanishing wormy chestnut and split rail fences register the loosening of the ties of people to land, as do the failing chestnut sheds and workshops dotting backyards throughout the region. As Elkins' elders shuffle off this mortal coil, he mourns the loss of memories, of wisdom, gleaned from gathering chestnuts under October moons, the kids so eager for a handful they stole out of bedroom windows and shook the trees until nuts rained down.

While TACF hubristically sets a timeline for its grand effort, Gary Griffin contemplates the one hundred years he calculates for chestnut's recovery as if he's a modern Methuselah, not a madman rushing to fix the world before dinnertime. The ACCF bases its schedule upon chestnut's biological clock rather than the lockstep cadence of humanity's march to doom. Indeed, if global warming plays out in the coming decades, Lucille's isolated patches of American chestnut, growing in Natural and State Forests in which they once held ecological dominance, might just survive with the trees spreading as their post-glacial predecessors had thousands of years ago to repopulate the US north into Maine.

Or else global warming will favor the kudzus, the gumbo limbos, invasive species adept at taking advantage of ecological disturbance and calamity. Gary Griffin also harbors such dark thoughts, realizing that chestnut restoration might never occur. He would be content with enough plantings to save the species in a much smaller way than it once lived.

Griffin's accumulated a massive amount of detailed information about the species and its ecology. Faint whisperings among chestnut advocates, particularly those committed to TACF's project, hint that Gary Griffin wants to avoid employing Asian stock in his breeding program because he has some strange, quasi-racist bias against foreign stock. I give little heed to their gripes. Griffin's urge to maintain a distinctive pure-American tree stems not from a dislike of other species but from his own deep respect for the American chestnut. Like a body builder spurning the use of steroids, he sees foreign stock as unnecessary and, potentially, dangerous. There's no need to go looking for foreign genes as this tough tree has the capacity to survive blight on its own, though a little human help might speed up the process. Without the odd survivors in the backcountry, Griffin would gladly turn to foreign stock for help. But he learned early, from Given and Dietz, that our own species remained—in very small numbers, but it remained. Trusting that those survivors hold a secret ignored by TACF, Griffins and Elkins pin their hopes on naturally-developed blight resistance.

As I prepared to head off for a week in the wilds of West Virginia, Gary, Lucille and I discussed chestnuts one last time over pizza and beer. Lucille subtly informed me that she was going to add me to her list of Cooperators. Over the week, we had discussed my interest in growing some trees. My labor's earned me a membership. In August, she'll send her annual letter which I could fill out to receive nuts which I hoped to grow on a handful of organic farms in southern Wisconsin.

Gary briefed me on a selection of his favorite wild places including the Cranberry Glades and the Dolly Sods, both in National Forest land on the eastern half of West Virginia. Griffin even copied maps at his office, with detailed descriptions of the sites. Though it's not chestnut country, he assured me that I'd find it rich with salamanders, and other enticing life forms, possibly blueberries if my timing was right. (It was.) I identify with Gary's urge to abandon human society for the wilds and relished the thought of collecting my thoughts after a captivating week with the couple and John Elkins. In my new Virginia Tech t-shirt, I backed out of their driveway and began my sojourn to a mountain wilderness I'd never seen before. We traded waves and I found myself alone with my thoughts.

I felt drained like an old battery left in the cold too long after spending two weeks of intense learning about chestnut. At the same time, I was energized as I hadn't been for years, blazing with newly gained knowledge that I needed to sort into a deeper understanding. Looking at the tremendous differences between the two organizations, one a hydra with its many heads patrolling the eastern seaboard, the other a mouse lurking in the midst of Virginia, unknown to many though leaving a trail the observant could follow. The third party, lurking in the backwoods—tiny sticks protruding from the soil to lone survivors more than a century old, remains oblivious to and unconcerned with human endeavors. Yet the humans continue to plot and plan in their insistence to offer a better solution for the near-extirpated trees.

My desire to drop in on the American chestnut 1,000 years in the future returns frequently, like a precocious reader who needs to know who-dunnit. I want to see what happens to the chestnut. Deep inside I believe that the best laid plans of chestnut researchers will have little or no impact upon the mighty tree which may already be plotting its own phoenix-like rise from its blighted ashes.

With all of Appalachia in my rearview mirror, I drove away from chestnut's past, present, and future. The true die-hards, the fanatic chestnut lovers quietly pass from this world, leaving barely a note of their lives, forgotten within time spans that compose an eye-blink in chestnut experience. I consider Gary, Lucille, and John, all in their sixties and wonder how long they will manage to continue their fights for chestnut. Ten years? Twenty? How will Appalachia memorialize these diligent activists? I can only conclude that their passing will go less noticed since most of chestnut's advocates have passed before. I hope that the Eric Hogans, the next generation of advocates for a species they've caught just a whiff of, will labor forward, amassing knowledge and applying it to preserve the uniquely American tree. I just doubt that it will ever be enough.

Like the architects of Giza or Mesa Verde, the ACCF will simply fade from public thought, its knowledge lost like the great library at Alexandria where the collected wisdom of the ages found its use as ash and smoke. Humanity in this alleged modern age simply lacks the ability or refuses to learn from its mistakes. While chestnut blight woke up Americans to ecological calamity, it alone didn't inspire the tough laws governing the importation of foreign stock. Once white pine blister rust and other plant diseases took a foothold, the US Senate began drafting legislation to require quarantine of plant materials making their way into our borders. But our problems with invader species continue, worsening in their impact upon our native ecological systems. The volumes of information learned from chestnut restoration will prove useful, if properly cataloged, in the spate of extinctions, extirpations, and ecosystem collapses to come.

I believe that scientists, both social and biological, should examine the ACCF and determine how their approach might prove useful elsewhere. Gary Griffin should be seen as an innovator, surveying scientifically important ground that others have avoided. Now, though, in an age where restoration ecology has become a field of study, where environmental ethics has grown in importance, where most Americans support environmental responsibility, we need to find tools and applications to save our embattled ecology. Griffin's work is vital given its complex comprehension of physical characteristics, interspecies interactions, and breeding for resistance. What a shame if every species restoration has to start anew, as if recoveries never happened before!

After sleeping on a dirt road hidden behind the county fairgrounds and the local animal shelter (where I'm fairly sure I saw canaries on the phone line), I arose with the sun to drive the final few miles to Dave McCurdy's tree farm in search of large chestnuts. Six days had passed since I left the Griffins, a near-week spent in the wilds of West Virginia contemplating the fate of American chestnut. This being my last mission in West Virginia, I felt a bit lost, knowing my chestnut adventure neared its end.

I discovered Dave early on a Friday morning opening the office. In a uniform similar to ones issued by the Forest Service, complete with a small chrome badge, McCurdy caught me off-guard. I imagined him as a farmer but he looked more like a Texas Ranger. For a minute or two, he was all business, wondering why this stranger wanted his attention so early in the day. But when I told him Lucille sent me and that I was interested in chestnuts, he smiled and directed me to his pickup. The farmer, proud of his crops, came shining through the governmental façade of the uniform.

Short and sturdy, Dave McCurdy had spent his last thirty years tending trees for the state of West Virginia. The last several years, he'd worked at the Clements State Tree Nursery, a farm once owned by Mark Twain's grandparents. The Clements mentioned in the name is not a misspelling of Clemens, though. Indeed, Clements was a more recent owner who sold West Virginia the land that sits north of Lakin's women's prison and a hospital. Ohio lurks across its namesake river to the West, beyond the massive cooling towers spewing their faintly disturbing steam. Point Pleasant to the south played unwilling host to the deceptive mothman recounted in a recent Hollywood movie.

McCurdy, who would have retired eight years ago if his wife had her way, maintained his employment status by telling her he'd retire as soon as they found a good home somewhere in Carolina. In truth, he has an attachment to his trees he'd rather not sever. The farm produces seedlings for use and sale within the state. American chestnut seedlings are grown especially for the ACCF and distributed to Cooperators throughout the United States.

He drove to several rows of pure Americans, many planted by Bruce Given in the early 1970s. Blight hit the trees starting in 1980. While some of the rows had seen much better days with trees either dead or tattered, more rows looked like they were raring at the bit to produce new nuts. Dave proudly informed me these very trees would put out their 25th crop of nuts that autumn. While other trees succumbed to blight within a decade, these trees thrived, despite visible cankers. Each row boasted a different breeding line—Gault #2, Pease, and others—with considerable differences in appearance. While leaf pattern, bark and other characteristics seemed fairly constant, it's the size and shape of the trees that varies substantially. McCurdy called me over to a row of Pease. The specimens at the end of the row, climbing to some 25 feet, dwarfed the 5 foot 8 inch Dave posing beneath them as I snapped a picture.

In contrast to most of Lucille Griffin's plots, these farm trees grow on a flat plat of land without the adventitious drainage found on sloped mountain and hillsides. Trying to picture the standard map of chestnut's range in my head, I asked McCurdy about their native range in Ohio. As I'd rolled downhill moving westward through West Virginia, the sites favored by the Griffins had petered out. Lower hills, with less extreme slopes, seemed less likely to house *Castanea*. Dave opened his tree guide and showed that chestnuts extended into the eastern fourth of Ohio. A finger of range climbed northward into Indiana from Kentucky, making evident the species' affinity for hills. Flatlanders were simply left out of the chestnut loop.

McCurdy assumes a cynical stance when considering American chestnut's restoration. Admitting that a lot of good minds work full-time to solve the chestnut problem, he argues, "We can be too smart for what we're doing." A story illustrates his meaning. Aspen, a prolific seed producer that McCurdy had tried to grow over the years, produces more than 7,000 seeds to a pound. The miniature seeds are sown by putting them in buckets of water and then splashing this liquid on the ground. Unfortunately, due to its feathery nature, the seed simply refuses to wet, riding safely on the water's surface. When one of his new employees suggested adding a bit of soap to the water to reduce the liquid's surface tension, McCurdy rejected the idea immediately, knowing somehow that the soap would kill the seed. He continued trying other ways that proved futile. Eventually Dave grew so frustrated with the difficult seed that he tried the soap solution. Amazingly, it worked and Dave learned a valuable lesson that he considers regularly—his built-in, trained ideas prevented him from solving the problem while a relative outsider, looking freshly at the problem, identified a solution quickly. Similarly, all the chestnut experts who've submersed themselves in the literature and their research share similar misconceptions that likely blind them to potential ways to revive chestnut.

In October, I discovered a bag of 25 chestnuts in my mailbox. In my new status as a cooperator, I held responsibility for the smallish nuts, taken from a tree in Lucille and Gary's backyard. Lucille wrote me that their diminutive nature will result in slow first-season growth, though the trees should rapidly catch up with their peers after that. Like a class of precocious kindergartners, these 25 have incredible potential I could not wait to witness directly. Organic farmer friends Sara Tedeschi and David Bruce would grow five of the nuts, while Judy Hageman and Bill Warner might fill out their woodlot with another five. Another five were destined for Milwaukee, where my good friend Glen Grieger would carry responsibility for the seedlings. The remaining ten would travel to five different locations, some public, some private, to begin their journeys through Wisconsin life. Each August, I'd summarize a report on the bunch, furthering the ACCF's research.

In 2004, the year Lucille claimed she doubted her ability to compete due to pain, she won the 400 meter individual medley (bettering her 2003 time by two seconds) and 200 meter backstroke, took second in the 100 and 200 meter fly, and third in the 100 meter backstroke.

Photo Gallery

The tell-tale burrs of the American chestnut in early October at the University of Wisconsin Arboretum, Madison

A cascade of male catkins, each swarming with pollen, and a visiting hemipteran

Fred Hebard employs his mobile office to plan future pollinations

A bag covers a pollinated flower to prevent other fertilizations

Mechanical mastermind Danny Honaker lends a bag from the bed of the big red truck

Volunteer Lou works the controls of the cherry picker to pollinate a

tree

Along the Appalachian Trail, a tiny American chestnut arises from much older rootstock

Lucille Griffin meticulously prepares a site for future American chestnuts. The pink ribbons keep deer from colliding with her plantings

Pith-helmeted Gary Griffin considers a plan of action

West Virginian John Elkins prepares for an afternoon of grafting

Elkins' dexterous hands in the act of grafting

Lucille Griffin pulls weeds from her chestnuts growing in Virginia's Lesesne State Forest

Dave McCurdy dwarfed by some of his 30-year-old chestnuts in West Virginia

Philip Rutter shows off some of his greenhouse chestnuts in southeastern Minnesota

Rutter's strange successes include this amazingly early flowering chestnut

Permaculturalist Mark Shepard leads a tour of his western Wisconsin chestnut stand

Michigan State chestnut guru Dennis Fulbright inspects blight-ridden chestnuts at West Salem, Wisconsin

ACF Board Member Bill MacDonald examines a canker in on-going research at West Salem

The blight has taken its toll, but this Michigan chestnut seems to be recovering, with healing cankers evident

Chapter 4

"The US Border Patrols and the US immigration and Customs Officials are unable to exclude either the introduction of thousands of tons of marijuana or the influx of hundreds of thousands of undocumented workers (not only from Mexico, but from many Latin American and Asian countries). Nor can they control the millions of birds that migrate back and forth between North and South America each year. That being the case, what are the chances that plant quarantine officials will be able to keep the spores of any number of diseases from crossing into the US from Mexico? The answer is obvious to any microbiologist."

—Dr. Norman Borlaug, cited by Curtis Byrd

A few miles outside of New Haven, a wandering black ant made itself known, scrambling across the tan dashboard of the Civic. Crossing west into New York, the creature reasserted itself, roaming freely around the border of the windshield. Newburgh, the Catskills, Binghamton—all new terrain to both me and the insect—passed by. I made a mental footnote to measure the beast which appeared a bit bigger than the average ant back home. In Cleveland, my concern as this hitch-hiker neared the open window led me to power up the windows and switch to AC. I apparently enjoyed its company since I rarely allow myself the luxury of air. 16 hours after I started, the ant made another appearance, framed by smokestacks in the Gary skyline. I wondered where it hid in those blank periods when I couldn't find it. Did it sleep?

The next day, the Connecticut ant entered America's Dairyland—more than a thousand miles from home. Its relatives would never see it again. The solitary pismire could go down in its species' annals as an Odysseus or Armstrong, or more likely a Laika. For me, though, it represented a much darker lesson as yet unlearned by most human travelers. But I digress.

Sandra Anagnostakis provided the impetus for visiting New Haven. She's the current chestnut expert working with the Connecticut Agricultural Experiment Station (CAES), the nation's oldest public agricultural research facility. Perusing her office as

I waited for her, I noted a broad selection of texts: mycological reference, a history of plant collector Frank N. Meyer the explorer who originally found the chestnut blight in Asia, the complete collection of Northern Nut Growers Association annual reports (which I'd been hunting down for a year). I'd been told by several sources that Sandy had the best collection of historical information available. Over the course of three days, I came to agree with these folks.

Her file cabinets are full of letters, clippings, receipts, and other odds and ends, almost all somehow connected to chestnut. Sandra strives to fill in any holes in her collection, keeping feelers out for disposed texts, 19th Century nursery catalogs, advertisements. Fred Paillet sends her regular updates on his study of pre-human history of chestnut, which she keeps safe. Libraries and researchers in wide-spread areas of biology know, when trimming their collections or finding seemingly non-interesting chestnut trivia, to send the material to Sandra. She even has the original glass slides, large panes used on a fore-runner to the overhead projector, from one of the visual presentations at the Pennsylvania Chestnut Blight Conference in 1913.

The white walls of the little square office host a variety of prints, a few featuring Smokey Bear and a variety of tree species, another above her antique rolltop desk entitled "Chestnut Morning." A series of individual photos have been seamed together to create a panorama of Sleeping Giant State Park, autumnal colors burying the obvious mammoth lying on his side. A large many-paned window looks out on Edenic greenery, a reason I'll find to return to Connecticut, a strange state where the trees, shrubs, and vines take precedence over buildings and advertising signs.

Sandra entered, clutching umbrella and sporting a knee-length raincoat. I recognized the researcher immediately from the group photo of the 1978 American Chestnut Symposium. Sandra's center-parted short mousy-brown hair and genuine smile stood out in the picture where she stood center-front. She was just one of three women fronting a crowd of male chestnut researchers. Her enthusiasm still abounds, though fits of coughing warned me that she was not in the best of health.

In a collection of older brick buildings, the type Nathan Hale might have known, the CAES began one year before the US Centennial. Arthur Graves had inspired Donald Jones, agricultural geneticist, to engage in chestnut breeding in the 1930s, developing a program that created new projects for plant breeders interested in chestnut. Richard Jaynes served as a graduate student in the 1950s, carrying on Graves' mission after the elder professor passed away in 1963. In 1966, Sandra Anagnostakis found her way to the Station after earning her Master's in Botany at the University of Texas at Austin.

Sandra does not have fond memories of Austin, recalling mostly that quite a few people carried firearms, including fabled Charles Whitman, the former Eagle Scout and Marine, who'd peppered the student body with rifle fire. Ducked behind a wall in the library, Sandra wondered why she'd wound up in Texas as Whitman fired from his high perch nearby. The relative quiet of Connecticut must have been a welcome change.

For her first few years at CAES, she worked primarily in mycology, studying the genetics of corn smut and the fungus killing the Dutch elms. In 1968, she began examining the chestnut blight fungus, an interest that has grown into the defining focus of her career.

Anagnostakis proves the kind of researcher who needs to look at all angles on the problems she studies. We discussed Evelyn Fox Keller's exquisite biography of another female scientist, Barbara McClintock, as Sandra drove me on a tour of the research farm. Contrary to the stereotypical male-dominated approach to science, where the researcher maintains a calculating distance—both physical and emotional—from the subject, Keller's portrayal of McClintock in *A Feeling for the Organism* exposes a scientist completely engaged with the corn she studied. Sandra delights in that book and that method, exhibiting an interrelational perspective of the trees we examined. Her feelings for chestnut have led her to succeed in ways others have failed.

Her duties, likewise, pull her in separate directions. She begins her day looking at emails, communicating with the various people seeking her knowledge. Quite often, folks will contact her to identify the chestnut from their backyard. With a multitude of odd hybrids abounding, getting a clear ID on a sample proves difficult for the average citizen. Sandra showed me a pile of dried leaves and flowers sent in by one curious party. With time, she'd look at leaf hairs under the microscope, perhaps placing the sample into one or another category, though a few leaves often prove inadequate.

She spends minimal time in the field, despite CAES' research farm, with a wide variety of chestnuts including a rare triploid, and the near-by Sleeping Giant State Park where Arthur Graves' legacy of breeding experiments lurk. As we drove through the site, I'd recognized the familiar white boxes full of honey-producing bees lurking beneath a stand of odd chestnuts gathered and manipulated by Graves. The buzzing pollinators keep the sting-sensitive Anagnostakis at bay.

A few times a year, tourists will find her to ask for growing directions for chestnut. The stories vary in details though the central theme remains the same: "We brought these beautiful nuts home from our global travels. How do we get them started?" Telling me of these fools who violated plant importation laws, Sandra summons a look on her face that I'd rather not have directed at me. Her response to these queries is simple and direct: "There are two insects and one disease in Italy that we don't yet have here. You could have brought them in. It is illegal for you to have brought these nuts in. I suggest you boil them to kill any organisms in them and then discard them."

One e-mailer thought he knew better than this veteran plant pathologist. He admitted to examining the seed he'd imported and finding no sign of insect or disease. In addition, he repeated his original request for growing information after she rebuked him. Sandra reported him to the Department of Agriculture. "I have a reputation of being a very tough person on people who do things like that," she explained matter of factly.

Of course, when one knows the story of the American chestnut, the profound impact that a few imported species can have on vast ecological systems becomes apparent. Dr. Anagnostakis has accordingly become a global spokesperson for following plant quarantine laws.

She knew, for example, that the chestnut blight fungus had recently been attacking eucalyptus trees planted on Japanese golf courses. A mycologist had noted cankers on the trees, tested them, and determined that chestnut blight caused them. When Sandra visited Australia at that country's invite, she made a point of telling as many scientists and officials as possible about the chestnut blight—eucalyptus connection, knowing that the blight could wipe out one of the key species of eucalyptus if the fungus gained a footing down under. "They had me record a little cautionary note that they put on the radio all over Australia, 'Don't import chestnuts because they could have chestnut blight inside the nuts and it could kill our eucalyptus.'"

Illegal importation occurs with even the most innocent of intentions. She discovered that Asian honeymooners to Australia accounted for a significant number of imported chestnuts. Wedding attendees, to promote fertility for the newlyweds, stash a share of chestnuts in the couple's luggage—chestnuts that inadvertently make their way around the world.

Then there's the case of that dreaded chestnut gall wasp, the same bug plaguing Hebard's chestnuts. That pest has become a case study for the deadly impact of intentional violations of plant quarantine law. I ask but Sandra refuses to give me the name of the individual responsible for introducing the wasp to American soil. He's still alive and she believes that, despite his imprudent actions, he deserves protection. But Sandra smirked in a knowing way as she explained how our native chinquapins seem immune, or at least resistant, to damage from the wasps. Potentially, someone might need to transfer some valuable genes from the chinquapins to American chestnut.

In relation to her work fighting foreign pests, Anagnostakis has worked diligently to catalog all the various introductions of chestnut stock in the United States. The US Forest Service's Forest Products Lab in Madison, Wisconsin, turned over all records they had inherited from other USDA facilities. In another building, CAES's library, she stores these index cards detailing each and every movement of chestnuts recorded—from a crop of trees planted on O.E. Beardsley's Walnut Grove Farm in western Wisconsin around 1870 to seed and scion wood shipped by Chinese interpreter and licensed guide Peter Liu who moonlighted for USDA from 1924 until the second World War. She's documented pre-blight breeding work described in Chapter 1. The work simplifies the identification of stock throughout the United States, particularly in Connecticut where she showed me some of the Japanese trees established 120 years ago. More importantly, this meticulous cataloguing allows researchers and breeders to find trees that might help in their efforts.

In the early 1970s, Sandra had been working with viruses in the corn smut disease. Only a few years earlier, scientists had determined that the kingdom of the mushrooms, like plants and animals, had viruses. Colleague Richard Jaynes came across one of French scientist Jean Grente's papers on hypovirulence. The staff all read this work. Grente's claim that some agent had changed the chestnut blight fungus caught the attention of both Jaynes and Anagnostakis who considered the possibility that a fungal virus might be responsible.

Excited, Sandra penned a quick letter to Grente, requesting some of his allegedly hypovirulent strains of fungus. She explained that she wanted to test his strains against American strains of chestnut blight to determine if hypovirulence might help rescue trees in the States. She sent her letter and, as she explained, "I didn't hear anything. And nothing, and nothing. Finally, I took my letter to one of my friends who's a high school French teacher. I asked her to translate this letter into French, using all of the right words that a woman scientist would write to a man scientist, and be really polite. So she translated it into French. I mailed it off and within the week I had cultures in the mail." Grente had intended to translate her original letter but missed the chance due to a busy schedule. When she communicated in his language, he could respond much more quickly.

With little difficulty, Sandra and Richard Jaynes proved that the three cultures Grente sent contained virus. The next step involved figuring out how to move the virus to new strains in the laboratory and see how American chestnut might react to hypovirulent fungi. "Dick and I did a test in the greenhouse—we had some small chestnuts in the greenhouse. We inoculated them with strains that we knew were killing strains and put in some of the white stuff at the sides of cankers." One of the three trees tested formed a large calloused canker and survived. The small tree, allowed the extra time to respond to an inoculation of deadly blight offered by the hypovirulent strain, walled off the infection so that xylem and phloem could still move water and nutrients through the plant. The scientists rejoiced, recognizing that hypovirulence might offer some hope for American chestnuts.

Having established hypovirulence as a product of a fungal virus allowed Anagnostakis and others to advance their knowledge of the mechanisms of hypovirulent fungi in fighting chestnut blight disease. Anagnostakis' work paved the way for Gary Griffin and the ACCF to examine potential uses of hypovirulent fungi in their work.

Nowadays, Sandra spends considerable time in her laboratory, plating out cell cultures of the blight fungus to test. Her lab lacks many of the high-tech apparatuses one would find in most modern genetics labs, but she does not need much to test the effect mutated viruses have on fungal colonies.

Sandra and others work to determine how a virus might impact the blight's virulence. Viruses remain on the verge of life; scientists debate whether they are living organisms or simply complex molecules that exhibit some interesting characteristics once believed to be restricted to living things. Viruses duplicate, much like living beings, but at much faster rates. Spontaneous mutations arise, leading to greater diversity and increasing the likelihood that certain strains will cause lethality.

Brad Hillman, who Sandra describes as "the genius who works on viruses," believes that the hypovirus is a single-stranded RNA virus that lives in a cell's cytoplasm. When replicating itself, the molecule forms numerous copies of itself in a double-stranded RNA form. Within the cell, the bits of virus are detected as foreign material. Cellular processes work to remove the tiny viral bits with the golgi apparatus walling off particles within bits of its membrane. These parts are then moved to the cell membrane, passed out, and given free reign to infect other cells, transmitting the virus throughout the fungus.

Sandra's challenge is to introduce hypovirulence to a tree so that the virus can enter fungal cells of lethal strains and convert them to non-lethal forms. Her work involves introducing hypovirulence to colonies. "It only takes a few virus agents, particles, to get through a bridge and into the cytoplasm and move to the next cell for that strain now to be hypovirulent," explained Sandra, who has faced some very difficult cases. In cases where the strains refuse to convert—primarily because they are of different vegetative compatibility groups, Sandra will plate out 50 or 100 cultures, adding the hypovirulence to each. Since all those bits of virus drift around from cell to cell, testing great numbers increases her chances of success. If even one colony becomes hypovirulent, or—in Sandra's language—experiences a "conversion event," she's created a strain to be used against that vegetative compatibility group. Sounding like some astute missionary, she takes pride in her persistence, noting "I have never found a strain that I couldn't convert eventually."

Unfortunately, laboratory successes do not translate to immediate successes in the field. While Europeans saved their chestnut orchards thanks to hypovirulent fungi, Americans have been less lucky. Sandra believes that quick discovery of blight in Italy by researchers allowed *C. parasitica* less time to evolve multiple strains. Grente and others had to come up with relatively few strains of hypovirulence to treat their trees. In the States, the fungus had more than 70 years and a much wider range to increase its genetic diversity. Thus, on a single tree, multiple strains of the blight will be found, representing vastly different vegetative compatibility groups. One treatment of hypovirulence will not convert all fungal forms on a single tree, let alone those in a stand of chestnut or chinquapin.

An interesting question arises: Why did this hypovirulence pop up in Europe rather than the United States? We cannot rule out the likelihood that hypovirulence did exist during the days of chestnut's demise, even the earliest days when blight was restricted to greater New York City. Unfortunately, the vast number of strains of blight would diminish hypovirulence's impact. Say a tree survived for a year or so due to hypovirulence. Statistically-speaking, that individual had a high chance of succumbing to another strain of virus. Genetic diversity of the virus combined with scientists' inability to detect hypovirulence given the stage of scientific knowledge led to the American chestnut's disappearance. Since blight appeared in Italy and threatened France decades after first being identified in the US, a period in which the understanding of genetics and pathology had advanced light years, a window of opportunity opened, allowing for the discovery of hypovirulence.

Anagnostakis' work on hypovirulence may play a small role in American efforts to rescue our native chestnut. TACF's approach has little room for concern over insect pests, let alone viruses. Griffin and his crew make new discoveries concerning hypovirulence but have yet to offer any cure for blight. Indeed, a wide-spread hypovirulent cure might never be developed, particularly given viruses' ability to mutate rapidly. Scientific innovations that saved the Italian and French chestnut economies might never pay off for Americans. Nonetheless, the work contributes to a wider body of knowledge concerning viruses, plants, and their interactions. Hypovirulence might find application in future plant blights and diseases, saving unidentified species from following American chestnut's fate.

Prevention, almost universally promoted as the cheapest way to address costly problems, has not found much deployment in our agricultural protection policies. Invasive species proliferate, skirting our borders like bugs through a torn screen. The chestnut gall wasp makes a new home in the United States, thanks to some fool's refusal to follow protocols for importing stock. While we fight a war against human terrorists, we maintain an antiquated system of customs that allows truckloads of insects, bacteria, and fungi purchase on our embattled ecosystems. Political forces push trade agreements through, though the ecological impact of such treaties remains ignored. Indeed, the concept of the nation-state has all but disappeared. Ecologically, though, the nation-state often proves the most realistic entity for protection of ecosystems because relative equilibrium has been achieved within such political bodies. Earth, though, does not fare well when the border between Thailand and Australia dissolves. Neither country's natural systems are ready for the influx of foreign organisms brought with rapid, frequent, constant exchange of goods and people. While Americans haughtily travel the planet, searching every nook and cranny for an authentic experience, they never stop to think of the effects such movement has for the other species we rely upon.

My friend, the ant—an anonymous six-legged explorer, helps me realize how easily my car, my shoes, a ship, or a jumbo jet can transfer parasites, disease-causing organisms, and weed species throughout the world. Sandra Anagnostakis' message concerning introduced species resounded in my mind as I tracked the ant's peregrinations. She bravely fights a losing battle, decrying the perils of indiscriminately moving species across borders—even as seeds. Sandra knows that she will never prevail in stopping those Italian pests from reaching US shores. It's just a matter of time before someone who thinks he or she knows better carries a family or population of destructive insects home in a suitcase. The next variation on the chestnut blight awaits us. Anagnostakis simply refuses to allow Americans to ignore the scientific facts she's pieced together. Foreign pests and pathogens will arrive on our shores whether in the belly of a ship or on the backside of a wandering insect. Given our propensity for free trade, we tear down international barriers with minimal awareness of the ecological roles such barriers play.

Chapter 5

> "Our understanding of the magnitude and gravity of species extinction has grown enormously in recent years, without, however, a corresponding growth in our knowledge of how to remedy the problem."
>
> —Peter Matthiessen, *Wildlife in America*, p. 275.

Driving up the pair of dirt tracks Philip Rutter calls his driveway, I caught a glimpse of the enigmatic nut breeder trolling through the knee-high grass fronting a row of chestnuts on his rural estate, Badgersett Farms. Arrayed in jeans and straw western hat, Rutter's six foot two frame remained fairly lean, due in part to the extended fasts he regularly enjoys. His neatly trimmed beard and mustache hinted at a style assumed decades earlier, in his academic phase. His eyes scanned the ground, as if he had dropped a small screw. Later I would learn he was just inspecting the parched soil.

Though colleagues dared to categorize Rutter the Graduate student as a mammologist, Rutter the Farmer admits he never really fit that mold. "Evolutionary ecologist" was the title he desired for himself, years before such an appellation was popular or likely possible. But selecting shrews as research subject pigeon-holed him in a discipline for which he had strictly tangential interest. Shrews just happened to exhibit behaviors that met his specifications. If mushrooms had met those requirements, he would have worked with them and faced his fate as a mycologist.

Academia has trouble with folks like Rutter who fail to fit into the accepted niches. "Cross-disciplinary," "unfocused," "generalist," and "rebel" are just a few of the pejoratives aimed at those broad-minded few who wander through the disciplines as their interests ebb and flow. In an age of specialization where the researcher delves deeper and deeper into a small body of information, the Rutters of the world, looking for the more expansive picture, feel not only out of place but also out of time. We no longer have many organismic biologists around. These researchers, people like Jane Goodall, committed their lives to understanding a select species and its interrelations to other species and the environment. Through extensive often isolated studies of their subjects, such researchers gained detailed awareness of the larger picture wherein human actions contributed to the destruction of the species. These scientists became social critics, not exactly a role favored by industrialists hoping to gather and transform resources from all corners of the globe. The last half century has brought a substantial decrease in funding for such research, pushing scientists into laboratory-based pursuits with less social impact.

I wouldn't dare categorize Rutter as an organismic biologist. True, he delves into the worlds of chestnut and hazelnut, but not to learn about only those species but to understand evolutionary process. A scientific maverick, Rutter remains discouraged by the average researcher's need to categorize and then behave as if constructed categories defined reality. Natural history, the unfolding of evolution, holds the nut breeder's interest, an obsession driving his work. Preferring to allow the natural world to reveal its oddities, he formulates ideas of how and why development occurred in that particular way. By refusing to examine nature the way scientists are trained to, Rutter is able to see traits to which others remain blind. He pays for his status as an intellectual hermit by sacrificing the credibility an institution and a discipline would bestow. For pragmatic reasons, he's selected chestnut and hazelnut as semi-profitable species to pay for his continued research outside of academics.

His self-claimed title begins to explain his current incarnation as a nut tree breeder. He's never really changed tracks even if some myopic others fail to recognize the train he conducts.

Hidden away in the undulating topography of southeast Minnesota, an anachronistic corner of the state often forgotten by denizens of the Twin Cities some 160 miles to the north, Rutter's acreage was purchased thirty years ago as a retreat from St. Paul graduate school for himself and his first wife. Saving a few thousand dollars in wedding gifts, the young couple heeded those older and wiser who regretted not buying land when it was affordable in their youth. While seeming millions gobbled up lake-access subparcels throughout Minnesota's north, Rutter focused his gaze on slightly warmer climes that would offer greater opportunities for his agricultural and botanical pursuits.

From the air, this driftless region—a one-time peninsula when glacial ice scraped clean the lake country to the north, east and west, but left these ridges and ravines undisturbed—lacks the ninety degree angularity, the grid work of squares and rectangles championed by Thomas Jefferson. Like Rutter, the terrain appears to struggle against any order humans might seek to impose upon it. Farm fields contour to the hills, often surprising drivers who see one row of corn mysteriously emanating from the tassels of the row directly below it. Crops snake along, following the agriculturalist's supposition of the most effective, efficient planting. Native greenery remains in those rare pockets too difficult or costly to till. Minnesotans can find a higher percentage of the state's biodiversity in these hollows and coulees—known to Laura Ingalls Wilder fans as "the Big Woods"—than found in the drier western part of the state and the colder north.

Wilder set her drama in Minnesota, but she really lived in Pepin, Wisconsin, north and on the opposite shore of the Mississippi from her fictional home. But folks in Rutter's rural district still call their land "the Big Woods." Further confusing matters, the Minnesota Department of Natural Resources uses "Big Woods" to denote an ecological zone stretching through the west-central part of the state. While some wildlife experts may claim they know all about Rutter's land, the truth is that this southeastern arrowhead remains a mystery to most in a massive state famous for its north woods and even more lakes than boasted on their license plates.

Years after building his one-room escape, Rutter contemplated a lucrative use for the land and, ultimately, himself. His courtship of academia, along with that of his first wife, soured after going ABD. Acute powers of observation, with which Rutter is obviously gifted, left him stunned after witnessing the cut-throat jealousies of the overeducated elite. Rather than slip into the stereotypical comfortable professorship that would have either destroyed him or cursed him to a life of comparative mediocrity, Rutter opted for the rockier road that's led him back to this land.

Institutions provide structures—rules, policies, and hierarchies serving to maintain the status quo—that diminish creativity and risk in their participants. One dare not go out on a limb if such a move threatens or challenges colleagues overseeing the approval of tenure. Senior faculty maintain control over their younger peers, staunching the flow of the creative and adventurous humours driving a fellow like Rutter. Instead, Philip chose the relative anarchy of private life, assuming the helm of his own destiny. Without institutional support, he faced possible failure, a compelling reason to fire his creativity and entrepreneurial skills.

Rutter removed his hat and wiped his brow with a sweatband as we lounged on white plastic chairs below a row of hybrid chestnuts. An orange cooler put forth delectably cool drinking water on an August morning where, as early as 10 am, radiant heat blurred the view to the horizon. It had been two months since rain graced these hills and some of the foliage showed signs of stress. Telling me of the trees, Rutter commented, "They're a lot smarter than I am." He began sharing decades' worth of knowledge that he'd mete out over the next seven hours. As parched for knowledge as the land was for moisture, I soaked it up like a sponge.

With fifty million years to develop its genetic constitution, the chestnut hides a history plagued with drought, fire, ice, flood, and numerous other natural calamities in its sequence of nucleotides composing 24 pairs of chromosomes. This tree species has out-competed extinct species and fended more animal attacks, predominantly insect, than the Fox network could imagine. While scientists have sketched out the general climatic dynamics for the last few thousand years, the fine details of specific history as well as the general climatic trends of most of the species' history remain speculative at best.

While many reductionists, scientists and non-scientists alike, hubristically believe that sequencing a species' genome reveals almost all that we need to understand a species—where 'understand' is oftentimes used euphemistically to mean 'manipulate and control'—Rutter's evolutionary ecology perspective forbids such formulaic understanding. Like a detective recreating the chronology of a car crash by examining skid marks and vehicle damage, Rutter focuses on the chestnut's genetics to detect its evolutionary history. The tree's phenotype—observable genetic traits—provides the bulk of his information. His trees have shown him that they are much more complex in their relationships to one another, other species, and their surroundings than any perusal of the genetic code might suggest.

He illustrated his argument with the case of what has come to be called "talking trees," an example that might seem to be ripped from the pages of a science fiction novel or James Randi's hoax-busting "*Skeptical Inquirer.*" Consider an industrious beetle that preys upon the chestnut. This insect, blown to the area on chance winds from a distant home, makes rare appearances, perhaps popping up once every ten years or so. Soon after the pest lands on one tree's trunk, that individual perceives the beetle's presence and begins producing a toxin to deter the invader. Since the beetle's visits come rarely, chestnuts evolve the capacity to only produce the toxin, which serves no other purpose than to deter this type of beetle, once the predator appears. Toxin production in non-beetle years, taking energy away from necessary cellular processes, would be wasteful and potentially dangerous to the tree. Rutter explained that researchers have found trees twenty or thirty feet away from the infested tree producing the toxin even though they have no direct contact with the beetles. Somehow infested trees communicate the coleopteran invasion to their peers.

To one-up this mysterious tale, Rutter detailed how some Finnish researchers discovered that beetles adjust their metabolism when necessary to permit digestion of the toxin. Chestnuts, not to be beaten at their own game, responded by exuding a second toxin to upset the beetle invasion.

The trees cannot be said to talk any more than a telegram can be said to sing. The term "talking trees" is unfortunate as it provides immediate fodder for the skeptic and literalist. Loosely speaking, trees do communicate in several accepted ways, not the least being by spreading, or "broadcasting," pollen to receptive neighbors. If communication can be simply described as the transmittal of information from a source to a receptor, then pollination exemplifies communication. Genetic information from one individual is transmitted to others and can be processed and stored in the genetic code of seeds. Perhaps in some yet unseen way, trees can transmit information concerning insect infestations. Whether that involves some transmittable plant hormone, mycelial networks, or pheromone-analogues remains to be understood. Suffice it to say that researchers have observed the very strange phenomenon of plants without contact to insect invasions developing a response to such an invasion.

The hybrids we strolled under as Rutter adjusted the strands of his web of chestnut intrigue were, like Frankenstein's masterwork, stitched together from American, European, Japanese and Chinese stock. The breeder reverently pointed out the sea-urchinesque burr of one specimen that carries traits of the Seguin, an odd tropical species from southern China that would never survive Minnesotan winters as a pure strain. Millions of years before this cloudless day, a progenitor filled the canopy of

Gondwanaland, a primitive ancestor who may have closely resembled one of today's existent forms or may have been quite different. We have little evidence of that ancient species though Rutter hopes to rediscover that progenitor's type in his breeding program. He insists that many of that ancient specimen's genes still lurk deep in the genomes of today's species and may be coerced into expressing themselves.

Waving me forward, Rutter bending beneath drooping branches scraped at the chocolate leaf-scar ridden trunk of a twenty-foot-tall tree. I expected the typical thick bark that protects most trees from girdling, impenetrable except through piercing. Rutter offered a surprise, though. A greenish layer lie beneath a thin, onion skin layer of darker tissue. The breeder smiled knowingly, explaining that the tree's entire surface was rich with chloroplasts allowing greater photosynthetic surface area than other species. While most terminal branches of deciduous trees are green, permitting some photosynthesis, older growth rapidly abandons this strategy. Deciduous trees enter dormancy in late fall, eliminating the need for photosynthetic tissue in the trunk and branches.

Chestnuts, though, at least one's like the hybrid Rutter used to emphasize his point, avoid dormancy, opting instead for a state of lower photosynthetic activity, akin to that of conifers or succulents. Another way Rutter explains this oddity is by noting that the tree transforms from living in mesic summer conditions, where water is readily available, to profiting from the desert-like xeric conditions of winter, where moisture stays tied up in its inaccessible solid forms, ice and snow. Capitalizing on winter's reduced solar insolation helped the American chestnut strive for the forest's canopy faster than dormant oak neighbors, perhaps providing a partial explanation for *Castanea*'s ecological dominance. In the time scale of evolution, even the most trivial adaptation may lead to fantastic developments.

Rutter has also thought long and hard on the chestnut burr, a structure possessing fascinating adaptations unseen in other species. Contrast the burr with cousin oak's acorn. Oaks and other nut bearers rely on mast years for their species' survival. In a typical year, critters consume nearly 100 percent of the acorns. Rutter rattled off a list of acornivores: chipmunks, blue jays, nuthatches, woodpeckers, mice, and squirrels. These animals love acorns and really see little need to plant a percentage of their haul to provide for the dietary needs of their descendants. The trees, somehow in coordination, have a mast year—a season where each tree produces a far greater amount of fruit than can be eaten by its voracious diners—to assure reproduction. White oaks, red oaks, and burr oaks will all overproduce simultaneously, creating a surplus to overwhelm the hungriest of consumers. (Once again, the synchronicity of trees sharing a mast year suggests some underlying shared information at the population level.) In this lottery, buried nuts stand a greater chance of germinating and developing into the next generation.

Non-mast years often find most acorns consumed before they are even biologically able to sprout. Chipmunks et. al. munch the green nuts right off the tree, littering the tree's apron with tell-tale caps.

The chestnut burr strategically eliminates the need for a mast year. Its tangle of spines can only be penetrated by two creatures, both weevils with sufficiently long proboscises. Even then, the burr, incidentally green and photosynthetic, does not contain nuts until late in its development. Opening an immature burr, an act equal to dissecting an enraged porcupine, reveals stunted, non-viable seeds in formation. By the time varmints can get to the seed, chestnuts have already escaped the burr, fertile and ready to start new trees. Moreover, groves of chestnut drop all their seed in synchrony, increasing each genetic package's chance of success.

The chestnut's arsenal of protections extends well beyond the burr. Saplings wield a host of protections as they quietly crouch among their predecessors' leaf litter.

Rutter boasted the young chestnut's ability to change its growth pattern as soon as a rent in the canopy appears. Saplings below shift in high gear to begin their race to the light. Whoever arrives first gains the sunlight and shades out its competitors, gaining an ecological ascendancy driven by evolutionary forces. Once the canopy is gained, the next five hundred years of growth only become easier as the canopy dwellers have more energy for growth and fighting off disease and pests.

All chestnuts, even saplings, share the capacity to produce shoots. Rutter's confounded by certain trees developing at a snail's pace. Often, when cut to the ground, though, the rootstock produces a shoot to challenge Jesse Owens as it rockets beyond the original tree's height in a matter of weeks. Fellow growers, remaining ever vigilant to protect their stock's central leaders, the predominant shoot containing the tree's apical meristem, underestimate the chestnut's versatility. Usually removing a plant's apical meristem—its focal point of growth—induces side shoots to develop, leading to bushiness rather than height. If one desires a taller tree, then the apical meristem must be protected. Hesitant tree lovers, though, remain two steps behind the chestnut which grows perfectly well without human interference, never resorting to undesirable bushiness. I began to understand what Rutter meant when he claimed the trees were more intelligent than he.

Rutter's chestnut hybrids result from crossing various species of chestnuts for selected qualities. While a pure Seguin (*Castanea seguinii*) will not survive Minnesota's harsh climate, stock with twenty percent Seguin genes might. Interspecies crosses produce great variability. Also they prove less stable genetically, given this variability. Two hybrid parents, selected for fast growth, may not sire fast-growing progeny; two slow growers might produce a speed demon. A wealth of unpredictability infuses Rutter's program.

But Rutter's goal is not to produce the next generation of American chestnut, blight resistant and chomping at the bit to repopulate its native range. The breeder has traveled extensively, laboring to find ways to give Earth's worst-off humans a fighting chance. While others seek to find ways to profit from the world's hungry, developing non-reproductive seed that brings the impoverished back for annual purchases, Rutter believes that self-sufficiency proves a morally superior option. His study of hybrid chestnuts pushes the limits of how one productive genus might be used to improve the quality of life for hungry agrarians in what Westerners term "developing" nations.

One row of hybrids is earmarked to illustrate the range of chestnut's uses and the ease of switching goals. A sunken stump surrounded by two foot high shoots provides graze for goats, cattle and other herbivores. If the shoots grow a bit taller, they can be gathered and stored for feed; the stump will readily produce more shoots. If a farmer needs poles for building, she simply culls some of the shoots to produce two inch diameter wood in little time. Of course, the tree can be grown out to produce nut crops, high quality timber and firewood. Rutter related an anecdote of village dwellers in India hiking miles to illegally harvest firewood from national parks. Their need for fuel threatens the protected areas of India. If the people had reliable chestnut trees, they might produce self-renewing fuel, cutting the reserves some slack, maybe enough to allow their populations to survive.

Given the global status of humanity—a burgeoning population stressed by depleted resources, epidemic disease, and imminent global climate change, the days of profiting from our world's poorest nations draw quickly to a close. Without agrarian visions like those proposed by Rutter, human populations will likely decline in numbers, precipitously and soon. Those terrifying Horsemen, Hunger, Disease, and War, will spread as the worst off face increasingly dire futures and become desperate enough to strike at those better off.

Self-subsistence will also pay off for inhabitants of wealthier nations where the oil economy may soon fail. Chestnuts offer some major benefits that our current agricultural staples do not. One day, we may all rely on chestnuts for our daily bread, as well as building materials, forage, and fodder.

Speaking of fodder, Philip and I moved our discussion to the kitchen table occupying the primitive cabin he built decades ago. As his new wife Meg grilled cheese sandwiches, Philip showed me slides on his laptop, while I tried to recall if any transmission lines ran to the house. Rutter's little home world seems radically anachronistic with the state-of-the-art greenhouse and research facility sitting a few hundred yards from this abode hidden back in the woods, next to the miraculously archaic solar, three-seated outhouse.

A picture of a miniature chestnut, an embryo in flower, caught my attention. Rutter claims that the odd specimen reveals ancient genetic traits expressed in one of his many breeding experiments. Accidental rarities pop up for Rutter rather often. Another shot captured strange behaviors of tissue-culture embryos. If Philip is right, he can uncover some of chestnut's hidden history, the secrets of the specie's genome never witnessed by humans. The unnatural conditions provided by tissue culture, where all the necessary nutrients are readily available to dividing cells, prompts severely early development. In the process, Rutter believes he gets a few snapshots of ancient history.

We ate our lunch with an aura of life's primordial ooze floating around us, a feeling of great, unknown potential brewing. I wonder if humans or chestnuts will stick around to experience the unfolding of that potential. Rutter has crafted a near-fantasy land for the plant enthusiast, opening up trap doors to reveal mysteries from talking trees to plants flowering before they set their first leaves.

Genetic variability increases a species' odds of survival. Within a population, the degree of genetic variability helps determine how the population will fare against such stressors as drought, heat, cold and insect infestations.

Chestnuts appear to employ genetic variability to improve the individual's chances of survival. Rutter's observations lead him to believe that each bud on the tree is genetically unique. Since buds persist at the base of every single leaf, each tree has thousands upon thousands of buds varying genetically due to a high rate of somatic mutation. Imagine if each of your toes and fingers possessed a different genetic constitution and you begin to understand.

Barbara McClintock earned a Nobel Prize for her work in explaining how a process she termed "crossing-over" created mutations in the cell. The chestnut seems to have a similar capacity for spontaneous mutations arising in the tree's regular non-reproductive somatic cells. Normally, such mutations would not be passed to offspring. Unfortunately, we currently understand little about genetic variation among nuts from the same tree to know how somatic mutations affect the tree or its progeny. Researchers like Brian McCarthy at Bowling Green University work to understand the adaptive advantages of genetic variability between an individual's cells.

What perplexes Rutter and others is the key question, Why could a species evolved over 50 million years, perched at the peak of ecological fitness, succumb so readily to fungal blight? Rutter rubbed sweat from his furrowed brow, vexed in his attempts to answer the question. "It just doesn't make sense," he explained, shaking his head.

Millions of individual trees, healthy, each with thousands of buds experiencing significant mutations, peppering hillsides in a swath covering 15 degrees of latitude and nearly 20 degrees of longitude, a grand variety of weather conditions in a kaleidoscopic topography of long degraded mountains, and *Cryphonectria parasitica* took them down like pins in a Milwaukee bowling alley. "It just doesn't make sense."

Often in science, answers appear where we are least likely to look. Rutter's insistence on paying attention to lesser known species populating his woodlot may offer some direction in explaining American chestnut's sudden demise.

Butternuts, also known as white walnuts, fell victim to their own fungal disease half a century after chestnut blight became known. In the late 1970s when he bought his land, Philip began monitoring the butternuts peppered throughout the woodlot.

Unlike American chestnut which had ecological dominance in its range, the butternut, *Juglans cinerea*, grows in far fewer numbers per acre, adding diversity to the forest as a minor player. In 1967, a canker-producing blight was discovered, not far from Rutter's property, in southwestern Wisconsin. (In fact, this blight first showed up close to West Salem, Wisconsin, home of the largest remaining stands of chestnut.) *Sirrococcus clavigignenti-juglandacearum*, the fungus responsible, attacked butternuts nearly as severely as chestnut blight had hit chestnut. To date, between 70 and 90 percent of butternuts have succumbed to the canker disease. But given butternut's relative obscurity, little public outcry has arisen to save the trees.

At Badgersett Farms, evidently infected butternuts have shown remarkable signs of recovery from the blight. Though many trees have died, others once marked by unsightly cankers now appear completely healed, as if the bark had never been affected. Philip offers photographic evidence of this intriguing rebound.

To what can we attribute the restored health of these nut trees? Rutter suggests three possibilities: genetic resistance in the butternuts, a less virulent form of the fungus on his property, or a local predator or disease attacking the fungus. Right now, he does not care that he has scant evidence pointing out the best explanation of the three. In the long term, he argues, the cause of the recovery does not matter. What does matter is the fact that trees are surviving, setting seed, and producing new butternuts.

He contends the key to the trees' survival lies in the fact that no one interfered with the butternuts. True, Rutter did his best to eliminate squirrels after the banner nut year of 1978, in an effort to increase the number of seedlings. Fewer squirrels results in fewer eaten nuts. He never touched the trees, though. While common historical practice requires the identification and removal of diseased trees to insure forest health and to aid uninfected individuals, Rutter left the sick butternuts to their own devices. He argues that a 30-year observation of diseased trees is necessary to assess the severity of the malady, to figure out whether it acts more like an influenza outbreak or a bubonic plague. Within those three decades, natural processes may favor the species' survival despite the loss of many individuals. "In watching our trees over the years," he observes, "it is clear that it may appear the fungus is winning for five years, then the tree for five years, then the fungus for four years, etc." Seeing the bigger picture requires a long time-frame that may benefit the tree species.

If Rutter had removed all infected stock, he would now have no butternuts; every single tree has had signs of the canker disease. Thus, the breeder has defined a policy he calls Rutter's Rule: "If it's not dead, don't kill it."

An understanding of evolutionary processes leads Rutter to recognize that individuals need to get sick to develop resistance in a population. When partially-resistant individuals breed, they may produce progeny with greater resistance that will only be recognized when those trees survive. Another possibility is that organisms that weaken or kill the disease-causing organism enter the area. They require significant populations of the disease—the sickest trees—to establish their own populations, contributing to the welfare of the trees. If those sickest trees have been removed, organisms antagonistic to the fungus will be much less likely to appear and establish themselves.

Rutter's butternut survival offers indirect evidence that those early opponents of chestnut blight, the rambunctious folks crying for action rather than further research, may have exacerbated chestnut's condition. In the early years of blight, the New York Botanical Garden's William Murrill and USDA's Haven Metcalf both trumpeted the need to treat diseased chestnuts by removing any blighted branches. While

Murrill focused on saving individual trees, his methods were later applied to save the species. A simple category error, treating the species the same way one would treat a sick individual, fueled activists' drive to rescue Eastern chestnut forests. But, just as different means are employed to confront a human disease in a population than in the individual, researchers may have benefited from developing a better plan to rescue American chestnut, the species. The early proposal to establish plots of American chestnut elsewhere in the world seems quite plausible now that we understand the tremendous value of genetic diversity and deeper gene pools. At worst, such plots would have provided stock for breeding programs.

Rutter believes that bad luck combined with greed helped wipe out the American chestnut. The misfortune lies in blight's reaching the US along Long Island. "As I recall," writes Rutter, "all chestnut populations north of Delaware were less than four thousand years old. That's very young in tree time—what it means is most of those populations were likely to be much less genetically diverse, from 'founder effects' of the originally invading trees." The "founder effect" involves a loss of genetic information; a small subset of a large population will lack some of the alleles available in the larger population. The American chestnuts of New England, established millennia later than more southern trees, would have had a smaller gene pool.

David Quammen, in his *The Song of the Dodo*, illustrates the founder effect's problems with a useful analogy involving packing for a trip:

> "When you pack hastily for a trip, groggy in the early morning darkness and grabbing socks at random, you're likely to miss the one flamingo pink pair. But what if your plane makes an unscheduled stop in Las Vegas on Halloween? Of course you'll wish you had them. The founder effect deprives small populations of rare and seemingly useless alleles that might later, under changed circumstances, turn out to be useful." (p. 518)

The blight ravaged the New England trees with their relatively shallow genetic pool. By chance, they might lack genes for blight resistance—the pink socks—while southern trees, with greater genetic diversity, might still have those genes. Years later, when the blight reached the southern chestnut forests with their significantly greater degrees of genetic diversity, Americans gave up and pragmatically sought income from trees that might have had the genetic means of surviving blight.

Of foresters, Rutter believes, "They'd spent all this time and energy on saving it; and it wouldn't be saved. All right then. Cut 'em all down; screw it." Unlike other forest species—like elms or butternuts—that have little economic value after death, the American chestnut's wood still brought top dollar as decorative wood or as tannic acid for the tannin industry. Tanners still employed chestnut as their primary source of tannic acid until 1968: "[The industry was] still going into the woods, and cutting those old 'dying' snags, and grinding them up. Nobody ever bothered to go harvest dying elms—the wood is basically worthless, and rots at the drop of a hat." So millions, perhaps billions, of trees earned their owners quick incomes. Left standing, some of those trees might have survived and produced blight-resistant progeny to repopulate the forest.

Rutter doesn't mince words in reminding me that we have failed to learn our lesson from chestnut so far: "This same thing is going on right now out west, where huge pine forests are dying from global warming and the invasion of the southern pine beetle—and the 'dead' pines are being 'salvaged.' Do you think the timber cutters are passing up that 'dying' tree? Hell, no. The entire mind set is 'dying'—not 'surviving.' They never think about it. We really need to change that." When immediate profits compete with the long-term survival of a species, the forester's eyes focus on dancing dollar signs for which we all pay the price. Rutter e-mailed me a news story detailing how Portugal fights the Pine Wilt nematode by cutting all pines in its southern and central forests. Portugal's Agriculture Minister Jaime Silva, quoted as saying, "Doing nothing would result in an embargo on Portugal's pinewood exports to the rest of the European Union, which is an extremely important source of revenue for Portugal," demonstrates Rutter's contention that short-term economic ends trump longer-term environmental goals almost every time. I can easily picture him shaking his head, astonished that some basic ecological lessons remain unlearned.

We cannot draw any definite conclusions from Rutter's work with butternut. The trees could all perish before the end of the year. Extended observation, though, might help us refine our practices and gain greater understanding of ecological and evolutionary processes in tree and fungal interactions.

Rutter's commercial arm distributes hybrid hazels and chestnuts while he runs frequent seminars at Badgersett Farms, drawing enthusiasts and professionals from across the country. He mysteriously earns enough to sustain his varied ventures. Though he barely maintains ties with TACF, he may still provide key discoveries that allow them to further their mission.

His operation stays too small and too far out in left field for Rutter to be a major player in chestnut recovery. The limelight has passed him by, to his benefit. Like the fabled butterfly favored by chaos theorists, a few beats of Rutter's wings—a minor observation, an accidental discovery he plays up—can reverberate throughout the chestnut world. The consequences of his butternut observations have yet to be seen, though people are discussing the work, building an awareness of Rutter's Rule. Methodically, the hermit nut-breeder releases his findings to a developing network, an academic underground, subtly influencing the underlying philosophy of the nut-breeding community.

The essential nature of Rutter's work only makes sense in light of the ACF's mission. Since Charles Burnham defined the back-cross method to bring resistance to the American chestnut, the ACF has mustered the bulk of its resources toward that goal. While Fred Hebard has a swarm of observations buzzing around in his head, the necessity of meeting challenging goals forbids him the time to record his findings.

While eager to answer my many questions, many tangential to the breeding program's goals, Hebard offered his educated views as if they were highly speculative and perhaps not within the realm of his duties as chief breeder. The constraints of his job sacrifice much of the knowledge he's gained through the decades.

Rutter, unfettered by institutional goals, can freely maneuver to explore the odd circumstances he encounters in the field and in the laboratory. While both men have much to offer chestnut recovery, Rutter has a greater chance to discover the little known facts that may make a difference down the line. If Rutter becomes curious about mycorrhizal relationships between chestnut and indigenous fungi, he sets up an experiment or two to deepen his understanding. If the study seems a dead end, he's still engaged in a score of other minor projects that might mushroom into major successes. Rutter's findings help us meet Matthiessen's call for greater understanding of ways to prevent extinction, offered in the quotation that opened this chapter. While the Hebards of the world are key in reaching measured goals, the Rutters provide vital information in their inventive freedom. Both work in tandem to create the solutions we need to rescue our forlorn planet.

Chapter 6

"The bulk of all land relations hinges on investments of time, forethought, skill and faith rather than investments of cash."

—Aldo Leopold, *A Sand County Almanac*

One hundred years ago, the American chestnut remained one of the essential flavors permeating life in the United States. Never a staple, more an eagerly awaited treat akin to today's fresh heirloom tomatoes or wild morels, chestnuts suffered from seasonality, relinquished to the winter holidays. After blight, American palates craved the disappearing nuts; the wealthy could still make do with chestnuts floated in from Europe. But, for the masses, the loss of the American chestnut meant the loss of a distinct flavor, a gourmand experience never to be enjoyed again. When the trees at the ol' Kentucky homestead died, the frugal tenant learned to do without, though a far-sighted many planted Japanese, Chinese, and European species around the house, hoping their kids might know the popular fruit once again.

Chestnut's demise pre-dated a paradigm shift in US food production. Decidedly non-native plants stepped to the fore of the 20th Century American diet. Corn and soybeans, championed by big business, eventually became the ubiquitous ingredients providing carbohydrates and protein for millions of commuters and fast-food regulars, conflating speed with quality. As food environmental writer Michael Pollan details in *The Omnivore's Dilemma*, farmers learned to play second-fiddle to the food industry. Archer-Daniels Midland and Cargill break corn and soybeans down into basic chemical building blocks which can then be reorganized into chips, pucks, tots, or any other food product consumers dare to eat. Food chemists synthesize new compounds that mimic the flavors we enjoy, from "apple-wood smoke" to "vanilla." These chemicals can then be patented, giving patent-holders a veritable monopoly on that food-type additive. The bamboozlers that figured out how to twist Mother Nature's largesse into privatized formula did more than make an economic killing; they hold much of the responsibility for a killing of a different nature, the current epidemic obesity.

Both corn and soybeans reshaped our agricultural and environmental practices. The family farm, during the tumultuous 1900s, all but disappeared, supplanted by the factory farm which took agriculture to new scales. While an extended family could work a few hundred acres, the factory system allowed a few growers to work vast tracts of land to produce the monoculture crops desired by the growing agribusinesses. Cheap oil made these enormous plantings possible, as James Kunstler explains in *The Long Emergency*, an extensive study of our society's oil dependence. Genetically invariant corn, once prone to devastation by insects or competition by weeds, could succeed given a strict regimen of pesticides and herbicides—both products made possible by the petroleum industry. Round-up™-ready soybeans survive doses of pesticide deadly to their undesired neighbors (at least until those neighbors evolve their own resistance as has happened with some amaranth). The wealth necessary for this scale of agriculture excluded small-scale farmers from the game, forcing them off the farm or into new economic ventures built around locally-grown and organic foods. Many mortgaged their farmsteads to afford heavy equipment that would allegedly increase their profits. For many, though, these reinvestments simply greased the rails to foreclosure.

Kunstler announces the imminent rise in oil prices. We balance on the brink of peak oil production globally. From here on out, oil only gets more expensive, with a few well-planned dips here and there to bolster voter turn-outs. Thus, industrial agriculture will only get more expensive. The days of abundant corn and soybeans grow fewer with each harvest. Prognosticators argue that we need to find the next wave of agriculture to survive the impending oil crises.

Mark Shepard foresaw many of these problems back in the 1970s, opting to study Ecology at Maine's Unity College in the early '80s. Graduation sent him and wife Jen to Alaska for close to a decade of hardcore homesteading. The Shepards sought ways to live sustainably in an unsustainable society. After years of contemplating a new approach to agriculture, Mark found solace in the developing permaculture movement.

"I realized that being concerned about the Earth's air, water, and wildlife was not enough so long as we eat food grown in an environmentally destructive way. Our agriculture should mimic nature's processes," he explains, justifying his search for new agricultural techniques.

Permaculture proves the antithesis of the common practices for growing corn and soybeans. Each spring, the corn grower starts anew, plowing and preparing the land with nitrogen fertilizers and fungicides, planting seed that requires a pharmacopoeia of chemical inputs to keep it alive, irrigating with water drawn from the near-empty aquifer, harvesting with titanic, costly equipment, employing the cheapest labor available—be it teenager or immigrant worker, and harvesting and shipping to the factory that makes Doritos. The key expenses in this system are the numerous inputs necessary to achieve economically-defined success. Permaculturists seek to minimize or, ultimately, eliminate as many of these inputs as possible, crafting an agriculture that enlists natural processes combined with human ingenuity to produce healthy, diverse foods to be marketed locally.

Thinking ecologically, Shepard looked for a surrogate to corn, a carbohydrate source that would fit into the ecology of the Midwest's savannah prairie ecosystems. Corn's ecological incongruence with prairie is the key reason it needs such a litany of inputs. A native species would already fit ecologically with the land. Such a plant would not need to be watered as it would have the extended root network to survive occasional drought by drawing adequate hydration from the deep soil. The plant would have natural defenses against indigenous insects. The near-by forest, a healthy community, never experiences devastation by insects, notes Mark, who argues that the natural cycles in the forest protect it. The trees and plants remain healthy because the soil and its biota remain healthy due to regular composting of natural materials. Only when humans disturb these natural communities in attempts to shape them toward human ends do the insects become a problem. We constantly upset the equilibrium of the system and then wonder why problems arise.

Shepard also realized that a perennial species would limit the energy invested in annual soil preparation and planting. The perennials with greatest longevity—trees—would offer the longest term agriculture, allowing the land to achieve an ecological equilibrium. Thus, Mark adopted the identity of "agroforester," an appellation with far more zing than "tree farmer."

Rural Wisconsin teems with a wealth of odd species particularly adapted to prairie savannah. Burr oaks, wild plums, raspberries, and hazelnut are some of the hardiest local plants. Unlike corn and soybeans, these species can withstand most of the tragedies distressing farmers employing traditional practices. The Shepards, relocating to southwestern Wisconsin in 1994 to put their permaculture plan into action, looked to these evolutionarily-adapted species for guidance.

Mark first considered the successional stages of plants in the region. A bare field, the earliest stage—the one favored by most farmers, invites rapid invasion by many of the species we consider weeds—quack grass, amaranth, lamb's quarters, dandelion. Any slight, wind-blown seed will gain purchase on open soil, developing quickly in those ideal conditions. Farmers spend a significant portion of their careers fighting off these adventitious plants evolutionarily designed to capitalize upon the open space. Grasses and shrubs next enter the area in waves of various species, followed by smaller tree species like burr oak and wild plum, which are then replaced in a succession that results in climax.

The knowledgeable farmer knows that succession works only in one direction. Once a later stage establishes itself, the earlier stages no longer prove competitive. A dandelion lacks the power to shade out a red maple; a shrub will not crowd out canopy forest.

The community remains at climax unless fire or other processes intervene. Shepard likes to quiz folks, asking them to identify western Wisconsin's key historic herbivore, the one in large part responsible for the region's current conditions. Most respond "buffalo" or "bison" but mastodons grazed this territory as recently as 7000 years ago, allowing the smaller shrubs and trees to adapt to the conditions, and preventing the climax tree species common in northern Wisconsin from settling the area.

On a drive, Shepard showed me a stretch of roadside—a triangular property too small for agriculture or other purposes—left to its own devices. Hazelnuts and wild plums proliferated, surrounded by smaller plants and grasses. These species adapted to survive Wisconsin's prairie and savannah conditions where regular burning favored them. Fires arrested the succession of ecological communities, providing a habitat in which shrubs and small, fast-growing trees thrive. The model for agricultural success, in Mark's assessment, lies in those forgotten weedy species, plants likely valued by the rare Aldo Leopold, not industrial agriculturalists.

Leopold, whose ramblings of Wisconsin's central sands a ways north of Shepard's land led him to design the land ethic, championed Wisconsin's undervalued species. He constructed prosaic paeans to secretive prairie relics like *Silphium* which he found only in undisturbed old graveyards. The land ethic, the cornerstone of environmental ethics, states that an action is morally correct "when it tends to preserve the integrity, stability and beauty of the biotic community." Consequently, any action harming such systems proves morally wrong. Dying young, Aldo Leopold never had the chance to formulate a complete rebuke of modern agriculture, though as the quote opening this chapter shows, he did not hold it in high esteem. People like Mark Shepard bear Leopold's torch today. The ecological crimes committed by modern farmers can be easily condemned using the land ethic; indeed, Shepard's practice composes a living argument against mainstream agriculture.

The Shepards enlisted hazelnut, a bushy native with a root network extending a radius of several meters out and a few meters down. The region experiences periods of scant rainfall when corn-growing neighbors face the choice of watering or losing their crops. Hazels, once established, could theoretically survive the most severe drought. Nutritionally, the hazelnut, also commonly called the philbert, provides dietary protein, Shepard's equivalent to the soybean.

Corn, though, did not have an obvious regional surrogate. The burr oaks, slow-growing smaller trees, produce acorns, but not in the numbers necessary to keep a permaculture operation afloat. Shepard examined the burr oak's family tree, noticing that the Fagaceae included chestnuts as well. Perhaps chestnut hybrids would provide the carbohydrate source he desired. Unlike their acorn cousins, chestnuts already earned reputations as delicious and nutritious nuts. Truly a dreamer's dreamer, Shepard envisioned a grandiose scheme which included local farmers pooling resources to start a chestnut pasta business, a winery, and other "value-adding" enterprises that would revive the rural economy. He could already see row upon row of prolific nut-producers, arranged in three-dimensional, multi-species plantings to maximize solar input. The up-and-coming agroforester turned to Philip Rutter, a distant neighbor in the Driftless Zone, hoping to coax the nutbreeder into entering a mutually beneficial business agreement.

Shepard's assessment of succession led him to focus on late successional stage species that need not compete with early successional weed species. He only has to worry about removing relatively slow-growing competitors, oaks and other large trees, from taking over his hazels and chestnuts. His corn-growing neighbors, involved with much earlier successional stages, end up fighting every fast-growing weed seed that finds purchase on open topsoil. To extend an analogy, Shepard jousts against a solitary bee while his neighbors battle against the swarm; ecologically-speaking, Shepard's approach offers the better chance at long-term, lowest cost success.

Arrayed in straw hat, a white work shirt, and rugged canvas pants, Shepard regularly leads groups of environmental and agricultural activists on tours of his gently rolling hills. Someone, usually a tag-along neighbor, warns the crowd to bring water bottles and other protections as Mark likes a captive audience. And he's never at a loss for words.

When I first visited the Shepards' acreage in 2003, many of the mighty chestnuts proved too small to see in knee-high grass. Others stood five or six feet tall, skinny saplings supporting a wealth of branches. Mark shared the tales of particular hybrids, explaining how a few grew so heavy with nuts that their branches lay on the ground. The little trees put out nuts in two or three years, quite a bit faster than expected. But, given Rutter's keen awareness of his trees, such early production could have been expected; Rutter selected hybrids for rapid fertility.

Rutter and Shepard found common ground in their shared mission to rescue global agriculture. Much of Rutter's work involves finding ways to employ chestnuts and hazels to improve the lives of Earth's poorest citizens. Forsaking the dependence model, where 3rd-world farmers regularly get seed from government-subsidized seed banks, he believes that people can grow their own food and cut their ties to agribusiness. A makeshift food drier he devised from a culvert pipe, plywood covers, and a hand-cranked motor allows farmers to lower the air pressure in the pipe, effectively speeding up the drying process of whatever crop they place inside. In higher humidity climates, the device extends the storage life of grains and nuts. Rutter understood why Shepard wanted to help devise permaculture systems and readily made his stock available. Perhaps the two will some day be recognized as the progenitors of a new Green Revolution, one that by necessity uses minimal fossil fuel inputs.

Walking Mark's land, one comes upon various experiments. The dead space at the ends of rows sports fruit trees companion planted with irises and other plants that break up the soil and draw deep-soil nutrients to the trees' root zones. Swales in the tractor paths catch and hold rain and snow, allowing the moisture to soak in to the soil rather than running off.

Rows of chestnuts climb the hillside, separated by various companion plantings that attract beneficial insects and pests alike. Shepard likes to point out that no plant disease or pest has ever been completely eliminated. His pragmatism leads him to speculate that to find a natural predator for a pest one requires a healthy enough population of the pest to sustain a population of predators. Thus, contrary to held dogma, he finds ways to invite the pests. Yes, his cabbage leaves have a few holes from cabbage loopers, but they're not a network of skeletonized leaf veins seen on other organic farms. His loopers eat a little and then get eaten, ultimately saving the cabbage without resorting to dangerous and costly chemical treatments.

He's also utilized the behaviors of certain species to perform work he'd rather avoid. To this end, the farm features small posts regularly planted every 30 feet, the perfect orientation for bluebirds who like to roost outside their nests. As Mark harvests his asparagus by hand, a squadron of bluebirds follows in his wake, devouring the delectable insects he's disturbed.

The chestnuts, while only a component of the Shepards' acreage, serve as the venture's backbone. Mark hopes to harvest enough nuts to keep the family alive. Some folks, though, think he's the real nut.

Ask any thriving orchardist to describe a tree plantation in three words, and they'll reply, "Uniformity, uniformity, uniformity." Apple orchards, almond groves, pine plantations—almost any mass growing of tree crops will maintain regular rows with similar trees standing at attention like soldiers in drill. Such uniform conditions allow for systematic pruning and mechanized harvest of the crop. To earn a living wage, most farmers need to maximize their production. Single size and age trees, it is commonly believed, permit the maximal harvest with the minimal waste.

Somehow, Mark Shepard missed this boat. Good luck finding two similar trees next to one another on his land. His ragtag mix of hybrids appears as a disorganized party of middle schoolers, some tall and gangly, others short and stout. Next to a handsome straight-boled 25 foot tree stands a runt chock full of burs. Some trees boast male flowers without females; others prove male sterile, the ones Mark claims give the best nuts. I try to visualize a corn field of foot-high stalks standing next to the "high-as-an-elephant's-eye" kind, wondering how farm machinery might address such diversity.

Michigan State plant pathologist Dennis Fulbright finds in such diversity an agrarian's nightmare. If other farmers adopt Shepard's ways, they'll be sadly disappointed and potentially economically spanked, he warns, when asked about the connections between TACF's work and the agricultural resurgence of chestnut. Fulbright states the agricultural rule of thumb bluntly, "If a tree is not producing as much as it could, it's a wasted resource." In other words, if Tree A does well and Tree B does poorly, the farmer should eliminate B and plant another A, at least if she wants to stay in business.

Fulbright's criticism focuses upon the difference between grafted cultivars and seedlings. Grafted cultivars, selected for production by agricultural researchers and breeders, supply the bulk of fruit and nut tree growers' stock. Nursery managers purchase tested cultivars, removing much of the guesswork from their missions. Seedling trees, on the other hand, have not necessarily been tested. What arises from the nut depends upon the chance combination of gametes rather than the product of agricultural engineering. Seedlings most often produce smaller, less consistent crops. They certainly fail to offer the uniformity most growers desire. One farmer in Ohio, Fulbright notes, grew 5000 seedling chestnuts and found maybe five worthy of grafting. 99.9% of his plantings failed to meet his needs and would be discarded. While Luther

Burbank or Fred Hebard might see in those five trees prize winners, the farmer taking the economic risk focuses on the 4,995 losses. Is the glass half-empty or half-full? In this case, that test of perception fails to note that one path leads to possible progress for a breeding program while the other ends in potential bankruptcy for an artisan working the land.

Fulbright reserves his concern for growers that don't understand the risks they're assuming. He discusses how representatives of chestnut-recovery groups enlisted the tender story of the American chestnut to leverage potential growers in Michigan and elsewhere to grow chestnuts. Growers could prove their patriotism by joining the mission to rescue "our" native chestnut. In Michigan, landowners wanting to do the right thing, while also succumbing to a bit of that "get rich quick" mentality, purchased thousands of dollars of Chinese chestnut seedlings from these groups. The trees rarely lived up to claims. Some growers swallowed their pride, killed their seedling trees, and reinvested in cultivars like *Colossal* that offer greater economic benefits. Others simply abandoned their plantings, writing off the loss on taxes.

While chestnut growing seems to be catching on again, researchers work to develop successful cultivars that will perform for growers. Shepard's trees are experimental, as he well knows. Perhaps that 25-foot, seven-year-old on his property will provide stock for future chestnut agro-forests. Today, though, any nursery operators assuming that they'll get a strong commercial crop from seedlings sold by organizations like the Chestnut Alliance will likely be unsatisfied. Fulbright mentions a Michigander proud of his 500 pound harvest from fifth-year trees. Elsewhere, growers grooved on their 14-year-old trees producing 1800 pounds of nuts, not knowing that others hauled in comparable sized harvests on trees half that age. With no standards of comparison, the chestnut entrepreneur has few ways to measure actual success or, what Fulbright fears is more likely, failure. Perhaps potential chestnut agroforesters could look to the success of apple growers for guidance.

Apple growers rely on a small number of proven cultivars—red and golden delicious, Granny Smith, Jona gold—to produce fruit for a discriminating market. The individual grower need not expend energy finding new apples to lure consumers. Instead, researchers, both for private companies and public institutions like the land-grant universities, develop new cultivars to tempt consumers and earn growers an income. Thus, researchers and orchardists, by dividing labors, ensure mutually beneficial outcomes while serving the greater needs of apple eaters.

To this end, researchers have provided a few cultivars of chestnut to growers. 'Colossal,' a Japanese/European hybrid, has proven itself in several trials, but one should remember that chestnuts are quite finicky. The success of any cultivar depends upon local conditions. Even in Lower Michigan, where Dennis Fulbright tracks chestnuts, a tree that thrives near Lake Michigan may flop 50 miles inland.

Growers commonly cite yield per tree in pounds as their prime measure of success. A number of other variables, though, go into selecting successful trees. One cultivar producing prolifically for ten years might gradually decrease production as it ages, reducing its value to growers. Some trees have bumper crops every two years, with the intervening year producing few nuts. And even the most prolific nut producer fails if its nuts taste like recycled fiberboard.

Researchers at the University of Missouri Center for Agroforesty, a leader in commercial chestnut production in the US, began long-term research to assess various cultivars in 1996. At their New Franklin-based Horticulture and Agroforestry Research Center (HARC), the group originally planted 20 kinds of chestnut and has since expanded to 56. They identify their objectives as finding "outstanding, locally-adapted cultivars that have traits suitable for commercial chestnut production," and setting field trial protocols to maximize the quality and yield of nuts. Besides selecting for flavor, nut size, storage potential, and consistency of yields, they catalogue important data such as the dates of bud break, flowering and nut fall, nut weight, and nut yield.

HARC's findings will primarily aid Missouri growers, though their data will help direct horticulturalists elsewhere. Northern growers, seeing that HARC's 'Qing' cultivars dropped nuts on the first three days of October, a time of likely frost, might opt for another cultivar such as 'Eaton' which drops fruit a week earlier. Likewise, their recommendation to abandon 'Willamette' prevents others from wasting growing space on the debunked cultivar.

Chestnut enthusiasts face a potential Catch-22, though, in developing strong cultivars. Until a profitable market for chestnuts exists, little money can be made from breeding strong cultivars. But a market will not develop until chestnuts become readily available to the public, the reason we need these successful trees. As Michael Pollan notes in *The Botany of Desire*, the apple, traditionally a source of alcohol as cider, needed a make-over to become the "apple-a-day" healthy fruit we perceive today. Once apple became a staple of the American diet, cultivators could earn big money developing favorable new apples.

A sizable gulf lies between American chestnut restoration and growing chestnut for a profit (or more likely, striving to break even, as the American agriculturalist knows). Hebard and the Griffins do not work to raise nut-producing cultivars; they want an American chestnut, a wild tree rather than a farm crop. Confined by economic reality, nut growers should not be expected to play roles in the recovery effort unless they receive substantial economic incentives and recognize that the trees may not be as productive as they desire.

Chestnut agriculture serves recovery efforts in an indirect but potent way—by keeping the word "chestnut" in the American vernacular. More people buying into the cult of the American chestnut leads to more people supporting recovery efforts. TACF needs to maintain a high profile so that volunteers and donors remain interested. When local farmers raising hybrid chestnuts make the headlines in small town newspapers, more folks learn about blight and enlist in TACF's mission. Shoppers finding the unfamiliar nuts in the produce aisle read the little cards with information and cooking directions, becoming much more receptive to the word "chestnut" as they navigate the various media in their lives.

Likewise, recovery also helps farmers hawk their chestnuts in the same way a war boosts flag sales. The American people want to support the American chestnut any way they can, be it by cutting a check to TACF or purchasing a pound of nuts to roast at home. A century post-blight, Americans partake in the rediscovery of the popularity, beauty, and savory flavor of chestnuts, climbing onto the bandwagon even though the nuts they enjoy ultimately come from China. The question bugging me is, Will this all prove a passing fad or has chestnut reentered our culinary tradition? The answer might not be evident for quite some time.

Ask Shepard and he'll be honest; his family might only scrape by working this land. That's why he keeps acres of asparagus, squash, and other market crops he can sell in town or to Organic Valley, the local corporate entity working to save the family farm. Like Iowa's corn farmers, Shepard has learned that farmers play against the house, giants like Archers-Daniels Midland and Cargill, and any astute gambler knows the odds always favor the house. Permaculture chestnuts and hazels might someday take over prime Iowa acreage once petroleum-hungry soybeans and corn become too expensive to grow. By that point, though, Monsanto or some other corporate monster will develop the facilities to process Shepard's produce. Instead of corn farmers going broke to keep the farm going, it will likely be permaculturists following in their footsteps.

Agricultural sanity left our agribusiness system long ago. We have devised corn that requires human intervention to continue, since almost all the seed sown is hybridized to maximize yield for only one generation. Many produce sterile seed. Corn farmers refuse to save their own seed, knowing that they'll only produce less volume, a suicidal notion in a system that forces all to search for all the tricky ways to increase harvests. Shepard and many organic growers seek to regain a measure of sanity, often wading against the undertow of economic forces trying to pull them out to sea.

The theory behind Shepard's practice remains sound. Hazelnuts and chestnuts provide the nutritional building blocks of American diets—protein, carbohydrate, fats, and more, just as corn has been engineered to do. But the tree crops require less energy and labor as they mature. Established chestnuts will put out more chestnuts whether or not Shepard pays them any attention. And the hazels will do the same. These two crops prove sustainable—they persist over the years with minimal inputs. In fact, they may be difficult to remove if Shepard ever wishes to change his mission. The rows boast more than a few hazelnuts that, due to undesirable traits, Shepard mows to the soil surface whenever the opportunity arises. He wants them out but they stubbornly refuse to take the hint, shooting up leaves faster than he can react.

So far, though, agroforesters remain in the backwaters of agriculture. Fertilizers, herbicides, pesticides—the entire agribusiness arsenal, along with government subsidies keeping the large-scale farmers afloat, keep the US swimming in an overabundance of cheap food. We even send troops to foreign soil to bolster the flow of oil keeping this destructive process moving. Shepard simply cannot compete with these forces. When the price of oil rises, though, his day may come—if he can last that long.

For Shepard, marketing remains a challenge. He awaits the day the food industry recognizes the true value of his crops. An agroforestry groundbreaker, he realizes that his revolutionary practice must wait for markets to catch up. Thus, he's become a zealous promoter of his project, presenting the basics of his permaculture to government agencies such as USDA, university groups, private corporations, and anyone else interested. While not earning what he could through standard agriculture, Shepard chooses to invest in a future that may never be realized.

Shepard's chestnut-based agriculture, while not key in reviving the American chestnut, does illuminate the ways in which a restored American species might re-enter the economy. Agribusiness can work the nut's nutritional wealth into its machine, pumping out various carbon compounds to flavor cereals, cement meat nuggets, or varnish cardboard boxes. Small-scale farmers can grow nuts for sale in local markets or for deployment in "value added" home-crafted beverages and foods. While I personally favor the latter approach, the incredible capital agribusiness could inject into serious chestnut recovery would allow for better results. The vision of Iowa covered by a canopy of hybrid chestnuts, nurturing a forest floor where diverse ecosystems persist, seems far favorable to the chemical-agriculture wasteland it has become in the last century.

Shepard's not the only entrepreneur seeking a living from chestnuts. Thirty-six Michigan growers have banded together to form Chestnut Growers, Inc., to promote their businesses collectively. They've enlisted the Michigan Agricultural Experiment Station staff as well as faculty at Michigan State University to help them establish their trees, promote their efforts, and develop markets for their products.

Ron Jeffries, proprietor of Jolly Pumpkin Artisan Ales in Dexter, Michigan, acquired some chestnuts from the group and produced his first chestnut beer. Instead of a corn- or wheat-based mash, Jeffries crushed chestnuts and employed their carbohydrates in fermentation. The beer, rich in chestnut flavor, sold out quickly, leading Jeffries and Chestnut Growers, Inc. to consider extending their business relationship. While the beer provides minimal exposure, it does introduce people to the flavors of chestnut. Dennis Fulbright, advisor to the collective, notes, "This is a new product and another source of income for our state. Though the amount of chestnuts sold right now is still relatively small, this shows that new Michigan-made products can be developed, processed and marketed from our natural resource base." A mere taste can hook return customers who spread the word throughout their social circles. Consider the popularity of herbs like basil and cilantro, known only by connoisseurs a few decades ago but now favored by many. Who knows? We might all be guzzling chestnut-laced beverages in a few years.

The University of Missouri's Center for Agroforestry (UMCA) also promotes chestnuts as a niche market for state farmers. In 2006, they sponsored the third annual Chestnut Roast, a multi-dimensional family-centered event designed to spread the word on chestnut and other nuts, demonstrate progressive agriculture techniques, and share the bounty of state-grown crops and products. By increasing the public's awareness of chestnut, project leaders believe they will create markets for chestnut products. Chinese chestnuts offer growers opportunity to open new markets for their crops. UMCA's promotional materials point out the benefits of chestnut. For example, chestnut flour is gluten-free, a healthy alternative for individuals with certain food allergies.

Whether we discuss petroleum, minerals, or agricultural products, the fact remains that raw materials afford one a minor income. The real money—the capitalist's quarry—comes from altering that raw item to produce a marketable good—a box of cereal, cutlery, kerosene. Farmers have been used for their raw goods for too long. Now, many Midwestern farmers pool resources to open commercial kitchens and small processing plants to add value to their raw materials. Dakota wheat growers banded together to form the Dakota Pasta Company. Now they grow the durum wheat and process it into an excellent dried pasta. Washington DC's *Agraria* restaurant, owned by a collective of farmers from across the US, offers a menu boasting all home-grown or gathered goods. Shepard and other chestnut growers might gain strength in numbers, pooling their resources to develop a larger chestnut-based agriculture economy.

For now, Shepard's farm and family survive by producing a diversity of quality products. Asparagus can bring in $1,900 per acre, limited mainly by Mark's ability to cut. With a few helping hands, he could double the acreage of asparagus. The potential for chestnut-fed pork, with swine vacuuming up fallen nuts greedily, may shape Shepard's future, as may cider and wine production.

The Shepards have developed a family-sustaining agriculture that benefits the land and its denizens. By allowing natural processes to unravel as they will, Mark can even afford week-long family vacations in the Boundary Waters during the peak of summer when his neighbors fret over their corn's fate. His solution may not be for everyone but one must credit him with plowing his own path and striving to better agricultural practices.

CHAPTER 7

"Sometimes I do see myself as a tree, even, rather grandly, as the ash Yggdrasil, the mythical world-tree of Norse legend. The ash Yggdrasil has three roots. One falls into the pool of knowledge by Valhalla, where Odin comes to drink. A second is being slowly consumed in the undying fire of Muspellheim, realm of the flame-god Surtur. The third is gradually being gnawed through by a fearsome beast called the Nidhögg. And when fire and monster have destroyed two of the three, the ash will fall, and darkness will descend. The twilight of the gods: a tree's dream of death."

—Salman Rushdie, *Shame*, p. 92.

Just like most housecats, the American chestnut remains indifferent to any name we wish to attach to it; the concept of species exists only in esoteric human categorizations of the world. Philosophers of science periodically try to remind biologists of this often ignored fact, though practitioners of the life sciences remain slow to pay heed. Indeed, we allow the goggles we call 'science' to influence greatly the way we witness and interpret the living and non-living entities populating our planet. We construct the boundaries separating closely related organisms and then act as if we "discovered" clearly defined divisions in nature. Even the little guidelines we coin to give our definitions their scientific allure fail given the odd instance dialed up by the blind watchmaker, evolution.

Species are supposedly separate kinds of organisms that cannot breed effectively outside their group, a rule facing few difficulties in differentiating badgers from weasels. But when scientists attempt to apply this simplistic alleged rule to chestnuts (and a multitude of other organisms), reality helps them fall flat on their faces. For example, pollen from southern China's Seguin chestnut pollinates numerous other chestnut species, producing fertile nuts that express hybrid traits when grown. Questions arise: Are the varied chestnut species failing to accord with theory really separate species? Are all chestnuts representative of one global species? Pragmatic as they can be, scientists rarely address these questions adequately, often offering swift *ceteris paribus* clauses to make exceptions accord to their system of rules. Despite their ability to interbreed and produce fertile progeny, we say the varied chestnuts belong to different species because they remain geographically isolated from one another. We conveniently overlook human efforts to interbreed these species, sticking to the needed fiction that all are separate species.

Despite millions of years of reproductive isolation, the American chestnut retains its capacity for hybridizing with historically geographically distant members of its genus. Thus, we might wonder why this alleged species, *Castanea dentata*, deserves rescuing. Are the other species insufficient for humanity's needs or are some larger principles in play?

From a simple human-centric perspective, a view environmental ethicists term 'instrumentalism,' American chestnut provides a number of services currently unavailable from other chestnuts. Putting aside contentious claims that our native nut's flavor exceeds that of all others, the American species' straight bole and comparatively greater height have not been duplicated in relatives, nor have many of its less popular morphological and ecological traits.

Perhaps these traits prove the true goal toward which breeding programs should aim. Arthur Graves historically and Sandra Anagnostakis currently support this pragmatic viewpoint which holds that the American chestnut's instrumental value lies in the wide variety of services and products the tree provided. An economic support for farmers, leather tanners, loggers, and homesteaders, American chestnut could only be replaced by multiple species and new technologies. Appalachia, characterized as an economically impoverished region, took a devastating economic blow when blight attacked. Recovery of the species might bring back some of the financial benefits, even though societal adaptations have diminished or eliminated markets for tannin, telephone poles, railroad ties, and even chestnuts. The nuts would almost certainly return in popularity to new connoisseurs.

Instrumentalism ultimately reduces the chestnut (or any other non-human) to the services and products it provides. For many, these traits—preferable though they are—do not suffice to explain fully chestnut's value. American breeders still want an American tree; we need to look at other reasons to explain this desire.

At first glance, one might succumb to the belief that an odd foliar form of nationalism pervades the chestnut establishment. The rabid need to rescue "our" tree has been expressed by many of the researchers. Fred Hebard and Gary Griffin, though, do not come off as dogmatists. They know their ecology and their chestnuts. Underlying their programs are deeper ethical and ecological callings.

For many, the American chestnut possesses a value irreplaceable by alternative species. One rationale for rescuing the native notes the species' unique evolutionary history. The species, more than a collection of traits, results from an age-old drama. Just as my Grandma Buege found a mysterious value in family heirlooms—a value involving the people and settings amongst which these objects moved, our tree cannot be supplanted with a look-alike species. Grandma would have never traded her crystal for duplicates from the antique store. Likewise, the people of greater Appalachia place "their" tree on a pedestal for the intricate connections it had with their lives. Japanese chestnut never established such a tight fit with American culture.

Outside my family, Grandma's dishes prove indistinguishable from others. The obvious difficulty with basing values on their history is their personal nature which remains elusive to outsiders. Rallying support for little known, localized species proves difficult, particularly given the cascade of extinctions faced on Earth. Every species has its own evolutionary history, as well as a record of human use and appreciation. It proves difficult to adjudicate your preferences as superior to mine. Moreover, ethics remains distinct from economics; the value I place on an entity may be quite different from the actual moral worth inherent in that being.

In discussions with old timers, I have discerned a deep appreciation for chestnut's aesthetic value. Tall flowering trees, appearing as if snow-covered, enter conversations as Virginians recall trees known in youth. The size of *C. dentata*, though slight in comparison to sequoias and redwoods, awed people in the east. But the giants gracing historical photographs were rarities occupying preserved lands. Those monsters, averaging 500 years old, will probably never be seen by humans again.

This aesthetic component also involves American chestnut's interrelations with other species. An ecological tapestry of interconnected organisms appeals to the Thoreauvian visitor aware of more than mere individuals. The turkey hunter favors chestnut because it serves to fatten up his prey. The mycologist treasures the intricate mycorrhizal connections between fungi and chestnuts. When one wants to expand ecological understanding of a woodlot, the possibilities may be endless as one examines the complex interplay of organisms from all five kingdoms with the abiotic components of the environment. In other words, the aesthetic value of chestnut may reach farther than humans are currently equipped to travel; future humans may unearth higher levels of complexity at which to marvel.

All of these perspectives—aesthetic, economic, historical—identify value in chestnut that depends upon human valuers. While not intending to minimize the importance of these instrumental values, I have argued as an environmental ethicist that components of the natural world can have another type of value independent of humans. This intrinsic value—literally, value in the thing itself—offers alternatives for grounding our actions in saving American chestnut.

The Griffins, Fred Hebard, Phil Rutter, and others have all spoken of righting wrongs committed by humans against American chestnut. By introducing blight and failing to stop the lethal fungus's march, Americans hold responsibility for nearly destroying another species. With strong senses of restitutive justice, researchers strive to rescue the species, returning it to its traditional ecological position throughout the eastern United States. In some respects, Gary Griffin's insistence on only employing American stock in the ACCF's mission stems from an urge to minimize the violation to American chestnut, while TACF sees the utilization of Chinese and Japanese genes as a pragmatic step toward a quicker recovery.

These different approaches imply that American chestnut in some way holds status as an ethical being. If an entity can be wronged and can deserve restitution, then it can be said to possess moral value of its own. The difference between this intrinsic value and instrumental value is illustrated in comparing laws that forbid killing a neighbor's dog. Instrumentalism identifies the damage as done to the neighbor as it is her property that is killed, while intrinsic value recognizes wrongness in killing the dog for the animal's sake.

Indeed, a tree does have interests. All living beings have an interest in being alive, in being healthy, in meeting biological needs. Acting out the code of the genome ties all living things together, provides a common goal. Acts that frustrate the unraveling of the organism's growth and development create stresses that force individuals and species to adapt, altering their genetic codes to deal with new circumstances. When humans prove the source of those frustrations, some conclude that the individual and species has been wronged. Someone holds responsibility for inflicting that wrong.

Does it make sense to say that a tree can be wronged? Do humans deserve blame for the millions of healthy trees cut down each year to supply housing, fuel, flooring, and other materials?

I remember my days in the Boy Scouts. On weekend camping trips or at summer camp, our leader held a strong prohibition on damaging any living trees. When a few firewood gatherers took down a half-dead pine, his terse lecture quickly extinguished any hopes for a fire that weekend. Like Rutter, he viewed the tree as "half-alive," contrary to our self-serving assessment. We knew that downed wood would suffice and, if it didn't, we needed to look farther or forego the warmth of the flames. Scoutmaster Kotlewski instilled in each of us a respect for and concern for the living trees. We had no doubt that a tree could be wronged. That wrong hinged upon damaging living trees unnecessarily.

To some degree, humans rely on wood for basic needs, a reliance more easily defended than wasteful use. The greater wrongs may lie in how we harvest our wood. Killing an individual tree that would be replaced through natural regeneration appears less morally reprehensible than destroying an entire population and denying the forest a chance to regenerate. Destroying the forest also removes and disturbs habitat for other species and destabilizes ecosystems.

Humans bear responsibility for introducing chestnut blight and spreading it throughout the American chestnut's habitat. Our lack of concern for the foreign stock we imported did wrong the species. If that seems a harsh judgment, consider how chestnut would have fared if humans had never entered their environment.

Unlike some areas of inquiry, ethics rarely offers us clean, clear solutions. Intrinsic value cannot be proven the way we demonstrate principles of physics or theorems of geometry. On the other hand, psychologists like Jim Rest recognize widespread levels of moral development, a progression that individuals undergo from predominating self-interest of infants to outward concern for others, as well as awareness of abstract ethical principles. Peter Singer, a highly respected ethicist, maintains that societies, including his case study—the Western European tradition, have evolved greater moral inclusion—his expanding circle—moving from moral status for only a privileged class of powerful landowners to include women, children, non-Europeans, the poor, slaves and ex-slaves, and animals. The civil rights movement of the 1950s and '60s demonstrates an advance in society's ethical development as do contemporary liberation movements. Expanding our realm of moral concern to include more entities can be seen as ethical progress.

If we view an ethic as a reasonable limitation upon members of a group in order to advance the well-being and persistence of the community, as well as the members, then the expanding circle of ethical concern makes sense. As human technologies have changed, the scale of consequences of human actions has also changed. While once we could only kill individual animals, we now can wipe out entire populations and species with ease. The relatively recent rise of environmental ethics in Western philosophy and environmentalism coincides with the recognition that human activity has significant impacts upon ecosystems and higher order ecological entities, likely including the entire Earth. We now need to develop environmental ethics to ensure the survival of human beings. If we fail to set limits on deforestation, soil loss, importation of plants and animals, pollution, expansion of agricultural and urban lands, resource consumption, and other large scale actions, we will ultimately pay the price in reduced quality of life, increased death, and a timely extinction.

An ethic can be devised by examining an action, determining the consequences that action is likely to bring, and assessing whether or not those consequences are desirable. John Stuart Mill's utilitarian theory provides an example of such an ethical framework. Kantian ethics, in some formulations, also examines the consequences of an action. Kant would okay any action if universalizing that action—allowing everybody to do it, would be favorable. On the other hand, if we can see we would like to do the action but would not want everybody doing it, we must assume the action is morally wrong.

An ethic, following Kant, can be seen as restraints on an individual's and a group's actions. Our economic system rarely rewards restraint; profit awaits those who rush headlong to exploit as much of a resource as possible in a short time. An environmental ethic would require restraint, thus coming in direct opposition to capitalist philosophy. At some point, we need to determine which should have greater influence on our decisions, ethics or economics.

Our foresight has already introduced several restraints that underlie what we might call our embryonic national environmental ethic. Starting with Yellowstone in 1872, we have created a system of National Parks that protect key natural treasures from various trespasses. Wilderness areas, national forests, and historic sites earn special protections against which potential exploiters must struggle. Legislative acts, like 1973's Endangered Species Act, can severely limit human impacts upon species categorized as threatened and endangered, protecting their habitats as a side benefit.

New globally-directed restraints have also been discussed, though the United States has not supported many of them. Bans on various weapons like landmines and cluster bombs earn a US veto despite support throughout the rest of the world. The Kyoto Protocol which begins to address human emissions contributing to global warming has yet to be signed by the US.

Economic forces push us away from the restraints designed to benefit future generations, as well as the natural world. We have entered an age in which the rush for more wealth, power and material goods eclipses concern for what we already have. We forget the incredible wealth we have (or had) in clean air, water, and bountifully diverse wild areas. Our failure to link cause and effect, our consumptive actions with a diminished environment, will precipitate our ultimate decline whether in quality of life or the continued existence of humanity.

With the development of environmental ethics, we begin to seriously consider the moral responsibilities humans have toward other non-humans. Formulating restrictions on our actions, we can begin to reduce negative impacts upon the natural world and ourselves.

Environmental ethicists have offered reasons for considering beings other than individuals as having intrinsic value. An intrinsic value inheres in the subject itself, regardless of humans or other sentient valuers. Species, social groups such as pods of whales or packs of wolves, populations, ecosystems, bioregions, as well as other evolutionary and ecologically determined entities, become candidates for special values, limiting the impact that humans can have upon them.

Rather than argue for the intrinsic value of American chestnut, I point out the consideration already shown toward the species. The groundswell of contributors, researchers, advocates, cooperators, and appreciators provides evidence of an existing environmental ethic respecting this high-profile species, as marches in Birmingham made evident the growing insistence on civil rights for African-Americans. Many consider the damage done to *Castanea dentata* as a wrong committed against the species itself. That species, in their view, must have intrinsic value.

Our developing environmental ethic will be called upon to do more than merely determine how species and individuals should be treated. Ultimately, it will address the value of the evolutionary process itself. A simplistic ethic that declared the value of all trees to be equal would surely miss important information. American chestnut co-evolved with other species to produce biological systems where species' interconnections promote the well-being of many different species. Replacing the chestnut with striped maple would change the complex system, favoring some species and harming others. Respect for the evolutionary process would prompt us to respect the natural development of the places we live and visit. Even those who deny the possibility of evolution may find value in the design they observe, realizing that disturbing that design has moral implications. The order and structure of the natural world, whether a product of divine labors or natural selection, can and should be accounted for in an adequate environmental ethic. The complexity, or more exactly the organic unity, of natural systems needs to be taken into account as I argued in a doctoral dissertation many years ago.

All species restructure their environments to their benefit. Only one species, though, has the cognitive capacity to control that restructuring. Ironically, that species has the greatest impact upon natural systems. Having the capacity to act ethically requires one to act ethically.

21st Century humans have not established a far-reaching, profound, and explicit ethic for the ways we treat non-human nature. Rescuing American chestnut, though, offers a workshop for examining our personal environmental ethics. We can learn and develop as moral people by examining the varied reasons for saving the chestnut. Given the growing urgency in addressing environmental problems, from invasive species to suicidal agricultural practices, we each hold responsibility for determining our own responses.

When we create an ecologically responsible society—an organized community where we learn to act responsibly toward nature as effectively as we learn to read, then most will stop smuggling foreign animals and plants, not out of fear of being caught, but through deeper understanding.

Our ethics often lag behind our activities. The Christian commandment forbidding killing followed many centuries in which killing provided employment and entertainment for many. Indeed, the millennia following the acceptance of this commandment have featured even more killing, most profoundly from those gathered beneath the aegis of Christianity. Formulation of an environmental ethic may prove similar with a wide number professing their concern for nature while few live by the principles agreed upon. The very failure to live up to an ethic is what makes an ethic necessary. Humans also need to learn how to help others abide by ethical decisions. We learn ethics through practice. American chestnut recovery offers a fantastic opportunity for more people to practice.

Even if chestnut recovery proves a longer range project than TACF predicts, a project as ambitious as American chestnut recovery has produced positive side effects. Given the massive disruptions of the Twentieth Century combined with a societal attention deficiency, the public wastes little awareness on last week's news cycle, dropping the events of last year into the same frame of reference as the Dark Ages, the Iran-Contra hearings, the fall of Rome, or the time of dinosaurs. Yet the American chestnut remains in the news, certainly pleasing older fans of the tree but also bringing new converts into the fold.

TACF issues press releases whenever an event of note occurs, with most press services staying savvy to the "chestnut agenda." Desperate for free news, local newspapers, and television stations round out their pages and telecasts with the latest results of the breeding program or new discoveries of hidden wild chestnuts.

Take, for example, Alabama's tallest known American chestnut, an 85-foot tall tree found in 2005 in Talladega National Forest. The Birmingham News (June 20, 2006) proudly reported the 14-inch diameter tree showing no signs of blight damage. Oddly enough, a genetic assay revealed the related chinquapin as a maternal ancestor, suggesting that chinquapin genes may help the tree survive blight.

In the spring of 2006, biologist Nathan Klaus made the news upon finding a stand of healthy 20- to 30-year-old chestnuts on a ridge not far from FDR's Little White House in Warm Springs, Georgia. Klaus speculated to the Associated Press, "It's either that these trees are able to resist the blight, which is unlikely, or Pine Mountain has something unique that is giving these trees resistance." Reports of newfound trees also surfaced in Maine and New Hampshire, suggesting that more survivors may exist throughout the chestnut's range.

Another popular theme for chestnut enthusiasts is the goofy tree climber who pollinates chestnut trees. The Asbury Park Press presented the story of Mike Ziroli, a TACF member in New Jersey, who volunteers his services to pollinate extremely rare surviving American chestnuts. At Holmdel Park, he worked his magic on the sole survivor on the 564-acre tract, a 25-year-old tree evidently suffering from blight but, hopefully, still capable of producing nuts. Passers-by gained an awareness of chestnut as did readers of the article.

For TACF, building public awareness makes sense. Thousands of volunteers will be needed to plant and care for their blight-resistant tree once it is ready. By spreading the word, an army of supporters will be ready for recruitment. Given wide-spread public support, American chestnut actually has a shot at new success.

Given the diverse groups and individuals struggling to find a new home for a revived American chestnut, resources continue to flow toward people laboring to rescue this species as they do for a slew of well-intentioned environmental groups convened to rescue other living beings and their habitats. Sectors of our society have little difficulty drafting the lay public into supporting ragtag coalitions and meticulously organized foundations promoting odd causes, from fighting extinction to keeping greedy industrialists out of preserved lands. Unfortunately, these groups often have trouble achieving long-term victories, a fact exemplified by the multi-annual attempts to open Alaska's North Slope to oil extraction. Activists and their efforts tend to recede quietly beneath the waters built up behind the dams of corporate America.

The American chestnut proves an odd case, though, as the ACCF, the ACF and others do not face organized opposition. The groups are not trying to limit the powers of Monsanto, Exxon, or General Electric—at least, not yet. People either remain absolutely ignorant of chestnut's existence or support its resurgence. But one would be mistaken to assume that American chestnut does not face threats.

Given the proliferation of so-called "free trade" agreements in the past few decades, the US Government has ceded much of its control over the importation of foreign goods, including plant material. By prioritizing trade over protection of our environment, we have widened the opening on a Pandora's Box of diseases and pests, many of which may spread rampantly as the chestnut blight once did. Legislation to protect our ecosystems from so-called invader species is trumped by the alleged need to expand our economy. For evidence, check out the annual flocks of weed-pickers combing the woods for garlic mustard, buckthorn, and all the other invasive nasties unleashed upon our environments.

But eclipsing the problems with free-trade agreements is the sheer mass of international traffic passing across our borders daily. When huge numbers of people hop the globe in search of new thrills, higher wages, escape, or asylum, the number of accidental and intentional introductions climbs drastically. While alleged security needs identify the threat of razor blade and box cutter, packages of seeds, insect-riddled fruits and vegetables, and fungus-toting clothes go unnoticed. Compounding this problem, our assumed neglect for rules and regulations that interfere with our personal freedoms dictates that we carry those tainted chestnuts through customs with our heads held high. No egghead scientist tells us what we can or cannot do! Folks who know better, who understand the ecological implications of such actions, have so far failed to educate the public or the officials who might push enforcement of quarantine laws. Of the millions of travelers coming and going, only one is needed to wreak ecological ruin, innocently to introduce the next chestnut blight or Dutch elm disease.

Even if these problems didn't confront us, we'd still suffer from global warming and an industrial complex aligned to abate any attempts to curb greenhouse gas emissions. Chestnut's native range has not only changed ecologically; it continues to change climatologically. Thus, sites formerly xeric become mesic or hydric. The grove of surviving American chestnuts reported in the spring of 2006 may owe their persistence to site-specific conditions that stopped the growth of the blight fungus. Altered climate may favor new forms of blight or even new pathogens with unforeseen impacts upon the recovered chestnuts.

Will newly planted trees survive catastrophic floods, hail storms, drought, hurricanes, and other calamities that threaten to increase in the coming age of extreme weather? We really have no idea. I have my doubts.

The century since the blight's introduction to Long Island has witnessed incredible changes in the landscape and the scale of impact humans have on the land. Considering only the technologies employed to cut timber, we have gone from individual loggers employing axe and saw, in many cases hauling logs out on horse-drawn equipment, to mechanical removal with big machinery that greatly multiplies the speed of extraction. These new technologies influence our conceptions of time. Perhaps we lack the patience for assisting chestnut that may take a lifetime to reach desirable size. Reforesting the Appalachians will take decades, if not centuries.

While Fred Hebard's generation might maintain the ability to undertake such long-term projects, younger generations crippled by the immediate rewards of video games and the shopping mall may not comprehend the importance of rescuing this once popular species. Unless we enlist future generations in this seemingly endless pursuit, chestnut's caretakers may be extinct inside of 50 years.

A bouncing four-year-old, with two eyes always interrogating the hometown outside our VW's windows, I quietly catalogued the world I witnessed, paying attention to details others missed. Seventieth Street, home to my hometown's central library, proved my favorite destination. The cathedral of elms stretching high overhead, meshed branches meeting in arboreal handshakes, evoked the safety I sought to engineer in couch-cushion fortresses and tirelessly excavated snow tunnels. No one ever pointed those trees out to me or remarked on the odd disease that waited to sweep in and wipe them from their urban grounding. Only years later, when I found vestiges of the same species north and westward in Fargo, North Dakota, did I revisit the serenity they had delivered to my pre-literate mind.

The Dakotan trees boasted thick circles of white paint, as if some knowledgeable bureaucrat sought to prevent drunk drivers from colliding with those weird survivors. The dirty white bands signified treatment—unknown chemicals pumped underneath the bark offered this island of trees a chance at limping into the Twenty-first Century. The analogy that popped to my mind involved amputees returning from war in a distant hostile nation. The elms would never be the same; they had sacrificed a chunk of their identity. Or, more accurately, humans had stolen their true nature, turning them into domesticated chemical junkies surviving to that next fix.

Perhaps only a child has the flexibility of mind to observe and accept the sudden disappearance of majestic rows of elms rising from curbside like so many living umbrellas. Most adults I know would be too busy to notice such changes, let alone think about them. Without witnessing first-hand the chainsaws ripping apart the heartwood of youth, leaving only dust and memories in their wake, I never thought about the trees' disappearances. Perhaps I laid down a mental footnote to figure out this calamity later in life. More likely, though, I just noted the loss and moved on. The elms comprised a mere stitch in a tapestry of biotic losses affecting my early life.

Vacations also alerted me to the not-so-gradual decline of American biotic diversity. Two trips to the Okefenokee Swamp serve as bookends for my developing environmental ethos. The first trip found me enraptured in the miasma of herptilian sounds billowing through the evening's failing light. Alligators bellowed in defense of their nests. Frogs and toads called out, a cornucopia of mating rituals, release calls, and what could only be an intense joy of existence in that riparian wonderland. Oh, to be amphibious in such a rich wilderness! I thought as a swamp novitiate at the undaunted age of 12.

Five years later, though, the dystopic reality of a burgeoning population milking the wild for every marketable resource weighed heavily upon me. I recoiled from the apparent decrease in amphibian voices, not knowing if their scarcity was a verifiable fact or a construction of my growing disdain for most things human. Adolescence left scars that still fester. The straws had piled up on this camel's back and I responded by rejecting my species affiliation. Like the race traitors attacked by bigots throughout abolition and the civil rights movement, I'd quietly renounced my identity as human, joining with those species upon which humankind built their empire. I devolved, gaining inspiration from a host of others abandoning the well-worn paths of that suburb-born religion, consumerism. I came to see society as a painfully destructive machine bulldozing a swath through the rest of their proclaimed "creation."

For decades, I held on to the flimsiest excuses for believing that the state of the world would improve. In fifth grade, my generation seemed eager to change our environment for the better. Kids hated pollution, cruelty to animals, deforestation and the other ecological calamities we discussed in class. Even high school found me hopeful though I'd noticed that the bulk of my classmates had sacrificed their concern for the world in exchange for mind-numbing bouts with alcohol, drugs and other destructive forms of pleasure. By graduate school, my hope had almost completely evaporated, leaving a crystalline cynicism in its wake. My people had veered from the paths we had envisioned in youth. Environmental issues became problems to ignore rather than challenges to overcome. The populace found a release from their consuming ennui and depression in the newly developed pharmacopoeia of prescription mood adjusters, devouring large enough doses to cloud out any worries about nature. "Consumption," once the common name for tuberculosis, now denotes a more pervasive ill that leaves most of us perpetually empty, searching for the imagined products that we feel might complete us.

Over this time, I also changed from an intrinsic part of cohesive social groups to a rugged individualist, often defining myself in antagonism with the people around me. The fluid dynamic of the playground, where diverse groups of children found commonality, was supplanted by the solipsism of adulthood, where one's needs and wants define the limits of one's social sphere. Adults simply lack the capacity to play well together. Each person strives so hard to rise above the pack that no one remains to watch the spectacle. Extravagant houses in the suburbs provide the isolated playgrounds to which my peers escape, somehow needing to define themselves outside the herd. Yet the content and satisfaction many crave never surfaces, hidden deep below the surface on which we focus.

Broken. If I had but one word to describe my experience of America's journey since my mid-60s birth, I'd wield the term "broken," like a hammer shattering a windshield or a team with too many losses. The rhetoric of school teachers held little power in disguising nightly images of the Vietnam debacle, Nixon's slow fall from power, a toppled statue that rejected gravity's insistent call. The signs of stress had shown on America's face.

Then I began to find the signs of collapse in the natural world. Pointless urban sprawl erased the wild places of my youth. Even if those spots were mere abandoned lots riddled with bike trails and weeds, they offered hope of escape. Drainage ditches proved good places to find grasshoppers or tadpoles until a dentist's office claimed them. Weeds would be replaced with monoculture sod, a green-on-green hue that said "Keep off," figuratively and literally, every time the lawn chemist plied the lawn with pesticides and little postcards declaring the space off-limits. A kid had nowhere to go to fire bottle rockets or chase rabbits.

The wild spaces of northern Wisconsin succumbed as well. Every last lot on the good lakes sold to anti-ecologists eager to rip out their riparian lakefront to install sterile beach. One had to burn more and more petroleum to reach the less-touched landscapes in which to get lost. And then came the age of ATVs and Jet-Skis. No longer was the cacophony of snowmobiles enough to satiate the under-stimulated weekend thrill seekers. Waterskiing paved the way for far more annoying craft that demanded little from their operators besides gasoline. The north woods became one long drone of infernal combustion. Nature's underappreciative visitors failed to find solace in peace, seeking disturbance from the painful act of contemplation. Throw in a few bottles of alcohol and even the most attuned minds shut down.

Millions of Americans seek this cyclic return to narcolepsy. Drive like hell to get out of the over-crowded, over-bearing city and make your destination indistinguishable from the hell-hole from which you crawled. The day I saw a young woman jogging around a lake with a Walkman, I knew that nature was doomed. Her insistence on drowning out the soundtrack of reality with ABBA made the hairs on my neck stand at attention.

In the droning, few paid heed to the loss of the elm, the natural, the quiet. Certainly, a minority mourned, but a minority in this society might as well not exist. The immoral majority holds power over all, paying little or no heed to the ruin they wreak.

Given this history, it should not surprise anyone that I remain quite skeptical of the American chestnut's chances in the hands of humanity. Were *Homo sapiens* to suddenly fall off the planet, chestnuts would return within a millennium, give or take a century. I believed this long before Gary Griffin voiced the idea. But humans prove an incredible speed bump on the way to saving the species.

We love nature but most refuse to sacrifice their immediate self-interest in nature's interest. Everyone loves the forests and meadows, bogs and lakes, but tourists fail to notice that their transgressions put the creatures they seek in permanent retreat, until they surrender and become suburban pests. Americans want their wild-ness but they also want to define exactly how the wild should appear and behave. Somehow, the contradiction inherent in such a view remains unheeded or unseen by many.

Compounding these immense problems is the low level of outdoors literacy in the general population, though more strikingly evident in the young. Johnny can probably distinguish between a plant and an animal, though if you ask him about an insect, he will likely be dumbfounded. Only a few generations ago, a time when American chestnut still populated Appalachian slopes, people gained knowledge of the varied species around them, identifying and gathering edible berries, tapping maple trees, harvesting wild scallops. Now we look at the lone mycologist in search of morels as a suicidal freak. Not understanding the kingdom of plants, we enter our default mode of fear, warning the children to stay away from the woods teeming with deadly ticks and poison ivy (which we cannot even identify).

The young reared their ugliest heads one Thursday morning as I attempted to engage a room full of freshman biology students in a viewing and discussion of Al Gore's "An Inconvenient Truth." Most of the kids elected sleeping, throwing paper, staring emptily into space, trading put-downs, and other forms of distraction over contemplating the future they might have a say in changing. Global climate change proved as distant as Hurricane Katrina had a year earlier. Apathy held greater appeal than serious contemplation of the world. I can only guess what it must feel like to be so young and so powerless to even engage with one's physical world. If these kids had had access to the Internet, they would have connected with the make-believe online world readily; it was reality they found repulsive.

I do not wish to overstate my case. Certainly, a wide number of people retain working knowledge of the biotic world. Hmong refugees in Wisconsin harvest watercress and numerous other free forages. Backwoods folk tap maple trees. Yet these people are exceptions to the rule. In a time of cheap, accessible food, most Americans remain ignorant of the ultimate source of their diet. We live without needing that information, thus, that information becomes lost.

Thus, for the majority, American chestnut recovery holds far less importance than Friday night's TV schedule or the number of visitors to one's myspace account. We have entered an age where fictional lives have gained ascendance over reality. It is within that framework that we should assess the likelihood of saving the many species we have wronged.

A semi-coherent group of individuals working toward any goal has limited ability to achieve their objectives. A concerted effort between organizations and agencies would offer greater potential for achievement. But we don't have that with chestnut. We have groups and individuals, while not quite stabbing one another in the back, at least refusing to cooperate with one another. Jealousy and selfishness prevail when camaraderie and selflessness would best serve recovery efforts. Chestnut's near disappearance proves a huge problem as the entire eastern third of the country was directly affected. Our solutions work at much smaller scales. It's like sending three doctors to treat 10,000 patients—too little to do too much.

To date, the Federal Government has remained blind to the chestnut issue. Given the massive failings of most of its recent undertakings, perhaps that can be seen as a blessing. On the other hand, the US Government has shown itself quite capable of winning the race to atomic weaponry and moonwalks. When a blight-resistant tree arrives, the time for government action will arise. What could be more patriotic than saving a distinct American species, and who better to trumpet that victory than our leaders in Washington?

By investing military branches in clearing and planting public lands and employing their grand fleets to move supplies, Congress could facilitate TACF's mission. Indeed, countless hometown patriots would rise up and join the action. Ten million saplings in the ground, one four-hundredth of the pre-blight numbers, might give American chestnut a foothold. Even if 5 million die, 5 million will survive. So far, though, such comprehensive plans have not materialized.

A species all but disappears. Humans rally to fix the situation. More problems arise, direct results of human short-comings. End of story.

Three brief sentences and a fragment might summarize the American chestnut story. At this point, we have far too little knowledge to predict the future of American chestnut. Will all this investment of time, labor, and money pay off in the long run or will American chestnut quietly follow in the passenger pigeon's wake? Do the rare survivors hidden in the netherwoods of Maine, Georgia and all states in between hold the secret to the tree's future, regardless of the machinations of humans? Would random mutation ultimately produce a blight resistant species? We simply do not know.

With an average human lifetime clocking in at fewer than 80 years, we have extremely limited awareness of longer term phenomena. Yes, astronomers have ingeniously employed tools to determine a rather accurate time for the big bang. Ice cores help us determine local, regional, and global climate trends. Our understanding of plate tectonics, barely 40 years old, dovetails with that of evolutionary science, a scant one-hundred years older, to allow us to sketch the movement of many species through pre-historic time. Yet, cognitively, we remain incapable of comprehending the scale of change that occurs in a million years. The fact that Earth's plates move conflicts with our observation of a minimally changing globe. We have yet to reach the defining event that will help us see deep time, an event analogous to the first pictures of globoid Earth from space that must have scared the wits out of members of the Flat Earth Society and which gave the rest of us a clearer conception of our home planet's shape and its finitude.

With our profound advancements in genetics, we've learned how to manipulate the very building blocks of life to create new beings, be they glow-in-the-dark rabbits or insulin-producing bacteria. The limits of this understanding, though, remain, despite our unwillingness to discuss them. The mapping of entire genomes of bacteria, mice, and humans still leaves us short of understanding these organisms. The tiny genetic difference between chimpanzees and humans astounds us, but we fail to comprehend the importance of our similarities. When we assess genomes from an evolutionary standpoint, we will reveal more of the picture needed for understanding the importance of those genomes.

Evolutionary scientists tell stories. Given an observed phenomenon, they construct logical histories that may have led to that phenomenon. So Venus flytraps developed the capacity for consuming insects because they could exploit low-nitrogen environments where few other plants grew. Orchids developed intricate flowers to lure specific pollinators. Likewise, each organism's genome results from millions of events, some dating to the earliest moments of life on Earth. Explaining how a gene developed or why redundant DNA populates the genome begins to unravel the larger stories of species, to bring finer fractal details into focus.

American chestnut, as a species, has more than 50 million years of evolution encoded in its genome. Before that, the ancestral species from which it evolved had amassed massive amounts of information, responses to various environmental stimuli, stored in evolving genomes, a portion of which would be transferred to *Castanea dentata*. Without the ability to decode this history written in sequences of purines and pyrimidines, geneticists can say they know the alphabet of genetics and maybe can figure out a few words, genes, but their reading comprehension scores prove quite limited when they look at sentences and paragraphs.

There's no money for sequencing American chestnut's DNA. We reserve those funds for money-making species, ones with patentable genes. Thus, breeders and plant geneticists know less about chestnut genetics than the high profile species of which we've sequenced the chromosomes. When Hebard talks of genes, he speaks of unknown, unquantified entities. The rumor that genes for orchard-growth and blight-resistance share space on a chromosome, still unsubstantiated or denied by evidence, helped shut down the USDA's chestnut breeding program. Nearly fifty years later, we still have little information about chestnut's varied genes and how they interact. We cannot even say how many genes work together to code for blight resistance.

Thus, a lot of chestnut breeding remains guesswork. Deeper issues involving chestnut's evolution remain unexamined, unexaminable. This highly developed species may have inherent abilities to overcome blight without human assistance. Indeed, our interference may have a net negative effect upon the species. Our eagerness to tromp through the woods in search of rare survivors might doom those individuals and, ultimately, the species.

Many of the American chestnut's genes express themselves only in certain crisis situations. Philip Rutter's odd speculations of talking trees and chestnut's encoded responses to pests allow us to begin to imagine some of the incredible information hidden in the species' genes. Rutter also pays keen attention to developing embryos which, he claims, occasionally flower at very early ages. Think of a baby walking or reading at two weeks to get the picture. Such odd, and rare, events, the breeder believes, betray ancient traits hidden well within the genome and expressed only under severe circumstances. He convinced me that deep, deep oddities hide within the genome that incrementally changed over perhaps more than a billion years.

The best plan for rescuing chestnut may be to think larger rather than smaller. If we can devise a way to prod the seemingly apathetic, underutilized majority into taking action to save chestnut, we might pave the way for a pervasive change toward environmental responsibility.

I have an idea. Imagine engaging every elementary student east of the Mississippi in the recovery. That's several million children. Smart and impressionable, kids often have the energy and passion to fix the world. If played right, we might enlist them to help save an American icon. By introducing young students to species recovery, we will gain activists ready to spend the remainders of their lives protecting and rescuing our natural heritage.

School children approach big problems with a freshness and positiveness rarely available to adults. With less experience, they avoid being cowed by a problem's size. They can also work in cohesive groups. By making chestnut recovery a group initiative, we allow the natural processes of peer interaction to make recovery "cool." Excited kids spread their enthusiasm to peers, building morale and interest throughout their social communities.

To carry out such a large scale project, a national committee needs to design the project, organize educators, maintain communication to and from classrooms, and develop and distribute materials. At present, likely groups to undertake such a mission include the National Science Teachers Association, the Forest Service, or the US Department of Agriculture. Perhaps an interagency committee with a budget substantial enough to achieve success would be the best bet.

The first component of such a program would involve introducing children to the story of the American chestnut. We need story books appropriate for varied reading levels—stories that allow children to understand how their actions can help the tree. Also, interested school teachers and community volunteers can read more extensive studies of chestnut to prepare themselves for questions from the children. Educators may identify elder members of the community or Cooperators that can explain their knowledge of American chestnut. Videos featuring the work of TACF and the ACCF may give older children a deeper understanding of the mission. The key is to introduce children to the loss of a species, to get them concerned about chestnut.

Perhaps a unifying experience, a Chestnut Week or some such Arbor Day-like event, can provide an annual framework in which American chestnut recovery enters the curriculum. Posters, public service announcements, and press releases can promote the event. Writing and art contests can build enthusiasm. During that week, all participating classrooms spend a chunk of educational time learning the science, as well as social and political issues, behind chestnut decline and recovery. As children get older, they learn more of the story, much in the way their understanding of mathematics or science develops. First graders might not learn about genetics, but middle schoolers could begin to examine the principles of back-crossing. The best time for such a week would be the spring, the period when American chestnut flowered and the soil becomes workable.

The next step would be to engage children in activities that directly aid chestnut. An adopt-a-tree program, where each child prepares a site, plants a tree, and oversees that tree's growth, provides a meaningful experience for each participant. Children can measure the sapling's growth, graphing their data, which contributes to learning science and mathematics. Like caring for a pet, care for a tree helps the child connect with nature. These kids would gain awareness of and concern for the trees, helping them develop environmental ethics. Children connected to nature in meaningful ways gain the ability to care for nature.

They could also connect with other schools via Internet resources. Software that tabulates and graphically presents student data such as Google's online mapping will allow students to construct a larger network in which their data allows for greater scientific discovery.

The National Science Teachers Association, along with chestnut experts, can be enlisted in developing age-appropriate curriculum. Lessons of varied lengths that meet the national and state benchmarks for science, social studies, language arts, and math education would be available to educators, along with any necessary materials. A teacher wishing to spend a week could employ one lesson; another looking to spend a month could employ another, more detailed set of lessons. The lessons would examine key areas of curriculum so that educators would not need to cut essential curriculum. For example, a unit on genetics in high school biology might focus on chestnut, ensuring that students learn both genetics and information about chestnut. Oftentimes, such "embedded" lessons help students bridge the gap between concrete and abstract thought. A chestnut tree is concrete; the gene proves more abstract. By providing a direct context for studying the abstract concepts, more students gain a working knowledge of science.

The organizing committee could also develop a geographically-based directory of chestnut speakers, helping educators find local volunteers to address their classes. School children will be interested in chestnut. Like Grente using a children's play as a hook for engaging chestnut growers in fighting blight, this project would draw in parents, grandparents, friends, and other members of the community, building strong local groups working to restore chestnut. Think of this as a fine tuning of TACF's state chapters.

While some American chestnuts could be grown in school yards, a great possibility because the children would have best access to them, each locality would also need other places to plant. Within rural areas, particularly in Appalachia, the Forest Service could clear areas of forest to prepare for trees planted by the school children. More urban areas might establish American chestnut parks. Fred Hebard recognizes the difficulties in finding public and private lands for chestnut recovery ventures. These difficulties could be addressed in relation to the large public school project.

While American chestnut's future may still be in question, some optimists and observant pessimists have noticed promise. At the end of summer, 2006, I returned to the West Salem, Wisconsin, stand of chestnuts. Last seen in their pre-leaf state a few years earlier, the fully foliated specimens proved a bit more interesting. I cruised the acreage in search of a different research team, noting the presence of burs in the canopy, plenty of sprouts bursting forth from the bases of still-living trees, dead crowns with green vitality below. These hillside trees clung to life as many colonists do in the face of adversity.

Eventually I heard mumblings bleed through the forest. The trio of experts patrolled one of the bramble-ridden transects, calling out data which scribe Andy Jerres recorded diligently. "Dead top. Epicormics go up 60%. Death at 10%. It's got burs. No basal sprouts," called out Bill MacDonald, West Virginia University plant pathologist and board member at TACF. Picture a tree, skeletal for twenty feet above its greenery which rises thirty feet. Epicormics are the branch-like protrusions that arise often below a canker. They produce leaves and act identically to branches, but while branch formation occurs systematically in trees, epicormics signal a stress faced by the individual—often severe pruning or death of the apical meristem, the growing tip. Blighted trees shoot up epicormics similarly to basal sprouts, of which this tree has none, as a chance to survive. While the specimen in question has burs, a good sign, one-tenth of the epicormic growth has died. Twenty feet away, Michigan chestnut guru Dennis Fulbright, vividly drawn in blaze-orange vest, pulled "diapers"—large sheets of toweling masking taped to the trees—from treated trees, toting the waste in a plastic garbage bag.

The three had traveled to measure the results of a hypovirulence study and to continue the research. The diapers covered sections of bark that were scratched and treated with virulent or hypovirulent blight fungus. Dennis pointed out how effectively some of the trees respond to the hypovirulent strains of virus, building callus through their lenticels in the treated areas.

A month earlier I had traveled by Lake Michigan ferry to visit Dennis on his home turf. As the moon set on the lake and the sun rose, I hopped in a Michigan State minivan to begin a lengthy day of chestnut observation. Dennis had implored my visit, frustrated that so many people contacted him yet none would accept his invitation to see the miraculously recovering trees of the Lower Peninsula. By the end of the day, my head would be spinning with new information and new possibilities for American chestnut.

Our second stop on an august August morning, what Fulbright coined the "County Line" site, not far from Thompsonville, illustrated the advantages of patience. In the 1980s, Dennis watched blight ravage the stand. Clean healthy trees swarmed with cankers, dead growth yearning skyward. As the Italians and French had done earlier, Fulbright and his crew treated the trees with fungus with a hypovirulent virus. Recovery inched its way through the stand, a mere few acres, with little observable success to report. But the last few years have brought significant change. While the old growth continues to fail, new shoots show greater capacity to withstand the blight. Dennis speculated as to whether the hypovirulence or genetics brings the renewed vigor and I suggested a combination would be the most likely cause.

A mile down the road, a 100-yard row of untreated trees wasted away. The hypovirus had yet to travel this minor distance. Diane Blocher, the landowner of both plots, beseeched Dennis to treat her trees. He agreed to see what he could do, and we took off for new pastures.

Michigan's diverse stands of chestnut, like the West Salem stand, offer outdoor laboratories to the chestnut crowd. Dennis says of West Salem: "We needed a place like that so we could all hatch our own ideas." After picking up some blueberries and Petoskey stones, we wended our way to another living laboratory, a hilltop stand lurking above the Chimney Corners Resort on the north shore of scenic Crystal Lake.

Dennis's first work on hypovirulence took place at Chimney Corners. I'd heard stories of a most creative yet failed technique for inoculating trees. Dennis related his plan to employ shotguns to blow inoculant-soaked pellets into the rough bark of the chestnuts. As with any good experiment, several candidates for a vector were tested—rice, millet, soybeans, and wheat. The wheat and rice simply blew apart, failing to make marks on the trees. Millet bounced off, while the soybeans held together enough to make crescent-shaped gouges. The flames escaping the gun's barrel left Dennis and other doubting whether the hypovirulent inoculum would survive. It did, though the researchers quickly learned that aiming directly at a tree blasted away too much bark. The wad had too much momentum so they elected for glancing blows that did the job. Alas, as ingenious as the technique may sound, the blasts annoyed Fulbright who cringes at the thought of bringing such reverberating racket to the quiet of the woods.

Though not on our initial itinerary, the Chimney Corners trees made the plan after Dennis saw my reception to his other trees. We scoured the stand, some of the largest trees I'd seen, finding abandoned ladders from decades earlier. Individual trees showed strong signs of recovery—healthy sprouts several years old, healing and healed cankers, and canopy greenery. Our visit, a mere still frame from an extended movie, offers us hope but provides no assurances for the future. Similar frames have popped up in all decades since chestnut blight hit these shores. Perhaps the greatest significance of these hopeful visits lies in their ability to bolster the Dennis Fulbrights of the chestnut world, dutiful workers eager to draw their labors to a close.

Walking the New Salem grove and collecting data, the four of us were joined by the dairy farming couple who own part of the land. While the trees seemed to be improving in health, the neighbors brought up a new threat to the stand. The dairy business barely keeps a farmer's head above water. These agrarians, hit with a series of misfortunes, faced possible bankruptcy and needed a quick infusion of cash to pay some sizable bills. They broached their concerns with Bill McDonald, saying they desired permission from TACF to go in and thin out the grove, leaving any significant trees. McDonald, understanding the plight of today's farmers, promised to look into the matter and assured the couple that they would be able to cut trees.

While contemporary humans have nearly forgotten the essential roles the kingdom of plants play in our lives, historical societies around the world held the great power of trees as fundamental. The Oromo of eastern Africa carried out important communal practices under the Odaa, gathering beneath the tree to formulate laws and discuss pressing social affairs. Indian groups on the subcontinent relied on trees to cure individuals suffering from various forms of possession. The patient underwent a ceremony, by which the offending spirit took shelter in a tree, agreeing not to harm the woody host. Lebanon cedars play important roles in the scripture of Christianity and Islam. Buddha himself traces his history from birth in a grove of Lumbini, enlightenment beneath the Bodhi tree, to death amongst a stand of sala trees. The druids, remembered as tree worshippers, found in their woody brethren many of the Elementals, pixies, and gnomes we still find in stories. They also enlisted the various species to perform many of the services needed to improve health and the quality of lives.

Perhaps the most significant role a single tree played comes from Norse mythology. Yggdrasil, some times translated as Odin's Steed, other times recognized as the World Tree from which the One-Eyed God hung for nine nights, provided the structure upon which Nordic peoples built their entire cosmology. Nine worlds, from Hel, Niflheim, and Muspelheim, where Yggdrasil's roots sought nutriment, to Ásgard, Álfheim and

Vanaheim, resting on the giant ash's branches, provided home to the varied gods and figures of Norse mythology.

At Ragnorak, Yggdrasil's shaking would signal the end of the worlds. Ultimately, the tree would fall when the frost giants and the dragon Nidhögg each severed one of its roots.

Yggdrasil symbolically provided sustenance, as well as shelter, for a variety of creatures, from the eagle and rooster roosted in its top branches, the squirrel Ratotsk who scrambled up and down the trunk delivering insults back and forth between Nidhögg and the eagle, to the four deer-like creatures eating of the ash's branches. For the northern Europeans, the mythology reflects a reality where humans and all creatures depended upon trees for shelter, food, fuel, and tools. The myth reveals ecological truth of interconnectedness of species, offering a view countering the individualism of anti-environmental thinkers.

Though having much different technologies and cosmologies, we of the 21st Century still maintain an absolute reliance upon trees for our existence. Our belief systems, amalgamations of our television technocracy, rabid individualism, and reductionist science, stress the ultimate reality of the minuscule—atoms, electrons, protons. What is a tree but extended chains of sugars, cellulose, arranged in three dimensions? How do we define the connection between human and ash when the electron microscope fails to reveal physical ties, elemental threads actually tying us together? Interrelationships have as little material reality as the invisible force of gravity that remains hidden in the mass of subatomic particles science has subdivided.

But interrelationships do exist and do structure our everyday lives. The broccoli I eat becomes part of me, while the carbon dioxide I exhale promotes the crucifer's growth. The forest of trees alters the immediate climate, providing the humid conditions needed for certain fungi which, in turn, route water and essential nutrients to trees'roots through mycorrhizal relations. While we can fathom how diverse organs such as heart and lungs work together to deliver oxygenated blood to the body's cells, we have less skill at seeing how ecosystems function similarly. The next step in human evolution requires us to step beyond the metaphor and myth of the individual organism to understand all living things as nodes in a larger web of life, to comprehend the life itself as a process rather than a product.

For the people of Scandinavia, the eventual fall of a tree signals the end of most of the gods, the giants, and all of creation, excepting two humans—Lif and Lifthrasi—who survive on Yggdrasil's dew and go on to repopulate the world. For us, the loss of American chestnut, or elm, or ash, or oak, or hemlock simply means replacement with another species that we can exploit until the time comes to replace it. Like the fish we learn to eat as soon as the tastier species' numbers decline from over-fishing, the trees replacing our American chestnuts, though less suitable, less pleasing, become the norm as we forget the beauty of former species. We become a people accustomed to weeds, learning to love the overlooked species through our own failure to protect the once favored. Settling for second, third, or seventy-fifth best, we rely on collective amnesia, fooling ourselves into believing that all species are created equal, a notion as simplistic as believing that all works of art possess equal beauty, that all philosophies share proportionate truths.

As we approach our own Ragnorak, an accelerating undoing of the complex natural societies we inherited from the evolutionary process, an unraveling of the careful relations among species, we have only ourselves to blame. If we wish to take responsibility for our actions, we need to consider the works of the American Chestnut Foundation, the Cooperators, and others, and build upon them. We need to learn from and expand their visions with greater understandings of ecological relations and genetics. To do otherwise is to continue on the same suicidal path we mindlessly trod, a path of comfort and least resistance where our wealth comes at the cost of unborn generations that inherit our spoils. It is up to each of us to decide if we dare leave our grand-children and beyond such a shaming legacy.

Our language hides small surprises for the nature lover. We still reserve the phrase "the tree of life" to refer to evolution's random wanderings, suggesting a deeper connection to trees than may be evident on the surface. A healthy individual can be called "rooted," a compliment stolen from our truly rooted brethren. Perhaps we can branch out and return vegetation to its central role in our mythology and daily lives?

I leaned my bicycle against a fence post and ambled into the grove. This time, I wasn't sure I would ever come out. I wanted to pledge myself to the trees, silent sentinels that would oversee the rise or the fall of humanity. This time, I left my expectations and misconceptions behind, hoping the trees would reveal the truth to me if they could.

INDEX

A

ABBA 170
Aesculus hippocastanium 35
Agraria 158
American Chestnut Cooperators' Foundation 59, 84-116, 133, 161, 166, 174, 179
American Chestnut Foundation 50-84, 96, 97, 134, 146, 153, 155, 161, 165, 166, 171, 174, 175, 179
Anagnostakis, Sandra 35, 44, 129-135, 160
Appalachian Trail 62, 107
Aughanbaugh, John 27

B

backcrossing 39, 40, 49, 56, 59, 70, 72, 74
Badgersett Farms 136, 144, 146
Barrus, George 31
Beadle, George 47
Beardsley, O.E. 132
Beattie, R. Kent 26, 38, 39
Berry, Frederick 41, 48
Bessey, Ernest 36
Biltmore Mansion 22
Biraghi, A. 44, 105
blight resistance 37, 39, 41, 48, 71, 72-73, 74, 75, 93, 98, 105-106, 112, 145, 173
Blocher, Diane 176
Bonaparte. Josephine 35
Borlaug, Norman 47, 129
Bowling Green University 143
Braun, E. Lucy 95-96
Brooklyn Botanic Garden, 42
Brown, Edmund 65, 68
buckthorn 166
Buddha 177
Burbank, Luther 35, 52, 154
Burnham, Charles Russell 47-49, 58, 70, 72, 74, 97, 146
burr. *See* chestnut burr
burr oak 140, 150, 151
butternuts 143-45
Byrd, Curtis 129

C

cankers 13, 27, 44-45, 57, 74, 93, 105, 114, 132, 144, 176
Cannon, Tom 62
Carleton, Mark 34
Carter, Jimmy 11
Case, Marshal 66, 71
Castanea crenata 22, 35
Castanea dolichophylla 18
Castanea pumila 22
Castanea sativa 44
Castanea seguinii 139, 141, 159
Castanea spokanensis 18
Castanea ungeri 18
Castanoxylon 18
Cherokee 19

chestnut blight 8
  discovery in Asia 38
  discovery of 21
  resistance. *See* blight resistance
  spread of 24-26, 44, 132
chestnut burr 12, 54, 139, 141
Chestnut Growers, Inc 157
chinquapin 17, 22, 47, 132, 134, 165
Clapper hybrid 39-41, 48, 56, 59, 78
Clapper, Robert 41
Clapper, Russell 39-42
Clements State Tree Nursery 114
Clinton, George 31
Cochran, M. Ford 59, 85
Collins, J. Franklin 24, 30, 46
Colossal cultivar 154
Columbia University 55
Concord College 98
Connecticut Agricultural Experiment Station 31, 42, 44, 58, 129
corn 48, 148, 149, 150, 151, 152, 153, 156
Cornell University 48
Cornett, Benji 61, 68
Corwin, Jason 68
Crab Orchard National Wildlife Refuge 39
Crick, Francis 111
crossing-over 143
Cryphonectria parasitica 44, 70, 75, 106, 134, 143
Cummings Carlson, Jane 13
Cupuliferoipollenites pusillus 18
Curtis, John 8
Cytospora 21

D

Dakota Pasta Company 158
Daniel Boone tree 36
Davies, Raymond Douglas 7
de Vries, Hugo 37
Dietz, Al 44, 91, 108
Diller, Jesse 39-42
Dioum, Baba 7
Discover 54
Dorsey, Judy 78
Driftless Zone 151
Dryocosmus kuriphilus 57
du Pont de Nemours, Eleuthere Irénéé 35
Dutch elm disease 167, 168

E

earwigs 54
Elkins, John 59, 85, 98-104, 106, 110, 111
Ellingboe, Al 70
Emerson, Rollins 48
Empire Chestnut Company 67
Endangered Species Act 163
Endicott, George W. 36
Endothia parasitica 46
environmental ethics 160-65
Environmental Protection Agency 89
eucalyptus 132
expanding circle 163

F

Fairchild, David 37, 38
Flannery, Tim 20
Forest Service 27, 40, 89, 174, 175
Forest Service's Northeastern Forest Experiment Station 42
Foster, Joyce 98-100, 103
founder effect 145-46
Fox Keller, Evelyn 131
Freinkel, Susan 54, 56, 65
Fulbright, Dennis 153-55, 157, 175-77

G

garlic mustard 166
genotype 72, 73, 75
George Washington National Forest 107
Ginkgo biloba 37
Given, Bruce 91, 102, 108
global warming 167
Goodall, Jane 136
Gore, Al 170

Gould, Helen 24
grafting 100-03
Gravatt, Annie 57
Gravatt, Flippo 39, 41, 47, 57
Graves, Arthur 15, 42-44, 47, 130, 131, 160
Great Smoky Mountains National Park 57
Greenwell, Ed 93, 103-05
Grente, Jean 44-46, 132-33, 134, 175
Griffin, Gary 59, 70, 85, 90, 92, 94-98, 107, 108, 109-13, 133, 134, 155, 160, 161, 170
Griffin, Lucille 86, 89-98, 101, 103, 104, 113, 115, 116, 155, 161
Griffith, Fred 67
Griffith, Linda 67
gypsy moths 26

H

Harshberger, J. W. 30, 32
hazelnut 150, 151
Hebard, Dayle 52, 59, 66
Hebard, Fred 51-84, 94, 132, 146, 154, 155, 160, 161, 167, 175
Hebard, Kyla 59
Hebard, Paige 59
Hepting, George 24
Hicks, Martin 8
Hillman, Brad 133
Hogan, Eric 106, 108
Honaker, Danny 51, 53, 55, 67
horse chestnut 35
Horticulture and Agroforestry Research Center 155
Hume, David 20
Hurricane Camille 44
hypovirulence 105, 106, 132, 134, 176

I

inarching 43
instrumentalism 160-162
intrinsic value 164
irradiated chestnut 44, 108
Irwin, Hugh 78

J

Jaynes, Richard 40, 43, 47, 49, 108, 130, 132, 133
Jefferson, Thomas 35, 137
Jeffries, Ron 157
Jerres, Andy 175
Jolly Pumpkin Artisan Ales 157
Jones, Donald 42, 130
Juglans cinerea 143-45

K

Kant, Immanuel 163
Kingsolver, Barbara 52
Klaus, Nathan 166
Kotlewski, John 162
Kubisiak, Thomas 78
Kunstler, James 149
Kyoto Protocol 164

L

Lebanon cedars 177
Leopold, Aldo 148, 151
Lesesne Foundation 43
Lesesne State Forest 43, 97, 108
Lewontin, Richard 77, 84, 96
Lifeson, Alex 9
Link, O. Winston 99, 108
linkage 41
Liu, Peter 38, 132
Long, W.H. 36
Lowe, Tim 69, 86

M

MacDonald, Bill 175
Marlatt, Charles 26
mast years 141
mastodons 150
Matthiessen, Peter 136, 147
Mayo, John 36
McCarthy, Brian 143
McClintock, Barbara 47, 131, 143
McCue, Charles 31
McCurdy, Dave 114-15
McDonald, Bill 177

McElwain, Jennifer 16, 17
Mediterranean fly 26
Mendel, Gregor 74
Merkel, Herman 21-23
Metcalf, Haven 25-26, 28, 30, 37, 46, 144
Meyer, Frank N. 37-38, 130
Michigan Agricultural Experiment Station 157
Michigan State University 157
Milburn, Margaret 47
Mill, John Stuart 163
Miller, Greg 67
Minnesota Department of Natural Resources 138
Moore, Rep. J. Hampton 33
Mountain Lake Scenic Area 86
Mount Rogers National Recreational Area 51, 61
Muir, John 61
Murrill, William 22-23, 28, 29-30, 32, 33, 144

N

National Climatic Data Center 19
National Fish and Wildlife Foundation 108
National Geographic 26, 59, 85, 102
National Science Teachers Association 174
National Wild Turkey Federation 108
New York Botanical Gardens 22
New York Times 23
New York Zoological Society 21
Niagara Gas Spraying Company 22
Niensteadt, Hans 43
Nixon, Richard 169
Northern Nut Growers Association 24, 130

O

O'Reilly, Bernadette 14
Oberlin College 57
Odaa 177
Odum, TR 69
Okefenokee Swamp 168
Organic Valley 156
Oriental chestnut gall wasp 57, 96, 132
Oromo 177
Outdoor Life 41
Owens, Jesse 141

P

Paillet, Fred 19, 87, 130
Pangaea 15
Paragon 36
Parry, Wililam 35
Parsons, S.B. 35
Patterson, Flora 21, 22
Peach-yellows 31
Pearson, Raymond A. 29
Peck, Charles 23
Pennsylvania Chestnut Blight Conference 130
Pennsylvania Chestnut Tree Blight Commission, The 27-35
permaculture 149, 150, 151, 156
phenotype 70, 72, 79, 139
Phytophthora 47, 97, 108
Pine Wilt nematode 146
Plant Quarantine Act 26
Pollan, Michael 148
Porter, Leon 69
potato wart 26
Project Village Smithy 43

Q

Quammen, David 145
Quercus alba 46
Quercus macrocarpa 140, 150, 151
Quercus velutina 46

R

Ragnorak 178, 179
Randi, James 139
Reader's Digest 41
Rest, Jim 162
Rhoades, Marcus 48

Roberds, James 78
Rockefeller, John D. 24
Roosevelt, Franklin Delano 166
Roosevelt, Teddy 24
Rushdie, Salman 159
Rutter, Meg 142
Rutter, Philip 49, 50, 57-59, 70, 72, 74, 83, 85, 97, 110, 137-47, 152, 161, 173
Rutter's Rule 144

S

Sagamore Estate 24
salamanders 87
Sargent, Winthrop 33
Seguin 139, 141, 159
Seliskar, Denise 79
Service, William 50
Shear, Cornelius L. 37, 46
Shepard, Jen 149
Shepard, Mark 153, 156, 157, 158
Sierra Club 89
Silva, Jaime—Portugal's Agriculture Minister 146
Simmons Bill 26
Singer, Peter 162
Singleton, Ralph 44
Sirrococcus clavigignenti-j uglandacearum 143
Sisco, Paul 70
Skeptical Inquirer 139
Sleeping Giant State Park 43, 130, 131
Slow Food 66-67
Smith, J. Russell 31
Smith, Ryan 69
Sober, Coleman K. 36-37
southern pine beetle 146
soybean 37, 148, 149, 150, 151, 156, 176
Stewart, Fred 30
Stout, William 50
succession 151
Sykes, George 67

T

Taft, William Howard 29
talking trees 139
Talladega National Forest 165
Tener, John K., Governor of Pennsylvania 27, 33
Tricolporopollenites 18
Tucker, Lowell 39
Twain, Mark 114

U

University of Missouri's Center for Agroforestry 157
University of Texas at Austin 130
US Bureau of Plant Industry 21
US Department of Agriculture 25, 131, 174
US Forest Service's Forest Products Lab 132
USDA's Bureau of Entomology 26
USDA's Division of Forest Pathology 38
USDA's Division of Pomology 47
USDA's Foreign Seed and Plant Introduction Section 37

V

Valk, Anne 43
van Fleet, Walter 36, 38
Virginia Department of Forestry 108
Virginia Tech 57, 89, 94, 106

W

Wagner, Anna Belle 57
Wagner, Cheri 57
Wagner, Jennifer 57
Warther, Ernest "Mooney" 99
Watson, James D. 111
Weimer, E.A. 33
West Virginia University 48, 57, 175
White, J.D. and Gladys 63
White pine blister rust 26
Whitman, Charles 130

Widriechner, Mark 58
Wilder, Laura Ingalls 137
Williams, I.C. 32
Willis, Katherine 16, 17
wooly adelgid 82, 95
World Conservation Monitoring
Centre 82

Y

Yellowstone National Park 163
Yggdrasil 159, 177

Z

Zea mays 48, 148, 149, 150, 151,
152, 153, 156
Ziegler, E.A. 35
Ziroli, Mike 166

32612017R00119

Made in the USA
Middletown, DE
11 June 2016